THE FLASH 8
GAME DEVELOPING HANDBOOK

Serge Melnikov

BPB PUBLICATIONS
B-14, CONNAUGHT PLACE, NEW DELHI-110001

FIRST INDIAN EDITION 2007
1 of 2

ISBN 81-8333-200-5

Published in India by arrangement with
A-LIST, LLC, USA

> NOTE: THE CD-ROM INCLUDED WITH THE BOOK HAS NO COMMERCIAL VALUE AND CANNOT BE SOLD SEPARATELY.

Distributors:

MICRO BOOK CENTRE
2, City Centre, CG Road,
Near Swastic Char Rasta,
AHMEDABAD-380009 Phone: 26421611

COMPUTER BOOK CENTRE
12, Shrungar Shopping Centre, M.G. Road,
BANGALORE-560001 Phone: 25587923, 25584641

MICRO BOOKS
Shanti Niketan Building, 8, Camac Street,
KOLKATTA-700017 Phone: 22826518, 22826519

BUSINESS PROMOTION BUREAU
8/1, Ritchie Street, Mount Road,
CHENNAI-600002 Phone: 28410796, 28550491

DECCAN AGENCIES
4-3-329, Bank Street,
HYDERABAD-500195 Phone: 24756400, 24756967

MICRO MEDIA
Shop No. 5, Mahendra Chambers, 150 D.N. Road,
Next to Capital Cinema V.T. (C.S.T.) Station,
MUMBAI-400001 Ph.: 22078296, 22078297

BPB PUBLICATIONS
B-14, Connaught Place, **NEW DELHI-110001**
Phone: 23325760, 23723393, 23737742

INFO TECH
G-2, Sidhartha Building, 96 Nehru Place,
NEW DELHI-110019
Phone: 26438245, 26415092, 26234208

INFO TECH
Shop No. 2, F-38, South Extension Part-1
NEW DELHI-110049
Phone: 24691288

BPB BOOK CENTRE
376, Old Lajpat Rai Market,
DELHI - 110006 PHONE: 23861747

Published by Manish Jain for BPB Publications, B-14, Connaught Place, New Delhi-110 001 and Printed by him at Akash Press, New Delhi.

Contents

Introduction _____ 1

   Vector Graphics, Flash Animation, and ActionScript_____1

   Interaction of a Flash Game with the Web Server or a Windows Application _____2

   A Brief Description of the Book _____3

Chapter 1: Starting Implementation _____ 5

Chapter 2: Importing and Creating Graphics in Flash _____ 9

   2.1. Setting the Application _____9

   2.2. Importing Graphics to Flash_____11

      2.2.1. Graphics for Squares _____12

      2.2.2. Graphics for the Background _____16

   2.3. Creating Clips Using Flash Tools _____16

      2.3.1. Creating the Background for the Game Pits _____16

      2.3.2. Creating Pit Borders_____18

      2.3.3. Creating Guidelines for the Pieces _____20

   2.4. Creating Button Clips_____21

   2.5. Creating Text _____26

   2.6. Creating Buttons_____29

Chapter 3: Creating Animation _____ **33**

3.1. Flash Timeline _____ 33

3.2. Layers and Key Frames _____ 34

3.3. Creating Animation Effects _____ 35

    3.3.1. The Motion Tween Animation _____ 35

    3.3.2. The Shape Tween Animation _____ 39

Chapter 4: Introduction to ActionScript _____ **45**

4.1. An Example of Displaying Text and Clips _____ 45

4.2. Variables _____ 48

    4.2.1. Creating Variables with Dynamically-Calculated Names _____ 49

    4.2.2. Type Casting _____ 49

    4.2.3. Scope of a Function _____ 50

4.3. Data Types _____ 55

    4.3.1. The *number* Type _____ 55

    4.3.2. The *string* Type _____ 56

    4.3.3. The *Boolean* Type _____ 58

    4.3.4. The *undefined* Type _____ 58

    4.3.5. The *null* Type _____ 59

4.4. Operator Precedence and Associativity _____ 59

4.5. Types of Statements _____ 61

    4.5.1. Conditional Statements _____ 62

    4.5.2. Loop Statements _____ 64

    4.5.3. The *break* Statement _____ 65

    4.5.4. The *continue* Statement _____ 65

4.6. Functions _____ 66

    4.6.1. The *arguments* Object _____ 66

    4.6.2. Passing Parameters to Functions _____ 67

    4.6.3. Global Functions _____ 67

4.7. Built-in Classes _____ 69

    4.7.1. The *Array* Class _____ 69

    4.7.2. The *MovieClip* Class _____ 71

    4.7.3. The *Sound* Class _____ 73

4.8. Built-in Objects _____73
 4.8.1. The *Key* Object _____73
 4.8.2. The *Mouse* Object _____74
 4.8.3. The *Selection* Object _____75
4.9. Event Handling _____75
 4.9.1. User Events _____75
 4.9.2. An Example: Creating Customized Mouse Pointer _____80
 4.9.3. Clip Events Related to the Movie _____84
 4.9.4. Scopes of Event Handlers _____85

Chapter 5: Coding the Script of the Game _____ 87

5.1. Final Preparations _____87
5.2. Writing the Data Section of the Game Script _____91
 5.2.1. Specifying Depths for Clips _____91
 5.2.2. Creating Arrays for Pits and Filled Lines _____92
 5.2.3. Coding Pieces, Check Arrays, and Piece Rotation Arrays ___93
 5.2.4. Coding the Splash Screen _____105
 5.2.5. Coding Score Display and Auxiliary Functions _____116
 5.2.6. Coding the Moving down of Pieces _____129
 5.2.7. Coding Motion and Rotation of the Pieces _____149
5.3. Continuation of the Theme _____155

Chapter 6: Interaction between the Game and the Web Server _____ 157

6.1. Installing and Setting PHP _____157
6.2. Installing and Setting the Apache Web Server _____158
6.3. Receiving Game Parameters from the Web Server _____160
6.4. Sending the Result of the Game to the Web Server _____166

Chapter 7: Integrating the Flash Project into a Program Shell _____ 177

7.1. Adding New Clips _____177
7.2. Updating the ActionScript Code for Work with the Shell _____187
7.3. Adding New Functions and Code to the Main Program _____197

Chapter 8: Creating a Key Generator   209

8.1. The Key-Generating Algorithm _____210
8.2. A Perl Key Generator _____211
8.3. A Delphi Key Generator _____214
8.4. A C++ Key Generator _____217

Chapter 9: Integrating a Flash Movie into a Delphi Program   219

9.1. Installing the Shockwave Flash Component in Delphi_____219
9.2. Writing the Program Shell in Delphi _____222
    9.2.1. The Type and Global Data Section of the Program _____223

Chapter 10: Integrating Flash Movie into a C++ Program   237

10.1. Getting Started with the Project _____238
    10.1.1. Precompiled Headers_____238
    10.1.2. Registering the Main Window Style_____239
    10.1.3. Creating the Main Window of the Program _____241
    10.1.4. A Message Loop _____243
    10.1.5. The Window Function _____244
10.2. Working with ActiveX Using ATL _____246
    10.2.1. Linking ATL _____246
    10.2.2. Loading the Shockwave Flash ActiveX Control _____247
    10.2.3. ActiveX and COM Interfaces _____249
    10.2.4. Finding Information about an Interface _____253
    10.2.5. Loading the Flash Movie _____254
10.3. Handling the ActiveX Component's Events _____255
    10.3.1. Sending Events from the Flash Control to Your Program Shell_____256
    10.3.2. Creating a Handler Class _____257
10.4. Creating a Shell for Tet-a-Tetris _____261

Chapter 11: Nim: Programming a Logical Game   265

11.1. A Description of Nim _____265
11.2. Preparing Game Graphics_____267
    11.2.1. A Game Board Square _____267

11.2.2. A Piece _____ 268

11.2.3. Buttons _____ 269

11.2.4. An Empty Clip for Event Handling _____ 271

11.2.5. Clips for Messages _____ 271

11.2.6. A Clip for Marking Pieces _____ 272

11.3. Writing Auxiliary Functions _____ 273

11.3.1. The Data Section of the Program _____ 273

11.3.2. The Code of the Main Program (without Functions) ___ 274

11.3.3. Functions of the Main Program _____ 276

11.4. Computing and Making Moves _____ 284

11.4.1. Recursive Functions _____ 285

11.4.2. The *computerMove* and *isWin* Functions _____ 288

11.5. Limiting the Depth of Skimming through Moves _____ 292

11.6. Adding Some Heuristic _____ 297

11.7. Continuation of the Theme _____ 301

CD Contents _____ **303**

Index _____ **305**

Introduction

Once you have mastered the Flash tools described in the following chapters, you'll be able to create Flash games for your Web sites — and at a charge — and write Windows applications capable of using the Flash Player (the Shockwave Flash component) installed in the system.

Vector Graphics, Flash Animation, and ActionScript

In bitmap graphics, each point of a bitmap requires one byte in a palette mode, and three bytes for red, green, and blue, in True Color mode. At the same time, vector graphics doesn't store colors for individual color points. Rather, it stores formulas describing strokes made while drawing. Thanks to this, the size of a vector graphics file created using a graphics editor is much less than that of a bitmap file with the same image. This is very important for the Web. In addition, vector images can be scaled and rotated without distortion.

What's more, an SWF file that contains a Flash movie stores only key frames, and animation between them is computed during the playback. The main object that undergoes animation is a *movie clip*. These objects are created in the Flash development environment, and are contained in a library that is also stored in the SWF file. A clip can be as complicated as the movie. It can contain sounds and other clips. When you attach a clip to another clip, the latter actually stores a reference to an appropriate library symbol. This saves the memory and allows you to change all clip instances of one symbol by changing this symbol. If you wish, you can break the link between a clip and its symbol, and edit the clip separately.

Not only can internal clips have their own motion, but they also move together with their master clips in their coordinate system — like, for example, a car wheel rotates and moves together with the car.

Flash offers you a full-featured programming language, ActionScript, which is similar to JavaScript. Scripts determine the behavior of clips and do some computation. They can be attached to clips, buttons, and key frames on Timeline. When the "player head" enters a frame, Flash Player executes all scripts in this frame, and then draws the contents of the frame. ActionScript includes commands for going to specified frames. This allows you to control animation. For example, it lets you arrange a loop playback. Using scripts, you can retrieve required clips from the library, and put them onto the work area of the movie. You can also change the properties of clip instances, such as the coordinates, the relative depth, scaling, the angle of rotation, the color, and the transparency. In addition, Flash MX allows you to draw clips programmatically, and have a clip be a mask for other clips. In the latter case, the user will see masked clips through the mask clip, like through a keyhole. Playing or muting sounds (in the MP3 and WAV formats) is also possible using ActionScript scripts.

You can attach event-handling code to clips and buttons. The code will be executed in response to certain events, such as moving the mouse pointer, clicking or releasing a mouse button, or pressing or releasing a key. This allows you, for example, to substitute the standard Windows mouse pointer with your own. There is an event that occurs with a frequency of the frame rate chosen when creating the movie. This event allows you to have code that will be played continually. For example, such code could move "enemies" in a game so that they encircle the character controlled by the gamer.

Interaction of a Flash Game with the Web Server or a Windows Application

ActionScript offers you functions that allow you to exchange data with the Web server, JavaScript code on a page, or an application that plays your Flash movie. For example, you can open a new browser window, load a specified page, or send a filled form to the server.

Flash allows you to output your movie to an EXE file, not only to an SWF file. In other words, you can turn the movie into an application for Windows or Macintosh. In this case, Flash Player will also be included in the file to play the movie. However, if you want your movie to work with files — to save a table of records, for example — you'll have to write a shell in C or Delphi. Then the Flash movie will become a full-fledged Windows application (e.g., a game or a screensaver), because it will interact with a shell capable of performing various actions. In such a case, the Flash movie is executed by an ActiveX component installed in the system (the same component that plays Flash movies in the browser window).

A Brief Description of the Book

Chapter 1. This chapter specifies a task to write a Tetris-like game. The game will have two game pits, in which two pieces controlled by the gamer will move synchronously. (This game, called Tet-a-Tetris, is available at my Web site: **www.gameintellect.com**). The chapter presents the game scenario. You'll see that the task isn't as simple as it might seem at first. You'll have to use your imagination and work hard.

Chapter 2. This chapter teaches you how to set up a Flash development environment, import graphics in GIF and JPEG formats, and use Flash tools to create text, clips, and buttons. In this chapter, the graphics for the game are created.

Chapter 3. You'll learn about the timeline, layers, and key frames. You'll create motion tween animation and shape tween animation, and attach actions to the clips, buttons, and frames created earlier.

Chapter 4. This chapter shows you examples of how text and clips can be displayed using ActionScript. You'll read about data types, operators and their precedence, built-in classes, and objects and their methods. I'll describe functions used in the game script and a mechanism for events and event handlers.

Chapter 5. In this chapter, the game (i.e., a splash screen, menus, and actions) is coded. Actions are attached to squares that make up pieces to implement explosions of the squares when lines in game pits are filled. I'll tell you how to code the pieces to rotate, move, and drop them.

Chapter 6. You might want to receive the gamer's name, residence, and score from the server, and to send his or her new score to the server. This chapter describes how to install a Web server, such as Apache, Perl, and PHP, on your home computer, and how to implement interaction with the server without connecting to the Internet. You'll write a simple PHP script to exchange data with your program. You'll set a five-minute restriction for each game for an unregistered gamer. To remove the restriction, the gamer will have to register and receive a registration key from you. Information about the registered users can be stored on the Web server or in a cookie on the client computer.

Chapter 7. By this chapter, you'll already have a functional online game. You'll update it a little so that it can work under a program shell like a Windows application. This version of the game displays a clip with the game rules and a table of records stored in a file in the game folder. It will display a form after five minutes of a non-registered play. The form will allow the gamer to enter his or her registration name and key to remove the time restriction. (The game will check the validity of the key).

Chapter 8. This chapter presents a key generator and its implementation in Perl, Delphi, and Microsoft Visual C++. The Perl key generator will work on your Web server or on the registration provider's. (The latter will receive payments from the buyers of the game). The other key generators can come in handy if you decide to send registration keys to the buyers on your own.

Chapter 9. This chapter presents a program shell that will start the SWF file with your game, and exchange data with it. In particular, it will exchange the table of records and the gamer's registration name and key.

Chapter 10. The chapter is similar to the previous, but the shell it presents is written in C++.

Chapter 11. This chapter describes the creation of a logical game that can "think" and search for a winning move, like chess programs do. You'll create graphics for a new game and learn about recursive functions. Being very small, they nevertheless can traverse the game tree and beat a person if they are allowed to analyze every possible move. After you write such a function, it will become impossible for a person to beat the computer playing this game. To make it interesting for people to play the game, you'll limit the depth of analyzing the computer's moves and introduce two game levels. To decrease the time, during which the computer is thinking (the time interval should be shorter than 15 seconds), you'll implement a good heuristic rule for analyzing game positions, and the analysis depth will decrease by five, from seven moves to two.

The book is accompanied by a CD-ROM that contains all source codes for the projects and programs described in the book.

Chapter 1: Starting Implementation

Of the all-time classics of the world of arcade games like Packman, Digger and Lode Runner, Tetris was the most popular of them all. It won five Oscars at a computer game contest held in London in 1986. Like many great and successful ideas, Tetris is simple: It is a computer program that could have been written by a schoolchild. Also like most great ideas, Tetris has spawned numerous variants with different playing pieces and rules. It might seem like all of the options have been covered and there's nothing new left to do with the original. This, however, underestimates the creativity of the programmer, whose imaginations can be boundless. Have you ever seen Tetris with two game pits? Neither have I. Do you like the idea? I'm going to implement the idea in a complete product, which will be called Tet-a-Tetris.

The point of having two game pits is simply to make the game more complicated and, as a result, provide more variety. When playing the traditional Tetris, a gamer doesn't think much about placing the next piece. In the two-pit variant, however, he or she will have to control two pieces simultaneously. If one of them cannot be moved or rotated, neither can the other. If one piece reaches the bottom and stops, the other will fall. This will call on the gamer to watch both game pits. If the gamer isn't able to do this successfully, one pit will filled up quickly, and the game will be over. This game helps the gamer develop better peripheral vision, which can come in handy. To avoid making the game overly complicated, the pieces should consist of one, two, or three squares. This will also simplify the programming process, which fits the book's goal of teaching you how to program a Flash game without getting lost in the labyrinth of the application. As you'll see later, the programming for the deletion of filled lines alone can be difficult, and not every game program will delete the lines properly.

If playing the game appears to be too easy or too difficult, there will be a trick in the program: You'll be able to adjust the probability of the appearance of pairs of pieces to optimize the difficulty level. Obviously, the most convenient pair would be two single squares, while the least convenient pair is a horizontal line of three squares on one side pit with a vertical line on the other.

There are nine possible pieces involved: one one-square piece, two two-square pieces (horizontal and vertical), four three-square "corners" and two three-square lines. Therefore, there are 81 possible pairings ($9 \times 9 = 81$), which seems like plenty to me. Each group of pieces consisting of the same number of squares will have a particular color and texture — the latter to make it easy for even a color-blind person to distinguish between pieces.

What will the gamer see on the screen? First, there will be two game pits (I'll discuss their sizes later). Second, there will be displays for the current speed, the gamer's score, the number of the pieces used and the number of lines filled. The points for the current pieces will also be displayed. This number will decrease as the pieces drift down, and a simple animation will have the number jump to the current score display and disappear, as if added to the gamer's score, before a new pair of pieces appears. Finally, the screen will contain three buttons: **New**, to quit the current game and start a new one; **Sound**, to turn sound on or off; and **Pause**, to interrupt a game (if, for example, the phone rings, or there is a fire) and resume it later.

There are two types of game. The first doesn't allow the gamer to move a piece after it has reached the bottom. The second does, thus simplifying the game. The original Tetris was created by Alexey Pajitnov on an Electronica 60 personal computer at the Moscow Academy of Science Computer Center. It was adapted to run on IBM PCs in the mid-1980s by Vadim Gerasimov, a student at Moscow State University. These examples didn't allow the gamer to move a piece once it had landed. An example of a game that does is Pentix. Because the game created in this book won't be simple, we'll allow the gamer to move a piece after it reaches the bottom, thus reducing the chance that he or she will smash the monitor with a hammer. However, it will only be possible to move both pieces if there are spaces for them.

The goal of the game is to get as many points as possible by filling as many lines as possible. To keep the gamer amused, we will include an animation to mark the deletion of a filled line: The squares in the line will explode with a bang. To make the explosions more natural, lightning will strike the filled lines. The lightning bolt, by the way, is the informal Flash symbol and is often present on the covers of books about Flash.

The startup window for the game will be the following: First, the game pieces will drop down to form the name of the game, Tet-a-Tetris, in the same way that this is done in Pentix. Then a bolt of lightning will strike the name, causing the squares to explode and disappear. Finally, a dialog square will appear asking the gamer to select the initial speed, and then start the game by clicking on the **Play!** button. A user-friendly program should allow for the startup window to be closed easily via the keyboard key or a mouse button, so you'll have to include this option.

After the gamer starts the game, a new pair of pieces will appear at the top of the game pits. If one of them overlaps an existing square, the game will end with the appropriate sound and the appearance of a dialog box containing the words **Game over!**. The speed-selection control and the **Play again? Yes** button will also appear. Otherwise, the pieces will drift downard at appropriate time intervals. The gamer will be able to control them — that is, rotate them counterclockwise, move them to the left or right, and have them drop. After a piece meets an obstacle, the program will wait for an instant, allowing the gamer to move or rotate the pieces, after which the next piece will begin to drop. Generally, the last step can be repeated several times, with the gamer able to move or rotate the pieces each time. After both pieces stop, the program will pause to check for filled lines. If it finds any, lightning will strike the squares, breaking them into pieces. Finally, the program moves the upper line down to close the gaps, and the loop will repeat with a new pair of pieces appearing.

When rotating pieces, you should check whether the piece can rotate, that is, whether it will overlap an existing square during rotation or when rotation completes. The manner of carrying out this check is described later, when we will discuss writing code for pieces in arrays.

Although the game itself is relatively simple, this does not mean that its implementation will be as well, so you might want to write the program first in your favorite programming language (e.g., Turbo Pascal), and then rewrite it in ActionScript for Flash.

Chapter 2: Importing and Creating Graphics in Flash

In this chapter, you will create graphics for the game using both imported images and Flash editing tools.

2.1. Setting the Application

Start the Flash 8 development environment, set the checkbox **Don't show again**, exit the program, and start it again. Flash will automatically create a document Untitled-1. If it does not happen, select **File | New...** menu item or press the <Ctrl>+<N> hotkey combination, and in the window that opens select **Flash Document** on the **General** tab. For our purposes, we only need the **Tools** window, the *work space* with the *work area* (which contains frames), and the **Library** window. You can close all of the other windows. To do this, open the **Window** menu, and uncheck every item except **Tools**, **Timeline**, and **Library**. Alternatively, you can use the hotkeys shown in the **Window** menu, which act as toggles. You can close all unused panels by right-clicking on their captions and applying the **Close panel group** menu item. In my program, all the panels are ungrouped, but it's a matter of personal preference.

Find the **File | Publish Settings** menu item and leave the **Flash** checkbox checked on the **Formats** tab. Check the **HTML** checkbox to obtain the HTML file in addition to the clip with the game. On the **Flash** tab, set the **Version: Flash Player 6** to make our game visible for as many gamers as possible and leave the **Protect from import** and **Compress Movie** checkboxes in the **Options** group checked. The movie will be compressed when generating an SWF (Small Web Format) file. If you want to know the sizes of the clips and other objects in your movie, check the **Generate Size Report** checkbox. Set **Jpeg Quality** to 80%. Set the **Audio Stream** and **Audio Event** parameters as follows: **Compression** to MP3, **Bit Rate** to **16 KBPS**, and **Quality** to **Fast**. You will be able to edit these properties later individually for each imported sound. To do this, simply uncheck the **Override sound settings** checkbox. On the **HTML** tab, set **Template** to **Flash only**, and **Dimension** to **Match Movie**. Uncheck all checkboxes in the **Playback** group, uncheck the checkbox **Detect Flash Version**, and then click the **OK** button.

Now it is time to set the preferences. Select the **Edit | Preferences** menu. On the **General** tab, select **New document** in the drop-down list **On launch** (or any option you find the most convenient), and set **Undo Levels** to 100 or greater. This number determines how many undo commands you can execute if you do something wrong. Leave the **Shift Select** checkbox checked. Set **Highlight Color** to light blue or turquoise. On the **Drawing** tab, check the checkboxes in the **Pen Tool** group and set all settings to **Normal**. On the **Clipboard** tab, set **Color Depth** to **24 bit color**. Set **Resolution** to **Screen** and **Size limit** to 500 K. Uncheck the **Smooth** checkbox. Set **Gradient Quality** to **Best**. Check all of the checkboxes on the **Warnings** tab. On the **ActionScript** tab, select the **Courier New** font with a font size of 10, or, should you prefer, a font and font size you like best. You may set **Coloring**, **Foreground**, and **Background** according to your own preferences. In my copy of Flash, syntax coloring is disabled, the background is black, and the foreground is gray. Now click the **OK** button.

Now we have to set the movie properties in the **Document Properties** window. To open the window, use the <Ctrl>+<J> shortcut or double-click on the gray box that reads **12.0 fps** (located below the timeline). You can also open this window using the **Modify | Document** menu or the pop-up menu that opens when you right-click on an unused place inside the frame work area. The document properties should be found through experimentation. Set the movie size to 769 × 564 pixels (in the **Width** and **Height** input boxes). Set the **Frame Rate** to 19. Select the background color you prefer. As for me, I prefer black or dark gray, so that the **Lasso** tool is visible. Click the **OK** button.

NOTE

Pixels are the colored dots on the screen.

You need a grid that makes it easy to place objects on the screen precisely. Because you'll make pieces from squares with a size of 23 × 23 pixels, this will be the best grid spacing value. In the **View | Grid** menu, select **Show Grid**, and then the **Edit Grid** submenu. Select the color gray for the grid, uncheck the **Snapping | Snap to Grid** checkboxes, set the size at 23 × 23, and set **View | Grid | Edit Grid | Snap accuracy** to **Normal**.

In the **View| Preview mode** menu, check **Antialias Text** to improve the quality of view. Uncheck all the checkboxes except for **Snap to Pixels**. If you notice that an object being dragged "sticks" to other objects on the screen, this means that these checkboxes (and **Snap to Grid**) are checked.

Save your project in a file. To do this, select the **File | Save** menu or press the <Ctrl>+<S> shortcut, and select a folder and file name.

NOTE

If you want to save the panel layout so that it is the same when you start Flash the next time, select the **Window | Workspace Layout | Save Current**, and choose a name for this layout. You'll be able to restore this layout later by selecting the **Window | Workspace Layout** menu and selecting this layout's name.

Copy the jikharev.ttf font file to the FONTS subfolder in the WINDOWS folder from the accompanying CD-ROM. If this does not work, reboot Windows. Open this folder using the **My Computer** menu, so that Windows can install the new font.

This font is used in the project, but you may opt to use another.

2.2. Importing Graphics to Flash

You should now import the images of the pieces for your project. These are nine small BMP files located in the \Examples\Chapter 2 folder on the accompanying CD-ROM. Each file corresponds to one piece. You could create graphics using Flash editor, but these pieces are three-dimensional, and were created in 3D Studio.

To import graphics, use the **File | Import | Import to Stage** and **File | Import | Import to Library** menu commands. You need, however, to create *movie clips* based on the imported images. These are objects that can be animated and controlled with an ActionScript program. So, first, you should create an empty clip, and then import graphics to it. Clips stored in a library are called *symbols*, and *instances* can be created based on these. Instances with new properties can be created when a movie is created in Flash or dynamically. For the latter, ActionScript is used while the movie is running.

2.2.1. Graphics for Squares

To create a symbol from scratch, select the **Insert | New Symbol** menu item or press the <Ctrl>+<F8> shortcut. You can also do this by clicking a plus at the bottom of the **Library** window. The **Create New Symbol** window will then open. In this window, specify the symbol's **Name** and **Type**. Check the **Export for ActionScript** checkbox (by clicking the **Advanced** button) so that it is able to control the symbol from an ActionScript program, and specify its **Identifier**, which will be its name in the ActionScript program. In your project, the names of the symbols will be the same as their identifiers.

NOTE

If you draw an image for a symbol in the main scene, you can always convert this drawing to a symbol. To do this, select all its components, right-click on it (or press the <F8> key), and select the **Convert to Symbol** item in the pop-up menu. On the menu bar, an identical command is present in the **Insert** menu.

Enter k0 into the **Name** input box, specify the **Movie Clip** type, and check the **Export for ActionScript** checkbox. The **Export in first frame** checkbox will be checked automatically, and the name k0 will be copied to the **Identifier** input box. This is what we want.

After you click the **OK** button in the **Library** window (if you don't see this window on the screen, press the <F11> key), the icon for the k0 symbol will appear. It will also appear on the **Scene 1** panel located above the timeline. You can now edit the symbol in the work space or create a new symbol. You should see a cross at the center of the work space where the grid lines meet. This is the symbol's *registration point*. The symbol will be scaled, bent, and rotated about this point, and the coordinates of the point are considered to be the coordinates of the symbol. You can view the sizes and coordinates of the symbols in the **Info** window. To open it, select the **Window | Info** menu item, or press the <Ctrl>+<I> shortcut. The first frame of the **Layer 1** layer on the timeline should contain an empty circle, indicating that this *key frame* is empty. If you don't see the circle, you can get it by clicking the first frame in **Layer 1** and selecting **Insert | Timeline | Blank Keyframe**, or by pressing the <F7> key. You need this frame so that you can import an external image to it.

Select the **File | Import | Import to Stage** menu item or press the <Ctrl>+<R> shortcut. In the **Import** dialog box that opens, select the \Examples\Chapter 2 folder, and open the k0.bmp file. Flash will "notice" that a few BMP files have similar names, but differ only in the associated number, and will suggest that you import all of these files to sequential frames of the symbol. Click the **No** button.

After importing, you'll see that the library contains a new object, of the bitmap type and named k0.bmp. It is related to the k0 symbol. Your screen should look like the example in Fig. 2.1.

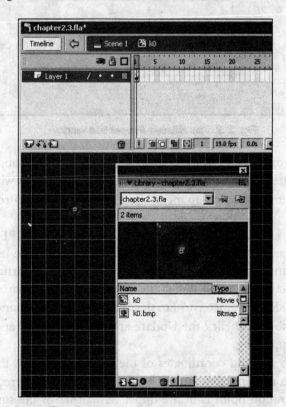

Fig. 2.1. Importing the graphics

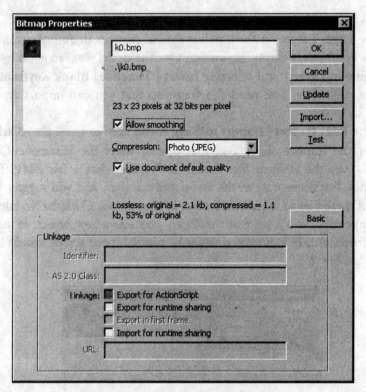

Fig. 2.2. The **Bitmap Properties** window

Double-click on the icon of a green tree next to the k0.bmp object in the library to see its properties. Alternatively, you could right-click in the window and select the **Properties** item in the pop-up menu. You'll see the **Bitmap Properties** window shown in Fig. 2.2.

You will now see that the k0.bmp file was imported in the JPEG format that is used for photos and scanned pictures. This format will also be used in this project for background images. It is compressed well, but distortions can appear. Because your picture is small and it should not appear distorted in the game, set the **Compression** parameter to **Lossless (PNG/GIF)**. Then uncheck the **Allow smoothing** checkbox and click the **Update** and **OK** buttons to apply the new settings for image importing.

You'll see the size and coordinates of the selected object in the **Info** window. In addition to correcting the square height, you should correct its cordinates so that the registration point is in the upper left corner of the square. You could, of course, drag the object with the mouse and watch the coordinates. However, it is much more convenient to enter zero in the **X** and **Y** in the **Info** window or in the **Properties** window activated by the hotkey combination <Ctrl>+<F3>.

NOTE

You can move selected objects precisely using the arrow keys. With the zoom level set to 100%, the movement step is one pixel.

Note that the circle in the first frame in the **Layer 1** timeline layer is now colored. This indicates that the key frame is no longer empty.

So you have now imported one square out of nine. To be able to edit the scene, click the **Scene 1** name. If there are several scenes in a movie, you can select the desired one by clicking the **Edit Scene** button to the left of the drop-down list of zoom levels.

Import the other eight images from the k1.bmp, ..., k8.bmp files in a similar way, and name them from k1 to k8. Do this as an exercise and take a break. Do not forget about the checkbox **Export for ActionScript** and about the registration point coordinates, otherwise your game will go weird! Also, do not forget to set the **Lossless (PNG/GIF)** import option and click the **Update button** every time. To change the properties of the clip, right-click its icon in the library window. If you are an experienced reader of computer books, you might have found the chapter2.2.fla file in the \Examples\Chapter 2 folder. In this case, don't take a break, and read further instead.

NOTE

If you imported a non-rectangular image, you will have to delete its background. This can be done by breaking the image apart using the **Modify | Break Apart** command (or pressing the <Ctrl>+<B> shortcut) so that you can edit the imported image. You should then use the **Lasso** tool to select background fragments and delete them with the <Del> key. You might need to increase the zoom level for the sake of convenience. To select background fragments of similar colors, you can use the **Lasso Magic Wand** tool's properties in the **Options** panel.

You should now arrange the objects in the library. Flash allows you to create folders, which is only logical, since objects in different folders cannot have the same names.

To create a new folder, click on the small yellow folder icon at the bottom of the **Library** window, and give a name to the newly-created folder — Images, for example. This folder will contain all of the objects related to import graphics (they have the "green tree" icon). Select all nine objects by clicking them while keeping the <Ctrl> key pressed, then grab one of them with the mouse, and drag them onto the icon for the created folder. Create a Squares folder in a similar way, and drag all of the squares onto it. It will be convenient to select the squares as follows: Click the k0 symbol to select it, and then click the k8 symbol while keeping the <Shift> key pressed to select the entire row. You have probably already guessed that you can open and close folders with double clicks.

2.2.2. Graphics for the Background

Now you should create background graphics for the game. The background will consist of two game pits and a panel with buttons and displays for the score, number of pieces, and so on. The game pits are contained in the bkgr1.bmp file, while the panel is contained in the panel1.bmp file.

Create a new clip named bkgr1. Don't check the **Export for ActionScript** checkbox, because you won't control the background from ActionScript code. You may set the **Type** parameter to **Graphic,** but this isn't a must: You can change an object's behavior whenever you like. Then import the image from the bkgr1.bmp file to the bkgr1 symbol. The JPEG format is best in this case because the image is dark. Set the origin of coordinates for this symbol to its upper left corner, in the same way as with the squares. Repeat the procedure for a new symbol with the panel1 name, and import the picture from the panel1.bmp file to the symbol. Everything is now ready for work with the editor tools to create the background for the game.

2.3. Creating Clips Using Flash Tools

Because the two game pits should be identical, it makes sense to create a symbol for one pit and then duplicate it. Jumping ahead, I'll tell you that the game pits will be 12 squares wide and 24 squares high. Therefore, you'll need to create two copies of the bkgr1.bmp picture placed horizontally and seven copies of it placed vertically.

2.3.1. Creating the Background for the Game Pits

Create an empty symbol and name it pit. Then grab the bkgr1 symbol in the library window (you can do this by clicking on its icon or on the preview window) and drag it to the work area. In the **Info** <Ctrl>+<I> or **Properties** <Ctrl>+<F3>

window, set its coordinates to 1 and 0. Then duplicate this instance in the work space until you obtain the background suitable for the pit. To drag the objects, use the **Arrow** tool, which is active by default when you start the application. Press the <Ctrl> key and keep it pressed while dragging the background instance down. You should obtain a picture similar to that shown in Fig. 2.3.

Because the element is 79 pixels high, you should set the coordinates of the new symbol to 1 and 79, so that it is adjacent to the upper symbol. Select both instances by clicking the unselected one while keeping the <Shift> key pressed. A rectangle will appear around them. Press the <Ctrl> key, and keep it pressed while dragging the instances downwards. Set their coordinates to 1 and 158, so that they are adjacent to the existing ones. Duplicate the three bottom elements of the background in a similar way, and set their coordinates to 1 and 316. The left part of the background for the pit is now ready. To create the right part, select everything you have on the work space (by pressing the <Ctrl>+<A> shortcut), and duplicate it by dragging it to the right. Set the coordinates of the new group to 139 and 0. If something goes wrong, undo your actions using the <Ctrl>+<Z> shortcut.

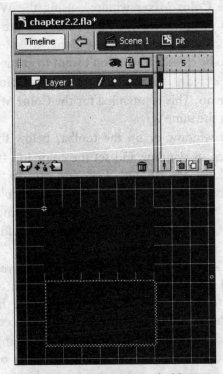

Fig. 2.3. Duplicating a symbol instance

NOTE

It may happen that there will be gaps between elements. In such a case, check the coordinates for each background instance and correct them. After you finish a stage of your project, save it on the disk. To revert to the saved file, use the **File | Revert** command.

You should obtain the 278 × 553-pixel background for the pit. However, you might have noticed that 23 × 12 is equal to 276, and 23 × 24 is equal to 552. This isn't a mistake. I intentionally selected the size of the bkgr1.bmp file with "extra" pixels at the sides and at the bottom to prevent the pieces from touching the borders of the pits. As for the borders, you are about to create them. To unselect, click an unused place in the editor work area or press the <Ctrl>+<Shift>+<A> shortcut.

2.3.2. Creating Pit Borders

Create a vertical strip of 6 × 559 pixels. This will be the side border. To choose a color for it, open the **Color Mixer** window, using the **Window** menu or the <Shift>+<F9> shortcut. If unwanted panels appear, you can close them by right-clicking on their captions and selecting **Close Panel** for the name of the corresponding panel that is to be closed. If you don't want to group the panels with each other, right-click the selected panel and choose **Group Color Mixer with | New Group** in the context menu. This is intended for the **Color Mixer** panel, but other panels are ungrouped in the same way.

In the **Color Mixer** window or on the toolbar below the **Colors** label, find the **Fill Color** tool. Open its window and set the color to #996600 (you can omit the # character) by clicking the <Enter> key. You can do this by specifying the hexadecimal value for the color or by selecting the desired color in the palette with the dropper. Then select the **Rectangle** tool, and draw a rectangle six pixels wide on an unused portion of the work area. The corner radius should be zero. You can set this parameter on the toolbar in the **Options** panel.

You might be wondering whether the border for this rectangle is necessary. In fact, it isn't — so delete it. In Flash, outlines and fills are different objects, even when they belong to the same instance. What's more, the outline consists of individual line segments. You will notice this if you select the fill and lines by clicking on them individually with the **Arrow** tool. When an image of an arc appears next to the mouse pointer, you can select the entire outline. Double-click on one of its segments, and press <Del> to delete the outline. Note that you could create a rectangle only with the fill without an outline (or, conversely, only an outline without fill). To do this, you should have clicked the **Stroke Color** tool, and then clicked the crossed white rectangle in the window that opened. Also note that identical **No Color** buttons are available on the **Tools** panel and in the **Color Mixer** window.

Now, create gradient fill as if the rectangle is illuminated from the left. Unselect all selected objects (if you haven't already done this), and select the **Linear** filling in the **Color Mixer** window. The default gradient is from black to white, so you'll need to select the color again. There are two sliders, for the light and dark gradient, under the horizontal bar indicating the gradient. Click on the left slider to select it. Then click the input box with the down arrow, and select or type in the #FF9900 color value. On the **Tools** panel, select the **Paint Bucket** tool and click the rectangle with this tool. If nothing happens, you will notice a lock next to the bucket cursor. Unlock this by releasing the **Lock Fill** button at the bottom of the **Tool** panel. Perhaps, the developers of Flash provided the lock to prevent the user from using the fill accidentally when an object is selected.

Set the filled rectangle's width and height to 6 and 559 pixels, respectively, and set its coordinates to –5 and 0. Actually, I obtained darker colors, #A0875F and #695B3E, in my project. Select the object and set the fill sliders to these color values.

You can scale and rotate the gradient fill using the **Gradient Transform** tool.

NOTE

Duplicate the selected strip using the <Ctrl>+<D> shortcut or the mouse, like in the previous section. Move the second instance to the right side of the pit, so that its coordinates are 279 and 0.

It is convenient to make the bottom border from the side border by rotating the latter through 90 degrees. To do this, duplicate the side-border strip, select the copy, and select the **Modify | Transform | Rotate 90° CW** command in the menu, or press the <Ctrl>+<Shift>+<9> shortcut.

If a selected object overlaps with other objects on the work space, drag it to an unused place before unselecting it to avoid spoiling those objects.

NOTE

Now you just need to set the horizontal strip's width to 278 pixels and its coordinates to 1 and 553. We should be pretty happy with the result! The pit is almost finished. To complete it, draw vertical guidelines so that the gamer can see where the current piece will "land". The pit is deep enough, and the guidelines are necessary.

2.3.3. Creating Guidelines for the Pieces

For the sake of convenience, create the guidelines on a separate layer above the pit's layer — **Layer 1**. I'll describe the use of layers later in the book. For now, you need another layer in the pit symbol to prevent the guidelines from crossing the pit background. If they do, it will be very difficult to edit the background should you wish to change it later.

To create a new layer, click the **Insert Layer** button in the lower left corner of the **Timeline** panel. Alternatively, you can execute the **Insert | Timeline | Layer** command. The **Layer 2** layer will appear above **Layer 1**. In order to draw on it, make it active. You can protect **Layer 1** from editing by clicking the circle located below the lock. A lock will appear, instead of the circle, in the layer's caption, as shown in Fig. 2.4.

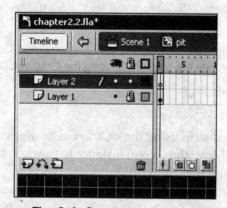

Fig. 2.4. Creating a new layer

First, open the properties of the current object using the <Ctrl>+<F3> shortcut. Then select the **Line** tool, and set the **Stroke Color** parameter to #606060. Unlike the fill color, it is set in the input box labeled with a pencil icon located under the **Colors** word on the **Tools** panel. On the properties panel, select the **Hairline** line type. This is a line one-pixel thick, regardless of the zoom level. While watching the **Info** panel, move the mouse pointer to the point with the coordinates 24 and 0, and draw a vertical line. It should be 552-pixel long, but you won't be able to fit it on the screen. Don't worry, because you can always set the line to the desired length. You should then copy the line and place copies of it at the coordinates (47, 0), ..., (254, 0). Remember that you can duplicate a number of instances simultaneously. The game pit is now finished.

Return to the main scene, drag the `pit` clip to the working area, and set its coordinates to 3 and 3. The upper left corner of the clip will move to that point. Set the coordinates of the second pit to 315 and 3. Place two instances of the `panel1` clip to the right of the pits, and set the coordinates of one instance to 605 and 3, and to 605 and 283 for the other. The result is in the chapter2.3.fla file on the accompanying CD-ROM.

2.4. Creating Button Clips

Create three buttons — **New**, **Sound**, and **Pause** — so that the gamer can quit the game and start a new one, turn the sound on and off, or pause (to go grab a coffee). Flash offers its users a symbol of the **Button** type. However, your buttons are going to be rather complicated, so it is best to use clips.

The buttons will be based on the same objects, and differ only with regard to their labels. This is why we create a base for them first. Press the `<Ctrl>+<F8>` shortcut to create a new clip. (Make sure to return from editing a clip to the main scene before doing so). Name the new clip `btNew`. Don't set the other parameters. In the clip, create two more layers — **Layer 2** and **Layer 3** — so that **Layer 2** is below **Layer 1**, and **Layer 3** is below **Layer 2**. You can move the layers by grabbing their captions and dragging. Rename the **Layer 1** layer to **Actions**. To do this, double-click on its name or open its pop-up menu and select the **Properties** item.

NOTE

The names of layers are just strings of letters and spaces. They don't affect anything.

Your buttons will have two states: active and inactive, depending on whether the mouse pointer is over a button. Therefore, the timeline will have two frames with two different images.

Move **Layer 3**, press the <Ctrl>+<F3> shortcut to open the properties window, and select the **Rectangle** tool. In the **Options** group, set the **Corner Radius** parameter to 7 pixels, set the stroke color to #D4D0C8, and disable filling. In the properties window, select the **Solid** stroke and a thickness of 1.5 pixels. Draw a rectangle with a size of approximately 60 × 24 pixels. Select the rectangle by right-clicking on it with the **Arrow** tool, and enter the size precisely in the **Info** panel. In the **Color Mixer** window, select the **Radial** fill, set the left color slider (marker) value to #9A8F7E, and the right color slider value to #585147. Click the center of the rectangle with the **Bucket** tool to fill the rectangle.

I'm afraid that I now have to ask you to jump to the next section and read how to create text on buttons. Once you have done this and returned here, create the **New** label on the lowest layer. Select any font you like, and set its color to #DDD7D0. Move to **Layer 2** and draw a Solid line one pixel thick under the "N" letter. The gamer will know that he or she can press the <N> key rather than click the button. Your button should look like the one shown in Fig. 2.5.

Jumping ahead again, I suggest that you enter some ActionScript code in the first frame of the **Actions** layer. Click this frame and press the <F9> key to open the ActionScript editor window. Move the left part of the window as far to the left as possible so that the editing area takes up the entire window. In the editor, type in the following line:

```
stop();
```

Fig. 2.5. Creating a button clip (size doubled)

Close the window. You'll see the letter "a" in the first frame of the **ActionScript** layer. This indicates that ActionScript code is assigned to the frame. The `stop()` function will stop the playback of this clip to display its first frame. Switching between the frames will be controlled by the main program, depending on whether the mouse pointer is over the button. You need the second frame, in which the button, its label, and the underline will have the `#FFFFFF` color. In other words, they will be highlighted. Click the second frame on **Layer 3** and insert the keyframe using the <F6> key or the **Insert | Timeline | Keyframe** menu command. Do the same for **Layer 2**. Notice that the contents of the first frame of these layers were copied to the second frame. In the second frame of the **Actions** layer, click <F5> to insert an empty frame.

Enter the second frame of **Layer 3**, unselect all, and double-click on the outline of the button to select it. Using the **Stroke Color** tool, make this outline white. Process the underlining strokes on **Layer 2** in the same way. Return to the second frame of **Layer 3**, select the text by double-clicking on it with the **Arrow** tool (or with the **Text** tool), and make it white. The button is now finished. When the gamer moves the mouse pointer over it, the second frame will be displayed programmatically and the button will become highlighted. When the mouse pointer leaves the button, the first frame will be displayed. You can check this by grabbing the pink box above the timeline that marks the current animation frame and moving the box to the left and right. Now we can proceed with the main scene.

It is easy to create the other two button clips. In the library window, right-click on the **btNew** icon and select **Duplicate**. Give the new instance the name `btPause`. Do the same for the `btSound` button. Edit the labels (**Pause** and **Sound**) on the new buttons. Their first letters are also underlined. Create an indicator for these buttons that will follow the label to show their current state (whether the pause mode and the sound are on or off). This indicator will be a clip named `check`. You could obtain the same effect by creating new frames for these buttons. You can see the clip in Fig. 2.6. I set its coordinates so that it is placed right next to the **Sound** and **Pause** labels on the buttons. You can do this by drawing a check in a new layer for one of the buttons, copying it to the clipboard (<Ctrl>+<C> shortcut), and pasting it to the same coordinates in a new clip with the **Edit | Paste in Place** menu command or the <Ctrl>+<Shift>+<V> shortcut.

Create a new clip using the <Ctrl>+<F8> shortcut and name it `check`. It doesn't need an identifier. The check is similar to the underline on a button: It also has two frames, and has the same colors, but its line is thicker. In the ActionScript editor, enter the following line into the first frame:

```
stop();
```

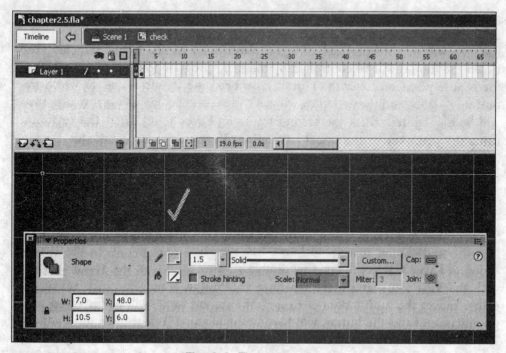

Fig. 2.6. The check clip

You can see this magnified four times in Fig. 2.6. By the way, in some cases Flash doesn't zoom in on a picture, but zooms out from the image of the grid. Don't worry, c'est la vie.

Insert the check clip into the btSound and btPause buttons. In the btPause clip, select the first frame in **Layer 2**, drag the check clip from the library onto the button, and set its coordinates in the **Info** window to the same values used when creating the clip (Fig. 2.6). These are 48 and 6. Repeat the procedure in the second frame. Do the same for the btSound button. To highlight the check, give it the name "s" in the btSound and btPause clips. You should specify it in the **Instance Name** input box in the properties window, which is opened using the <Ctrl>+<F3> shortcut. Click the check to select it, and specify its name in both symbols. Make sure the name is specified in both frames.

Note that the check clip isn't highlighted in the second frames of the buttons. This is natural, because this clip uses its own timeline.

Before a new game starts, a panel for game speed selection should be displayed. It will contain ten button clips with speed values from zero to ten. The gamer will be able to select the speed using the mouse or an appropriate key. He or she will be able to move among the buttons using the arrow keys. The button, on which the focus is at present, will be highlighted. We will now create this button.

Create a new symbol, and name it speedval. Check the **Export for ActionScript** checkbox (the speedval name will appear in the **Identifier** input box). Select the #FFFF00 fill color and draw a rectangle of the size 23 × 23 pixels, without an outline, with a small corner radius (e.g., 3), and with the coordinates origin in the upper left corner. Create **Layer 2** above **Layer 1** and the **Actions** layer above **Layer 2**. In **Layer 1**, create the second keyframe. In the frame, set the #FFFFD5 highlight color for the rectangle. In **Layer 2**, create a text field that will be used in ActionScript code for displaying the speed value for each instance of the speedval button clip. This text field should have the **Dynamic Text** type with the **_sans** font, 16-pt font size, and the black color. Create this and enter "9" into it. Click on the **Align Center** button in the properties panel (<Ctrl>+<F3>). The digit should be centered on the button. Delete the digit so that an empty field is left. You'll need to enter some text in the field, as it should have a name, so type "t" in the **Var:** input box. Move to the second frame of **Layer 2** and press the <F5> key to create a new frame. It should contain an identical text field. In the **Actions** layer, assign the following action to the first frame:

```
stop();
```

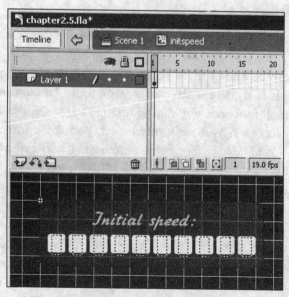

Fig. 2.7. The initial speed selection panel

Create a panel for speed selection based on this button. This will be a clip named `initspeed`, with the same identifier, so that you can control it with ActionScript code. The clip will be a semitransparent rectangle with rounded corners. To draw this rectangle, select the `#FF0000` stroke color value. In the **Color Mixer** window, set the **Alpha:** parameter to 70%. This is the transparency level (to be more precise, this is non-transparency). Select the `#996600` color value for both the fill and the alpha. Type the static text `Initial Speed:` with the `#FFCC00` color value and include ten `speedval` clips, by duplicating their instances from the library (Fig. 2.7).

Important: To enable access to each instance of the `speedval` button, you will have to assign names to them. Names are given to instances in the properties panel opened using the <Ctrl>+<F3> shortcut. Here you will find the **Instance Name** input box below the **Movie Clip** parameter. Select the leftmost button and name it `d0`. Name the next button `d1`, and so on through to `d9`.

Compare your results with the chapter2.4.fla project. In Flash, you can open several projects simultaneously and move objects between them using the drag-and-drop method or the clipboard.

2.5. Creating Text

Create a few text labels on the panel. These should be the following: `Speed`, `Score`, `Pieces`, and `Lines`.

In Flash, text can be one of three types: *static*, *dynamic*, and *input*. Static text isn't changed, and it is usually written in a large font. *Antialiasing* is applied to this text. With a small font size, antialiased text isn't readable, so it is best to use dynamic text in such cases, as it isn't antialiased. You can control dynamic text using a program. Input text is free from antialiasing and can also be accessed programmatically.

A font or some of its characters used in a movie can be included in the resulting SWF file, so that the user sees exactly the same text as the developer. When **Device Fonts** are used, in order to make it smaller, they aren't included in the resulting file. In this case, the same (or similar) fonts are selected from those installed on the user's computer. Flash uses three built-in fonts with names beginning with the underline character: **_sans** (Arial-like), **_serif** (Times-like), and **_typewriter** (Courier-like).

Flash allows you to rotate and scale the text without affecting its properties: You can continue editing it. In addition, you can break text into individual characters (using the **Modify | Break Apart** menu command or the <Ctrl>+<B> shortcut) and assign each character individual attributes (e.g., font, color, etc.). The next time you press the <Ctrl>+<B> shortcut, the characters become graphic objects. You can edit them using graphic tools, but they are no longer text elements.

To create text, use the **Text** tool, which is a button labeled A. There is a **Text** menu for selecting the font, size, and other attributes (I have never used it).

You can type text in the same layer as the background, but I recommend that you create another layer above **Layer 1**. Just click the **Insert Layer** button. Then click the **A** button on the **Tools** panel (the mouse pointer will take the shape of a cross next to a letter "A"), and click on the top part of the panel (Fig. 2.8).

An input box with a circle in the upper right corner should appear. This input box is for static-type text. The circle means that the width of the text field will change as the text length changes. If you grab the circle and specify a text size, the circle will turn into a square, indicating that the width of the text field is constant.

Dynamic and input-type text fields have squares in the lower right corner. Their widths cannot be changed.

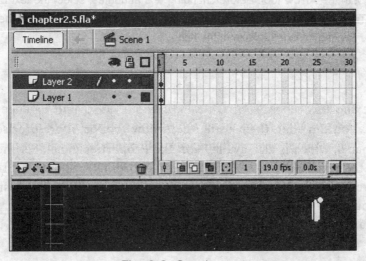

Fig. 2.8. Creating text

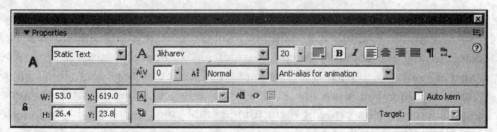

Fig. 2.9. Text attributes

To work with text, open the appropriate window using the **Window | Properties** menu command or the <Ctrl>+<F3> shortcut. Select a font, such as Arial. This, however, isn't the best font for games, and you can install a more appropriate font, such as Jikharev, on your computer. Set the font size to 20 pt and select the **bold** font style and the #B59B84 color. In addition, the text should be of the static type and be left-aligned (Fig. 2.9).

Type the word Speed in the newly-created field.

NOTE

To be able to edit text, click the text field with the **Text** tool or double-click on this field with the **Arrow** tool. Before changing text attributes, select the text by dragging the **Text** tool over it. Using the box or the circle in the upper right corner of a text field, you can change the size of the text.

Create the text labels Score, Pieces, and Lines, and arrange them in a column. You can align them using the **Arrow** tool or, more precisely, using the **Info** panel, which is also available in the **Properties** panel. Set the X coordinate of the text fields to 612, while the Y coordinates should be 14, 49, 84, and 119, respectively. You can set the X coordinates to all the labels simultaneously if you select them.

Compare your work with the chapter2.5.fla project.

2.6. Creating Buttons

Like in any interactive program, buttons are required to allow the user to select, confirm, or cancel certain actions. Starting from the Flash MX version, clips are generalizations of buttons. In other words, you can create a clip that behaves exactly like a button. However, it is easier and more convenient to create buttons, because they have built-in responses to mouse clicks and moves of the mouse pointer over them.

The timeline of a button consists of four frames: **Up** (the initial state of the button), **Over** (when the mouse pointer is over the button), **Down** (when the button is pressed down during a click on it), and **Hit** (the button's active area). A few words are in order concerning the last item: The active area is one where the button's action is triggered when this area is clicked. It doesn't need to coincide with the button, and it is drawn using the **Rectangle** tool.

Create the btPlay button that will start the game. Press the <Ctrl>+<F8> shortcut, and select the **Button** behavior and **Export for ActionScript** with the same name. The button should look like the one shown in Fig. 2.10.

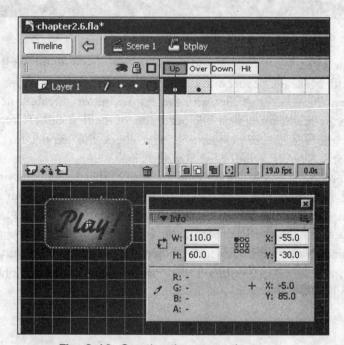

Fig. 2.10. Creating the btPlay button

Fig. 2.11. The menu clip

Press the <F6> key in the second frame to copy the contents of the first frame to the second. Make the border and the text a bit lighter.

Based on the initspeed clips and the btPlay button, create a new clip: menu. This will be the menu available at the beginning of the first game. Create a clip with the menu name and the same identifier and check the **Export for ActionScript** checkbox for it. The clip window is shown in Fig. 2.11.

You should then give a name to the instance of the initspeed symbol in order to access the buttons, and then assign them the speed values from zero to nine. In addition, you should assign an appropriate action to the btPlay button to start the game. Make the instance of the initspeed symbol active and enter is in the **Instance Name** input box in the object properties panel. Right-click on the btPlay button and select **Actions** in the pop-up menu. In the ActionScript editor, enter the following code:

```
on (release)
{ _root.startGame();
}
```

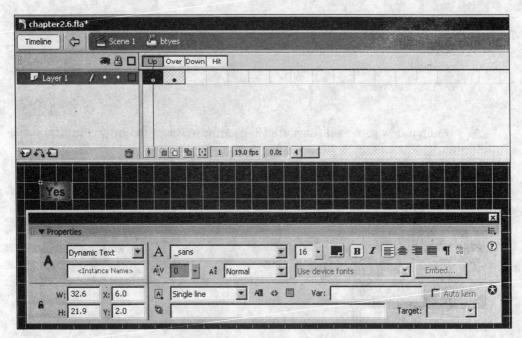

Fig. 2.12. The btYes button

The startGame() function will be defined in the name program. Here, it is called when the gamer releases the mouse button after clicking on the btPlay button. Close the code editor window.

Now, you need only to create the **Game Over!** panel that will appear at the end of the game. You'll be able to create a few remaining small clips later, as necessary.

Create the **Yes!** button for the panel so that the gamer can play again. This button is similar to btPlay, but its size is 45×25 pixels. Name the button btYes, and don't check the **Export for ActionScript** checkbox. The button is shown in Fig. 2.12.

Create the **Game Over!** panel, which should be similar to the menu panel. Start a new clip and set its name and identifier to gover. Drag the initspeed clip to the newly-created clip and draw a rectangle in the same way as for the initspeed clip. Drag the btYes button into the rectangle. Create a new layer above **Layer 1** and write Game over! and Play again? on this layer. Give the instance of the initspeed symbol the is name in the properties panel. Select the instance of the btYes button, open the code editor window using the <F9> key, and enter the following code:

```
on (release)
{ _root.startGame();
}
```

As a result, a new game will start after the gamer releases the mouse button on this button. The gover clip is shown in Fig. 2.13.

Compare your results with the chapter2.6.fla project.

Now that you have learned how to create clips and buttons with a single mouse movement, it's time to study animation.

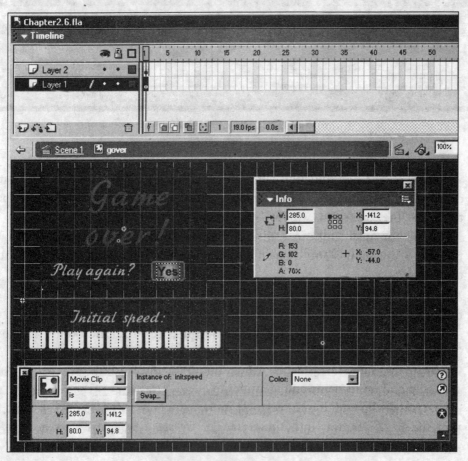

Fig. 2.13. The gover clip

Chapter 3: Creating Animation

In this chapter, you'll get acquainted with timelines, layers, and frames in Flash, and learn how to create animations of shape and motion.

3.1. Flash Timeline

In Flash, *timeline* is a convenient way of working with the frames that make up a movie. The frames are numbered, starting with 1, which allows the animator to view and edit the contents of individual frames. Each clip has a timeline similar to the timeline for the entire movie. When the clip is displayed, its timeline is synchronized with the timeline of the movie. The frame rate (**19.0 fps** in this project) is the same for the movie and all its objects, and you cannot change the rate once you have begun work on your movie. For this reason, you should choose a rate that will allow the quickest movement in your movie to be displayed smoothly. You should balance this concern against the fact that the higher the frame rate, the higher the load will be on the processor, which has to compute the next frame while the present one is being viewed. If it can't manage this in time, certain frames will be skipped and the playback will be jerky. The same is true for the sound.

The timeline is set using a button located in the upper right part of the timeline. It allows you to preview objects in the frames, but this isn't really necessary for your purposes, so the standard view of the timeline will do here.

3.2. Layers and Key Frames

Creating a movie in Flash is somewhat like creating an animated cartoon. Animators draw intermediate postures for characters on transparent plates. The plates are then stacked up to obtain a movie frame. The more talented animators usually draw key frames, while less talented animators draw "tween" frames.

Objects in the upper layers cover those in the lower layers. In Flash, a clip or a button can hold clips or buttons inside it (a button inside another button, however, hardly makes any sense). This is why a movie layer containing a compound clip of this type is divided into sub-layers. In addition, you can create clips programmatically and transfer them from the library to the work space. When doing so, you should assign the new clip a layer number in the form of an integer. All objects created programmatically are placed above those objects created with the editor. One layer can contain only one animated object or group of objects. (However, several instants of the objects can be animated in one layer, those placed on this layer during the development.) Objects created programmatically can be removed programmatically. To remove objects created with the editor, insert a blank key frame on their layer (using the **Insert | Timeline | Blank keyframe** command or the <F7> key). However, when frames containing an object on the parent timeline are exhausted, the object ceases to exist.

In Flash, you can create guide and mask layers. *Guide layers* are used to guide the motion of an object on the underlying layer. To do this, the animator draws the object's trajectory on the guide layer. An object in a *mask layer* is something like a hole, through which the objects on the underlying layers can be seen (these layers are "masked"). Flash offers you a feature that allows you to make clip masks programmatically. This feature, however, isn't necessary for the project at hand. If you are interested in this feature, you should study the examples that came with your copy of Flash.

As you already know, key frames are marked with a circle. You change the contents of the layer in a key frame, using the development environment tools, and Flash player then computes the contents of tween frames. The "tween" frames aren't stored in the movie file, which is why SWF files are relatively small. (In addition, this is a vector graphic.)

Just as in Adobe PhotoShop, you can hide layers and prevent them from being edited. An eye icon and a lock icon are used for this purpose. There is a square box to the right of the lock icon that allows you to display only the outlines of the objects on the layers. What's more, the outlines on different layers can be given different colors. If you click on one of these icons on a layer while keeping the <Alt> key pressed, the property corresponding to the icon will became active in all the layers except this one.

You already know how to create and drag layers. To delete a layer, use its pop-up menu or drag the layer to the recycling bin located at the right side of the layer-creation panel.

3.3. Creating Animation Effects

In Flash, you can animate an object's position, angle of rotation, size, distortion, color, transparency level, and shape. You can transform one object smoothly into another. In the game you're creating, the animation will involve the following: The squares in the filled lines will disappear, the "value" of a new pair of pieces will be displayed before the pair appears, and lightning will destroy the filled lines.

3.3.1. The Motion Tween Animation

Let's start with the squares that are already contained in the library in the appropriate folder. Double-click on the k0 square so that you can edit it. Set the zoom level to 400%. As I pointed out earlier, the squares are going to break into halves that will rotate, grow smaller, fly away, and then disappear.

First, create three layers above **Layer 1** (from the bottom up): **Layer 2** and **Layer 3** for the animation of the halves, and **Actions** to use a program to control the animation. Nothing should happen from the first to the third frames. A square instance is only waiting for a command from the main program to start animation. If you do not set it up this way, all of the squares will explode simultaneously and damage the screen. In **Layer 1**, enter the third frame and press the <F5> key to create a common frame. There will be no more frames in this layer, so the square will cease to exist beginning at the fourth frame. It will be replaced with fragments flying away. Then, copy the contents of the first frame of **Layer 1** to the fourth frame of **Layer 2**. To do this, select only the first frame of **Layer 1**, right-click on it, and select the **Copy Frames** item in the pop-up menu. Right-click on the fourth frame of **Layer 2**, and select the **Paste Frames** item. As a result, this frame will receive the same square and become a key frame. It is a good idea now to zoom in four times on the fourth frame.

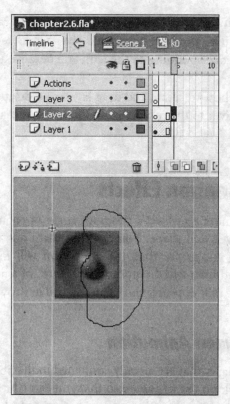

Fig. 3.1. Breaking a square apart

Currently, the imported images are indivisible objects that cannot be edited partially. In order to edit a square's fragments, you need to convert the square into a bitmap by selecting it and executing the **Modify | Break Apart** command (or the <Ctrl>+<B> shortcut). The square will be covered by a white grid. Select the **Lasso** tool, unselect the square, and draw a rugged line dividing it into two parts, as shown in Fig. 3.1 (the background on the figure is gray so that the line is visible).

When you release the mouse button, the right part of the square will be selected. Use the **Arrow** tool to move the halves of the square apart and upward (Fig. 3.2). (If the object moves unevenly during dragging, uncheck the **View | Snapping** checkbox in the menu.) You have now created the first frame of the exploding square.

Now, move one half of the square to **Layer 3**, as each half will rotate in its own way. To do this, select the right fragment by clicking on it, select the **Edit | Cut** command (or press the <Ctrl>+<X> shortcut), click the fourth frame of **Layer 3**, press the <F6> key to put a key frame there, and select the **Edit | Paste in Place** command (or press the <Ctrl>+<Shift>+<V> shortcut). You shouldn't use the **Paste** command or the <Ctrl>+<V> shortcut in this case, because you need to place the object at the same coordinates that it had in the **Layer 2** layer. Then look at the properties of these two fragments in the properties window, which is opened with the <Ctrl>+<F3> shortcut. You will see that the fragments are now called **Shape**. When you broke the square into two parts in **Layer 2**, its connection to its parent symbol, k0, was broken, so the square became a shape. Unfortunately, shapes cannot be animated for movement or rotation, so you need to convert them to clips. To do this, right-click on the left fragment, select the **Convert to Symbol** command, and give the fragment the name k01 and **Movie Clip** behavior. A new symbol with the same name will appear in the library. Drag it to the Squares folder. Carry out the same procedure for the right fragment, and name it k0r.

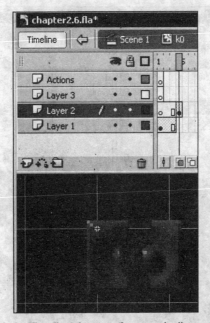

Fig. 3.2. The first frame of an exploding square

NOTE You could try to create animation without converting the shapes to clips, and Flash would convert them on its own. It would create symbols in the library and name them Tween1, Tween2, and so on. It will be more difficult, however, to create proper animation in this case.

Now click on the tenth frame of **Layer 2**, and press the <F6> key. A key frame will appear. It will be a copy of the fourth frame, and the frames from the fifth to the tenth will have a gray background, indicating that there are no changes between the two key frames. In the tenth frame, move the left fragment up and to the left, so that its center is approximately one grid cell to the left and two cells above the upper left corner of the original square. Execute the **Modify | Transform | Scale and Rotate** command on this fragment (you can use the <Ctrl>+<Alt>+<S> shortcut). In the window that will appear, set the scale to 40%, and rotation to 179 degrees. After you confirm this transform, the object will become 2.5 times smaller and rotate a half-turn. Select the fourth frame, right-click on it, and select the **Create Motion Tween** command in the pop-up menu. An arrow connecting the fourth and the tenth frame will appear against a blue background (Fig. 3.3).

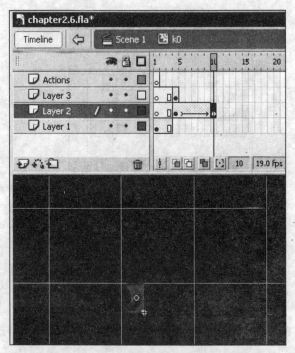

Fig. 3.3. Creating the **Motion Tween** animation

You can grab the pink rectangle above the timeline and move it to watch frame-by-frame animation. If you select the fourth frame and open its properties window using the <Ctrl>+<F3> shortcut, you'll see the properties of the newly-created animation. Using the **Ease** parameter, you can control the speed at the beginning and end of the motion, while the **Rotate** parameter allows you to specify the rotation direction and number of turns.

Process the right fragment in a similar way. Set its rotation angle to −179 degrees, so that it rotates counterclockwise.

You can speed up your work by creating the tenth key frames in both layers simultaneously, by pressing the <F6> key, but first be sure to select both tenth frames using the <Shift> key. What's more, you can create animation in both layers simultaneously. To do this, select both fourth frames and right-click on one of them. If you make a mistake when creating animation, you can simply create it again. First, you should remove it, using the **Remove Tween** item in the frame pop-up menu.

If you don't remember the procedure for creating the **Motion Tween** animation, you can get a little more practice by carrying it out for each of the other eight squares. After doing this, you should be able to create the animation with your eyes closed (or at least screwed tight). For the other squares, try to move their halves apart a bit differently than for the k0 square, to avoid uniformity. You will need to put some code onto the **Actions** layer, but I decided to postpone this to a later chapter to avoid confusion. Now you're ready to animate digits that show the score, the number of pieces, and the number of filled lines.

3.3.2. The Shape Tween *Animation*

First, create ten consecutively numbered clips. Use the same font as for the **Speed**, **Score**, **Pieces**, and **Lines** labels, that is, **Arial**, with a font size of 20 pt and the #B59E84 color. Press <Ctrl>+<F8> shortcut, name the clip d0, and check the **Export for ActionScript** checkbox. Then, select the **Text** tool and the appropriate font and color, and type the following static text: 0123456789. Press the <Ctrl>+<B> shortcut twice, and the text will first break into individual characters, and then into shapes. Unselect the digits, right-click on "1", and select the **Convert to Symbol** item in the pop-up menu. Name the symbol d1, and check the **Export for ActionScript** checkbox. The registration point should be at the center of the symbol. Convert the other digits to symbols in a similar way. In the d0 symbol, select the unnecessary digits from one to nine by clicking on them while keeping the <Shift> key pressed, and delete them using the <Del> key. You need to align the zero. To do this, select the **Modify| Align| Vertical | Center** command, or press the <Ctrl>+<Alt>+<2> shortcut, and then select the **Modify | Align | Horizontal | Center** command (or press the <Ctrl>+<Alt>+<5> shortcut).

The digits are all in order and the image in each clip is a bitmap shape that can be edited. The **Shape Tween** animation is for this type of object. You will now animate the color and the digits will move upward by 105 pixels. (The current score will be 35 pixels lower than the **Lines** label, whereas the digits will need to jump to the **Score** label, that is, $35 \times 3 = 105$ pixels). Before the next pair of pieces appears, the points for the dropped pieces will flash white and move upwards, gradually fading out until they merge with the total next to the **Score** label.

So far, so good. Enter the window for editing the d0 symbol by double-clicking on its icon in the symbol library. Select a zoom level of 200% or, better still, 400%. Leave the first frame, because it is the base image of the digit displayed on the **panel1** panel. Enter the second frame on the timeline, and press the <F6> key. The second frame will become a copy of the first. The zero will be selected. Select the **Fill Color** tool on the toolbar or in the object properties window, and specify the #FFFFFF color. The zero in the second frame will become white. Then click on the eighth frame to select it, and press the <F6> key. A copy of the white zero from the second frame will appear in the eighth frame. Set its color to #735B46. Then look at the **Info** window (you still can open it with the <Ctrl>+<I> shortcut). In my project, the **Y** coordinate is equal to –7.3, or sometimes to –7.2. In your project, the value might be different. Subtract 105 from this, and enter the result in the **Y** input box. The zero will move upward by 105 pixels. You may already have guessed that you now need to create an arrow from the second frame to the eighth. In this case, the arrow will show against a green background, indicating the **Shape Tween** animation. There is no appropriate command in the pop-up menu, so you'll have to open the properties window (with the <Ctrl>+<F3> shortcut). Click on the second frame, and select **Shape** in the **Tween** drop-down list. An arrow against a green background will appear. Move the pink rectangle along the timeline to watch the animation (Fig. 3.4).

In addition to the **Ease** parameter, with which you are already familiar, the properties panel contains the **Blend** drop-down list, containing the **Distributive** and **Angular** items. This parameter is used for *morphing*, that is, the gradual transition from one shape to another. When the **Distributive** blend is selected, the intermediate shapes are rounded and, so to speak, less correct. With the **Angular** blend, angles and straight lines are maintained. If your symbol library contains sounds, you can select a sound for this animation. In this project, however, all sounds will be issued in response to the program's commands.

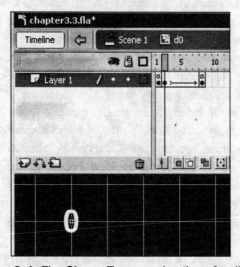

Fig. 3.4. The **Shape Tween** animation of a digit

It's now time to specify actions. Click on the first frame and open its **Actions** window. You can do this either in the properties window (notice a circle with an arrow) or by pressing the <F9> key. Enter the following command:

```
stop();
```

If you don't do this, animation of the digit will start as soon as the digit appears in the work area, and the digit will jump up, changing its color. In this project, animation starts programmatically in the second frame of the movie. In the eighth frame, the digit should disappear. There is a convenient command, `<clip name>.RemoveMovieClip();` for this purpose. In ActionScript, you can use the `this` keyword to access the object on this object's timeline. Thanks to this option, the code for each digit is the same:

```
this.removeMovieClip();
```

Enter this code in the eighth frame, and close the code editor window. Unfortunately, you have to repeat the same procedure with the other digits, so that they jump and disappear like the zero. To avoid typing the `#735B46` color value repeatedly, save it as a swatch in the **Color Swatches** window, which can be opened from the **Window** menu or using the <Ctrl>+<F9> shortcut. Open this window, scroll the palette upward, and you'll see a gray strip. Generally speaking, it might already contain a few color swatches. After you select a color you would like to save, move the mouse pointer (which looks like a bucket) to an unused space on the strip, and click the left mouse button. A square similar to those on the palette will appear. If you move the mouse pointer to this swatch, the pointer will take the form of a dropper. From now on, you can select saved colors and gradients with a click on the toolbar next to the **Fill Color** tool, so you can close the **Color Swatches** window. For the sake of convenience, copy the `this.removeMovieClip();` line of code onto the clipboard. After all the digits are ready, create a folder in the library, name it Digits, and move them to that folder. You can select the entire range by clicking the left mouse button while keeping the <Shift> key pressed. Right-click on any selected element, and select the **Move to New Folder** command in the pop-up menu. Name the new folder.

You should now create a lightning bolt. It will also be an animation of the **Shape Tween** type. First, the lightning will be small, with its length being equal to the width of the square (23 pixels). Then it will quickly grow longer, and branches will appear. By the fifth frame, it will be as long as the pit's width (12 squares). Moving toward the eighth frame, the lightning will grow shorter and move to its end, finally disappearing in the eighth frame. The animation will last approximately 0.35 seconds. The registration point of the lightning will be in the upper left corner of the first square in the line being struck by the lightning. First, draw the fifth frame of the lightning bolt, where it is at its longest. You will then obtain the starting end images by scaling the lightning horizontally.

Create a new clip symbol using the <Ctrl>+<F8> shortcut, name it `lightning`, and check the **Export for ActionScript** checkbox. Set the zoom level to 200% and the **Stroke Color** parameter to #CCFFFF. Select the **Pencil** tool, open the properties window, and select the **Solid** line type and a thickness of 2 pixels. In the **Options** panel, set the **Pencil Mode** parameter to the **Ink** value. With this setting, Flash won't sharpen or straighten the drawn line, leaving it unprocessed.

Draw a curve 12 squares long with one gesture, as shown in Fig. 3.5.

Now decrease the stroke thickness to one pixel, and draw about ten branches (Fig. 3.6).

Honestly, I'm not happy with my lightning, because its branches are too short. I believe yours is better. I hope that the short lifetime for my lightning will mean that its flaws won't be that noticeable.

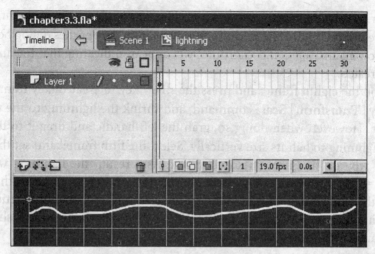

Fig. 3.5. The trunk of the lightning

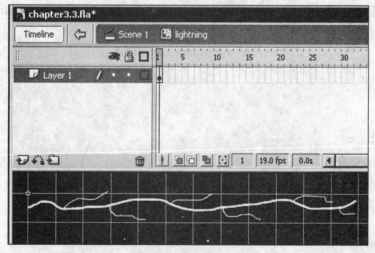

Fig. 3.6. The lightning

Click on the fifth frame, and press the <F6> key. In the first frame, select the **Modify | Transform | Scale** command. A rectangular box with nine handles on the perimeter and a circle in the center will appear around the lightning. Place the mouse pointer on the right non-angular handle, and drag it to the left until the lightning shrinks to the width of the cell. Scale the lightning to half its vertical size in a similar way, by dragging the lower non-angular handle. Click on the first frame on the timeline and set the **Shape** animation type in the properties dialog box.

An arrow against a green background will appear, indicating that the animation has been created.

Click on the eighth frame, and press the <F6> key to create a key frame. Select the **Modify | Transform | Scale** command, and shrink the lightning to the width of one square. However, when doing so, grab the left handle and drag it to the right. Scale the lightning to half its size vertically. Select the fifth frame, and set the **Shape** animation type on the properties dialog box. As a result, the lightning will grow longer up to the fifth frame, and then shorter (at a faster rate) up to the eighth frame, all the while moving to the right. In the eighth frame, open the ActionScript editor (using the <F9> key), and enter the following command, which should already be familiar to you:

```
this.RemoveMovieClip();
```

As a result, the lightning clip will disappear in its eighth frame.

The game animation is complete. Compare your results to the contents of the Chapter3.3.fla file.

Chapter 4: Introduction to ActionScript

In this chapter, you'll start programming in ActionScript. You'll get acquainted with ActionScript data types, operations, and operator precedence. You will also study a few useful examples.

4.1. An Example of Displaying Text and Clips

First, I suggest that you create a movie that displays a simple **Hello!** in the **Output** window. Start a new project, select the first frame on the timeline, and press <F9> to open the code editor window. Click in the window, and type the following code:

```
trace('Hello!');
```

Select the **Control | Test Movie** menu command or press the <Ctrl>+<Enter> shortcut. An empty window of the new movie and the **Output** window will appear on the screen. The latter will read **Hello!** You can hide or display this window using the <F2> key. The `trace()` function is a built-in Flash function that outputs its argument to the **Output** window. The argument should be a string. Close the movie window by clicking on its close button (the one with a cross), clear the code editor window, and type the code from Listing 4.1.

Listing 4.1. Output of variables to the Output window

```
a = 'Hello ';
b = 'World!';
trace(a + b);
```

Press the <Ctrl>+<Enter> shortcut. The **Output** window will display the phrase **Hello World!**.

You first created two variables in this code with the names a and b. You then used the = operator to assign them string values. In the trace command, you concatenated these strings using the + operator. (The string concatenation operator looks identical to the addition operator, and ActionScript correctly interprets the + character in relation to the type of operands). The trace() function outputs the value of the a variable, followed by the value of the b variable. The trace() function is very useful during debugging. For example, you can learn the type of the a variable by adding the following command to Listing 4.1:

```
trace(typeof a);
```

(You don't need to enclose the a argument with parentheses in this case). In the output window, you'll see string, which is the type of the a variable.

Unfortunately, the **Output** window is available only during debugging. The browser and the Flash player don't display it. To obtain the result of your work as SWF and HTML files, save the current project in the hello.fla file, so that the resulting files appear in the same folder. Then, select the **File | Publish** menu command, or press the <Shift>+<F12> shortcut. Start the hello.swf and hello.html files, and you'll see an empty window.

To display some text in a movie's window, you need a text field for dynamic text (or text of the input type). Create a text field somewhere in the work area. The field should be wide enough to avoid the truncation of the text. Select any font (e.g., **Arial**), open the properties window of this text field (using the <Ctrl>+<F3> shortcut), and select a size and color to your liking. Notice the **Var:** input box; it attaches the text block to ActionScript code. In this input box, you need to type the name of the variable that you want to output programmatically. Type t in the input box, and type the following line in the code editor window:

```
t = 'Hello again!';
```

This greeting will be displayed both in the Flash player and in the browser.

To add some ActionScript code to the first frame, first click on the frame on the time-line to select it.

Create a clip with a text field. Press the <Ctrl>+<F8> shortcut, give the symbol the name clip, and create a dynamic text field in the clip. Place the upper left corner of the text field in the registration point of the clip. (The point is indicated with a cross). In the text properties window, type the name t in the **Var:** input box. Enter the main scene, and drag the clip from the library to the work area under the text field. If the old text field is selected, click on an unused space to unselect it, and then select the instance of the clip symbol. In its properties window, you will see **Instance of: clip**. The **Instance Name** text box is under the instance behavior drop-down list. This text box attaches the instance of the clip instance to ActionScript code. Type the iclip1 name in this text box, and add the following line to the program:

```
iclip1.t = 'Hello from iclip1!';
```

When the movie starts, you'll see one more greeting.

You can create as many symbol instances as you like. Drag the clip to an unused space in the work area, and name its instance iclip2. Add the following line to the code:

```
iclip2.t = 'Hello from iclip2!';
```

Start the movie to see this greeting.

ActionScript allows you to call clips from the library to the desk using the attachMovie() function. It takes three parameters: idName — a string with the name of the clip in the library, newName — a string with the name of the clip's new instance, and depth — the depth of the instance. The depth is specified by an integer starting from zero, and is similar to a layer in the timeline. The larger the number, the closer the clip is to the viewer. You should assign different depths to the clips. If depths of two clips are the same, the newer clip will substitute the older example.

Right-click on the icon of the clip symbol in the library, and check the **Export for ActionScript** checkbox with the clip name. Add the following lines to the program:

```
attachMovie('clip', 'iclip3', 1);
iclip3.t = 'Hello from iclip3!';
```

When you start the movie, you'll see the greeting from the `iclip3` instance.

Change the coordinates of the clips. The coordinates are measured in pixels, with regards to the zoom level starting from the upper left corner of the movie window. The X coordinate is stored in the `_x` property of the clip, and the Y coordinate is stored in the `_y` property. The underline character is used to distinguish between the library properties of the clip and the properties defined by the programmer. Add three more lines to the code:

```
iclip1._x = 0;
iclip3._y = 100;
```

The clips will change the coordinates. This example is in the hello.fla file.

In the next sections, I'll provide an overview of the ActionScript language. If you're familiar with JavaScript, you'll see many similarities, because these two languages comply with the same standard. Flash incorporates online help (opened using the <F1> key) that contains a complete description of methods and properties of objects (see *ActionScript Dictionary*), along with many examples.

4.2. Variables

In programming languages such as Pascal, variables are declared after the `var` keyword, and a variable's type is specified in the declaration. It is impossible to use a variable before it has been declared. Like other scripting languages, ActionScript isn't as strict. When its interpreter encounters a new name in the script, it automatically creates a new variable (according to the autovivification principle). It is a good practice, however, to declare variables before they are used. You can assign a variable a value when declaring it:

```
var
  a1 = 100;
  a2 = 'text';
```

The type of variable isn't specified, and the interpreter detects this from the variable's value. The type can change if you assign the variable a value of another type. If you don't assign a variable a value when declaring it, the variable (and its type) will take a special value — `undefined`. The names of variables should comply with a certain standard: An identifier can consist only of letters, digits, and underline characters, and you cannot use certain reserved words (`true`, `object`, `array`, etc.) as names for variables. Unlike other scripting languages, ActionScript isn't case-sensitive, so `a1` and `A1` identifiers, for example, refer to the same variable.

4.2.1. Creating Variables with Dynamically-Calculated Names

ActionScript allows you to create a variable for which the name will be computed dynamically. The set operator is used for this (Listing 4.2).

Listing 4.2. Using the set operator

```
i = 3;
set('var' + i, 'flash');
```

This code creates a variable with the name var3, and assigns it the 'flash' string.

4.2.2. Type Casting

You can assign variables data of any type (Listing 4.3).

Listing 4.3. Outputting types of variables

```
a = 1;
trace(typeof a);                        // number
a = '1';
trace(typeof a);                        // string
attachMovie('clip', 'clip', 100);       // assuming that the clip exists
a = clip;
trace(typeof a);                        // movieclip
a = [1, 2, 'Hello!'];
trace(typeof a);                        // object (an array)
a = 1 + '1';
trace(typeof a);                        // string
a = '1' + 1;
trace(typeof a);                        // string
a = 1 - '1';
trace(typeof a);                        // number
a = '1' - 1;
trace(typeof a);                        // number
a = a + '1';
trace(typeof a);                        // string
a = true;
trace(typeof a);                        // Boolean
```

As you see in Listing 4.3, when numbers are added to strings, the + operator is interpreted as a string concatenation, rather than an arithmetic addition. Before the concatenation, the numeric operands are automatically cast into strings.

In addition to implicit type casting, there is also an explicit form:

```
trace((123.2).toString());      // 123.2
a = '234.5';
trace(Number(a));               // 234.5
trace(Boolean('0'));            // false
a = 4.7E5;
trace(String(a));               // 470000
```

Note that a string that is not empty, usually cast to zero, is cast to `false` in ActionScript.

ActionScript offers you one more elementary data type: `null`. It differs from `undefined` in that a variable with the `null` type exists, but its value is not defined.

Aggregate data types are the following: `array`, `object`, and `movieclip`. Action-Script functions are objects and can have properties. You can define a property for a function, and the property will behave like a global variable maintaining its value between calls to the function. Programmers seldom use this feature, however.

4.2.3. Scope of a Function

Variables can be created in scripts attached to the frames of the main timeline, clip instances and buttons on the timeline, the frames of a clip's timeline, instances of clips and buttons located inside other clips, and so on. When the player encounters the next frame, it executes the script attached to this frame and the scripts attached to the current frames of all clips on the timeline before it displays the frame. Therefore, if you create a variable in the second frame, at first it doesn't exist in the first frame. However, if Flash returns to the first frame after it displays the second, this variable will exist in the first frame.

Variables attached to the frames of the main timeline are available in all nested clips and buttons via the `_root` reference to the timeline. Variables of this type are referred to as variables of the `_root` level.

Consider the example4.2.3.fla project. It creates a clip named `clip`, for which the timeline consists of three frames. The following code is attached to the first frame:

```
trace('1st clip frame. _root.a = ' + _root.a);
var b = 'bbb';
```

The code attached to the second frame is the following:

```
trace('2nd clip frame. _root.a = ' + _root.a);
```

The third frame's code is:

```
trace('3rd clip frame. _root.a = ' + _root.a);
```

The first frame of the `clip` clip outputs the value of the `a` variable defined in the first frame of the main timeline, and creates the `b` variable, to which the `'bbb'` string is assigned. The second and third frames output the `a` variable again.

The main timeline consists of two frames. The following code is attached to the first frame:

```
var a = 'aaa';
trace('1st frame. iclip.b = ' + iclip.b);
```

The code attached to the second frame is the following:

```
trace('2nd frame. iclip.b = ' + iclip.b);
```

The first frame creates the `a` variable with the `'aaa'` value, and outputs the value of the `b` variable of the `iclip` instance of the `clip` clip. (The instance is also placed in the first frame).

If you begin playback of this movie, you'll see the following lines in the **Output** window:

```
1st frame. iclip.b =
 1st clip frame. _root.a = aaa
2nd frame. iclip.b =
1st frame. iclip.b =
 1st clip frame. _root.a = aaa
2nd frame. iclip.b =
```

The lines will be displayed repeatedly until you close the movie window or an overflow takes place in the **Output** window.

NOTE

In the Flash environment, a movie is played in a loop unless you put the `stop();` command in the last frame of its timeline. In the browser, this behavior is set with the `loop` parameter in the HTML file, which is controlled using the **Loop** checkbox available in the **File | Publish Settings** menu item on the **HTML** tab.

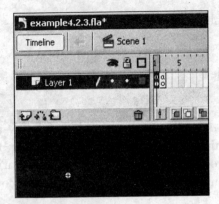

Fig. 4.1. The scope of variables

Let's examine the output. Flash player enters the first frame of the movie, cre-ates the a variable, assigns it the 'aaa' string, and outputs the value of the b variable of the clip clip that doesn't yet exist. The value of a non-existent variable is an empty string, which you can view. Because the iclip instance of the clip clip is associated with the first frame of the main timeline, the player enters the first frame of the clip clip, outputs the value of the already-existing movie variable a, and cre-ates the b variable with the 'bbb' value. The player then enters the second frame of the movie where the clip clip doesn't exist because you have only moved it to the work area in the first frame. This is why the value of the iclip.b variable is also an empty string.

Now consider a slightly different example. On the movie timeline, create the **Layer 2** layer below the **Layer 1** layer, enter the first frame of **Layer 1**, select the in-stance of the clip, and press the <Ctrl>+<X> shortcut to cut it and place it onto the clipboard. Then, return to the first frame of the **Layer 2** layer, and paste the clip there using the <Ctrl>+<Shift>+<V> shortcut. The result is shown in Fig. 4.1.

Start the playback of the movie, and close the **Output** window a few seconds later. The output will be as follows.

```
1st frame. iclip.b =
    1st clip frame. _root.a = aaa
    2nd clip frame. _root.a = aaa
2nd frame. iclip.b = bbb
    3rd clip frame. _root.a = aaa
1st frame. iclip.b = bbb
    1st clip frame. _root.a = aaa
```

```
2nd frame. iclip.b = bbb
    2nd clip frame. _root.a = aaa
1st frame. iclip.b = bbb
    3rd clip frame. _root.a = aaa
2nd frame. iclip.b = bbb
    1st clip frame. _root.a = aaa
1st frame. iclip.b = bbb
    2nd clip frame. _root.a = aaa
2nd frame. iclip.b = bbb
    3rd clip frame. _root.a = aaa
1st frame. iclip.b = bbb
    1st clip frame. _root.a = aaa
```

In the second frame of the movie, the `iclip.b` clip variable already exists. Notice how the clip frames are synchronized with the timeline: These is a current frame for each clip, and this frame will be played synchronously with the next frame of the main timeline. First, two frames of the `clip` clip are played simultaneously, because the frames of child clips are processed before the frame of the parent timeline.

If you remove the statement

```
var b = 'bbb';
```

from the first frame of the clip and insert it into the second frame, you'll see in the output window that the `iclip.b` variable doesn't exist in the second frame of the movie. It only appears in the movie after the player enters the third frame of the clip.

Now, add the following command to the code in the third frame of the clip:

```
stop();
```

Examine the output:

```
1st frame. iclip.b =
   1st clip frame. _root.a = aaa
   2nd clip frame. _root.a = aaa
2nd frame. iclip.b =
   3rd clip frame. _root.a = aaa
1st frame. iclip.b = bbb
2nd frame. iclip.b = bbb
1st frame. iclip.b = bbb
2nd frame. iclip.b = bbb
```

You will see that the playback of the clip stopped in its third frame. If you add the following command to this clip:

```
iclip.play();
```

its playback will resume from the next frame.

NOTE

If you move the `stop()`; command to the first line in the third frame of the clip, the output will be the same. This might seem strange. Why was the code of the third frame executed after the `stop()`; command? Flash executes all the code attached to the current frame and only then executes commands that stop the playback or move it to another frame.

You could remove the `iclip` instance from the main timeline and add it programmatically by adding the `attachMovie('clip', 'iclip', 1)`; command to the first frame of the timeline. However, before you do this, you will need to check the **Export for ActionScript** checkbox for the clip clip in the library and set the `clip` identifier. The resulting output in the **Output** window won't change.

So you have learned that you can access a variable belonging to the main timeline from any frame in this timeline, just by the variable's name. You can access the variable from any clip or button using the absolute path `_root.`*`the_variable_name`*, much like when you specify the absolute path to access a file. You can access the `b` variable of the `iclip` clip instance from any clip using the absolute path `_root.iclip.b`. If the `clip` clip contained, for example, another clip instance named `iclip1` with the `c` variable, you could access the `c` variable as follows: `_root.iclip.iclip1.c`.

In addition to the `_root` property, Flash offers you another property, `_parent`, which refers to the timeline, to which a particular clip instance is attached. Links that use the `_parent` property are relative. For example, you can access the `a` variable of the main timeline from the `clip` clip as `_parent.a`. If the `clip1` clip was attached to the timeline of the `clip` clip, you could access the `b` variable from the `clip1` clip's timeline as `_parent.b`, while you could access the `a` variable as `_parent._parent.a`. As you see, you don't need to know the names of the parent clips, and the code in child clips is universal. However, you should remember that a clip's variables only live while an instance of this clip is on the work space (inside another clip, for example).

Like any other programming language, ActionScript features local variables that are declared inside functions. They exist while the function executes.

4.3. Data Types

As you already know, ActionScript supports the following data types: number, string, boolean, undefined, null, array, object, and movieclip. In the following sections, I'll describe them in detail.

4.3.1. The number Type

This type refers to integers, floating-point numbers, and special numeric values. Examples of integer literals are –55, 0, and 1,000. Examples of floating-point numbers are 2.45, –10e3 (which is –10,000), and 2E–2 (which is 0.02). Flash uses the double-precision representation of floating-point numbers, which is about 15 significant digits.

If an integer literal begins with a zero, the number is considered octal, for example, 0010 is 8, and 015 is 13. To write a hexadecimal literal, use the 0x (or 0X) prefix. For example, 0xFF is 255.

The special numeric values are the following: NaN (Not a Number), MIN_VALUE, and MAX_VALUE. The last two are the minimum and the maximum positive numbers. (The negative value with the maximum module is equal to MAX_VALUE). Two more special numeric values are Infinity and -Infinity. For example:

```
a = 0/0;
b = 1 - 'abc';
```

The a and b variables will have the NaN value and the number type. Note that a isn't equal to b. This makes sense, as equality is valid only for finite numbers. To find out whether a variable has the NaN value, use the isNaN(value) Boolean function.

Since the bit depth of any processor is limited, the range of the numbers is also limited. The Number.MAX_VALUE value is used to check whether the value of a variable is a valid positive number:

```
a <= Number.MAX_VALUE && a >= -Number.MAX_VALUE
```

The same can be done using the isFinite(value) Boolean function. If the result of some computation is greater than Number.MAX_VALUE or lower than -Number.MAX_VALUE, it is represented with the Infinity and -Infinity literals, respectively.

ActionScript offers you convenient access to common irrational numbers via the Math object. For a list of these constants, refer to the online help related to this object. The online help also contains built-in mathematical functions. Here are useful methods associated with the `Math` object:

- ❑ `Math.abs(x)` — Returns the absolute value of the x number.
- ❑ `Math.ceil(x)` — Rounds the x number up to the nearest greater integer.
- ❑ `Math.floor(x)` — Rounds the x number down to the nearest lower integer.
- ❑ `Math.max(x, y)` — Returns a maximum of two numbers.
- ❑ `Math.min(x, y)` — Returns a minimum of two numbers.
- ❑ `Math.random()` — Generates a pseudo-random number from 0.0 to 0.999.
- ❑ `Math.round(x)` — Rounds the x number to the nearest integer.

4.3.2. The string Type

A string is a text data type. String literals should be enclosed by apostrophes or quotation marks. A string literal bracketed by apostrophes can contain quotation marks as common characters, and vice versa. For example, `'I said: "Hello!"'` or `"Can't read"`. If you need to include a delimiter or a backslash in a string literal, you should put a backslash before that character (i.e., mask the character). For example: `'I said: "Can\'t read"'`. An empty string (a string containing no characters) is written as `''` or `""`. This is not the same as a string containing one or more spaces, because a space is a character.

ActionScript uses the ISO-8859-1 (Latin-1) character set. To output characters that are missing from the keyboard, you can use Escape sequences that are either Unicode-like or have a shorter format. For example:

```
trace('\u00a9');
trace('\xa9');
```

Both lines output the copyright character. In addition, you can use the `chr` global function:

```
trace(chr(139));
```

The argument is a decimal. The comparison operators for strings are the same as for numbers:

```
'Abc' == 'abc'        // false
'Abc' != 'abc'        // true
```

The <, >, <=, and >= comparison operators compare the characters on the same positions within the strings until the first difference is encountered or one of the

If no value is given to a variable when it is declared, its value is `undefined`. Unlike in JavaScript, `undefined` is converted to an empty string.

4.3.5. *The* null *Type*

The `null` value is assigned only with the assignment statement. It indicates that the variable is defined, but doesn't contain data. The `null` and `undefined` values are equal:

```
var a;
b = null;
trace(a == b);          // true
```

4.4. Operator Precedence and Associativity

The *priority* of operators determines the order of their execution if the operators follow each other. When the operators have the same priority, the order of their execution is determined by the *associativity* rule. For example, the from-right-to-left associativity of the assignment operator (=) allows you to assign a value to several variables simultaneously: a = b = c = 0.

Table 4.1. Operator precedence and associativity

Operator	Priority	Associativity	Description
x++	16	Left to right	Post-increment
x--	16	Left to right	Post-decrement
.	15	Left to right	Access an object property
[]	15	Left to right	Access an array element or an object property
()	15	Left to right	Group
function()	15	Left to right	Function call
++x	14	Right to left	Pre-increment
--x	14	Right to left	Pre-decrement
+	14	Right to left	Unary plus
–	14	Right to left	Unary minus

continues

Table 4.1 Continued

Operator	Priority	Associativity	Description
~	14	Right to left	Bitwise one's complement
!	14	Right to left	Logical NOT
new	14	Right to left	Create an object or an array
delete	14	Right to left	Delete an object or an array element
typeof	14	Right to left	Type of an object
void	14	Right to left	Return undefined value
*	13	Left to right	Multiply
/	13	Left to right	Divide
%	13	Left to right	Modulo
+	12	Left to right	Add or concatenate
-	12	Left to right	Subtract
<<	11	Left to right	Bitwise left shift
>>	11	Left to right	Bitwise right shift (signed)
>>>	11	Left to right	Bitwise right shift (unsigned)
<	10	Left to right	Less than
<=	10	Left to right	Less than or equal to
>	10	Left to right	Greater than
>=	10	Left to right	Greater than or equal to
==	9	Left to right	Equality
===	9	Left to right	Strict equality
!= or <>	9	Left to right	Inequality
!===	9	Left to right	Strict inequality
&	8	Left to right	Bitwise AND
^	7	Left to right	Bitwise XOR
|	6	Left to right	Bitwise OR
&&	5	Left to right	Logical AND
||	4	Left to right	Logical OR
?:	3	Right to left	Ternary conditional

continues

Table 4.1 Continued

Operator	Priority	Associativity	Description
=	2	Right to left	Assign
+=	2	Right to left	Add and assign
-=	2	Right to left	Subtract and assign
*=	2	Right to left	Multiply and assign
/=	2	Right to left	Divide and assign
%=	2	Right to left	Modulo and assign
<<=	2	Right to left	Bitwise left shift and assign
>>=	2	Right to left	Bitwise right shift (signed) and assign
>>>=	2	Right to left	Bitwise right shift (unsigned) and assign
&=	2	Right to left	Bitwise AND and assign
^=	2	Right to left	Bitwise XOR and assign
|=	2	Right to left	Bitwise OR and assign
,	1	Left to right	Comma

4.5. Types of Statements

ActionScript scripts consist of statements. Generally speaking, each statement should end with a semicolon, but this rule isn't strict. As a result, confusing situations can arise. For example, the following function returns undefined:

```
function f() {
  return
  100;
}
```

However, the following example returns 100:

```
function f() {
  return 100;
}
```

A construction containing one statement can contain several statements enclosed between-braces { and }.

ActionScript comments are similar to comments in C and JavaScript:

```
// A one-line comment
```

All the characters between two slashes and the end of the line are ignored.

A comment enclosed by the `/*` and `*/` character sequences can consist of as many lines as you like:

```
/* A multi-line
comment */
```

4.5.1. Conditional Statements

There are several types of the `if` statement. A simple `if` statement executes a statement or a block of statements if the condition is true:

```
if (condition) {
  statement
}
```

or

```
if (condition) {
  statement1;
  statement2;
  ...
}
```

NOTE

In this and the subsequent statements, the condition is any expression. It will be evaluated, and the result will be converted to the Boolean type.

A compound `if` statement has the `else` branch, which is executed if the condition is false:

```
if (condition) {
  statement or block of statements
} else {
    statement or block of statements
}
```

Using the `else if` clause, you can divide a script into many branches:

```
if (condition) {
  statement or block of statements
} else if (condition) {
    statement or block of statements
  } else if(condition) {
      statement or block of statements
    } else if(condition) {
        statement or block of statements
      } else {
          statement or block of statements
}
```

This code executes the block, for which the condition is true. If all the conditions are false, none of the statements is executed.

In Flash MX, a convenient substitute for `else if` was included. This is the `switch` statement:

```
switch (expression) {
  case label1: statement;
          break;
  case label2: statement;
          break;
  case label3: statement;
          break;
  default: statement;
}
```

The expression in the `switch` statement can be of any type. Labels are literals or names of variables. This statement executes the first branch, for which the label matches the condition with consideration for the data types (the label should have the same type as the expression). If you omit the `break` statement, the next `case` branch will be executed. If no label matches the expression, the `default` branch is executed. This branch is optional, so you can omit it.

The conditional ternary statement has the following syntax:

```
condition ? condition1 : condition2;
```

If the condition is true, the statement returns the result *expression1*, otherwise it returns the result *expression2*. This statement is convenient used in combination with the assignment operation.

4.5.2. *Loop Statements*

The `while` pretest loop executes its internal statements while the condition is true. It has the following syntax:

```
while (condition) {
  statements
}
```

If the condition is false when the loop starts, the body of the loop won't be executed.

NOTE

If a script in a frame runs for more than 15 seconds, the ActionScript interpreter will output a modal window with an appropriate message and buttons allowing you to cancel scripts in this movie or continue execution of the script.

The `do-while` post-test loop executes the body first, and then checks the condition. If the condition is true, the loop body is executed again, and so on.

```
do {
  statements
} while (condition);
```

In the `for` loop, the header contains initialization of the loop variable (or variables), condition, and modification of the variable.

```
for (initialization; condition; modification) {
  statements
}
```

For example:

```
for (i = 0, j = 5; i < 6 && j >= 0; i++, j--) {
  statements
}
```

The initialization section is executed once when the loop starts. The condition is then checked. If it is true, the loop body is executed. Otherwise, the statement that follows the loop is executed. When the loop body execution ends (if no `break` statement was encountered), the modification section is executed. The condition is then checked, and so on.

There is a `for-in` variant of the `for` loop. It enumerates all of the properties of an object:

```
for (property in object) {
  statements
}
```

For example:

```
var
 o = new Object();
o.size = 100;
o.color = 0xFF;
for (prop in o)
 { trace('Property '+prop+', value '+o[prop]);
 }
```

The result is the following:

```
Property color, value 255
Property size, value 100
```

In each loop iteration, the `prop` variable is assigned the next property name as a string.

NOTE

For built-in objects, the `for-in` loop can fail to enumerate all of their properties.

4.5.3. The break *Statement*

In a loop body, the `break` statement interrupts the loop and passes control to the statement that follows the loop. In a `switch` statement, `break` passes control to the statement that follows the `switch` statement.

4.5.4. The continue *Statement*

In a loop body, the `continue` statement interrupts the current iteration and starts the next. In the `while` and `do-while` loops, control is passed to the condition check, and in the `for` loop it is passed to the loop variable modification section. In the `for-in` loop, the next iteration starts with the next property of the object.

4.6. Functions

Functions are fragments of code written in a special way so that it is possible to execute them repeatedly with different values for their parameters. The scope and life span of a function are similar to those of a variable. To create a function, you should write:

```
function function_name(parameter1, parameter2, ...)
{ statements
}
```

The parameters are optional. To call a function, write its name and list the parameters in parentheses. The function terminates when the end of its body is reached. Control is then passed to the statement that follows the call to the function. To terminate a function prematurely and/or return a result, use the following statement:

```
return;
```

or

```
return expression;
```

ActionScript allows you to create function literals and assign them to variables. You'll use this feature later to create dynamic event handlers. A function literal doesn't have a name:

```
var f = function (parameter1, parameter2, ...)
{ statements
}
```

You can call this function as follows:

```
f(actual_parameter_list);
```

4.6.1. The arguments Object

Before entering a function, the interpreter creates an `arguments` object that contains all actual parameters specified in the function call (regardless of how many parameters were declared), the number of the actual parameters, and the function name.

❐ `arguments[0]` — The first actual parameter

- ☐ arguments[1] — The second actual parameter
- ☐ ...
- ☐ arguments.length — The number of actual parameters
- ☐ arguments.callee — The name of the function being called

4.6.2. Passing Parameters to Functions

Simple data (such as variables, array elements, or object properties) are passed to functions by value, that is, the function receives a copy of the data. If you assign values to these parameters inside the function, this won't affect the data outside the function. Aggregated data (such as arrays or objects) are passed to functions by reference. Therefore, the function operates with the data themselves, rather than with their copies. For example:

```
var m = [1, 2, 3];
function f(p)
{ p[0] = 100;
}
f(m);
trace(m);              // 100, 2, 3
```

As soon as you assign a value to a parameter passed by reference inside the function, the link to the actual parameter will be broken:

```
var m = [1, 2, 3];
function f(p)
{ p[0] = 100;
  p = [4, 5, 6]; // A new array p different from the m array is created.
}
f(m);
trace(m);              // 100, 2, 3
```

You can pass functions to functions as actual parameters.

4.6.3. Global Functions

Global functions are built into ActionScript and available to any script of the movie. In addition, there are built-in functions that are methods of objects and, therefore, should be called using the objects. Here is a description of a few useful global functions:

- ❏ escape(string) — Returns the URL-encoded value of the string string. However, it converts a space into %20 rather than +.
- ❏ unescape(string) — A function opposite to escape(). It returns the URL-decoded value of the string.
- ❏ fscommand() — Sends a message to the master of the Flash movie. For example:
  - fscommand('quit') — Quits the movie and exits the Flash player.
  - fscommand('showmenu', 'false') — Disables the pop-up menu in the movie window.
  - fscommand('allowscale', 'false') — Disables the scaling of the movie when its window is resized.
  - fscommand('fullscreen', 'true') — Enables the full-screen mode for the movie.
  - fscommand('trapallkeys', 'true') — Disables the menu commands of the Flash player, prevents the user from exiting the full-screen mode using the <Esc> key. This function is convenient at the beginning of the movie.
- ❏ getURL(URL), getURL(URL, window), or getURL(URL, window, method) — Loads a document with the specified URL into the window or frame of the browser. Here, window is the name of the window, the frame, or one of the following reserved words: '_blank', '_parent', '_self', '_top'. The method parameter is the 'GET' or 'POST' literal.
- ❏ getTimer() — Returns the number of milliseconds elapsed from the beginning of the movie.
- ❏ gotoAndPlay(scene, frameNumber) or gotoAndPlay(scene, frameLabel) — Continues the playback of the movie from the frame with the specified number or label (which is a string). If the scene parameter (the scene name) is not omitted, the playback continues from the specified frame of the specified scene.
- ❏ loadVariables(URL, target) or loadVariables(URL, target, method) — Requests a file (script) by its URL address and receives variables from it. Here, target is the path to the clip that defines the loaded data. For the current clip, target is an empty string. The method parameter is optional. It is the 'GET' or 'POST' literal. The default is 'GET'. If no variables with the specified names are defined, they will be created. The text received by this function should be URL-encoded. For example:

```
name1=value+1&name2=value+2&...
```

The `name1` variable receives the `'value 1'` value, and the `name2` variable receives the `'value 2'` value. The values are sent as text, even when they are numeric. Spaces are substituted with pluses, and all characters that aren't uppercase or lowercase letters are encoded with hexadecimal codes in the `%xx` form.

❏ `.stopAllSounds()` — Stops all the sounds in the movie regardless of whether they were started from ActionScript code or the timeline. The function doesn't affect the sounds started later.

❏ `#include path/file` — Is a directive for the interpreter to include the contents of the specified file in the script. The path can be absolute or relative; a slash is used rather than a backslash. Note that the directive doesn't end with a semi-colon. For example:

```
#include "outerscript.as"
#include "inc/outerscript.as"
#include "C:/FlashGames/Tetris/outerscript.as"
```

You'll use this directive because it is more convenient to edit large files with scripts in FAR than in the built-in ActionScript editor.
Note that the use of apostrophes in this directive, rather than quotation marks, is incorrect.

The **Check Syntax** command in the code editor window doesn't check external scripts. You shouldn't rely on this check anyway, because it fails to find all syntax errors.

4.7. Built-in Classes

ActionScript is aware of the following classes: `Array`, `Boolean`, `Color`, `Date`, `MovieClip`, `Number`, `Object`, `Sound`, `String`, `XML`, `XMLNode`, and `XMLSocket`. Some of them are already familiar to you. Consider a few more classes that you're going to use. For the others, refer to Flash online help.

4.7.1. The Array Class

An array is a data structure consisting of elements that can be accessed by their numbers (indices). The elements are numbered from zero. It is possible to name elements like in hashes, but I won't describe this feature. The elements are independent of each other and can have different types. You can create an array using the constructor. For example:

```
var m = new Array()
```

This creates an empty array, and a reference to it is assigned to the m variable. Another example:

```
var m = new Array(10)
```

Here an array with ten empty elements is created.

You can also create an array by assigning a literal to a variable:

```
var m = ['abc', 2 + 2, getTimer()]
```

Arrays can be multi-dimensional:

```
var m = new Array([1, 2], [3, 4])
```

or

```
m = [[1, 2], [3, 4]]
```

A two-dimensional array is created here. The m[0][0] element will contain 1, and m[1][1] will contain 4. The m[0] element will contain the [1, 2] one-dimensional array.

An array has the length property, which is the number of the array's elements, including empty ones. If an array is multi-dimensional, the length returns the number of its sub arrays with the maximum number of dimensions. You can assign new values to this property, thus changing the numbers of elements in arrays. You can also add new elements, using the assignment operator if you specify an index value greater than or equal to length.

Here are a few methods of the Array class:

❑ push(element1, element2, ...) — Adds one or more elements to the end of the array and returns the new array length.

❑ unshift(element1, element2, ...) — Adds elements to the beginning of the array and returns the new array length. The indices of the original elements are increased.

❑ splice(start_index, number_of_deleted, element1, element2, ...) — Inserts new elements and/or deletes elements. start_index is the start index for the insertion or deletion of the elements. *number_of_deleted* is self-explanatory. The optional parameters *element1*, *element2*, ... specify a list of elements to insert.

- ❑ concat(*element1*, *element2*, ...) — Adds elements to the end of the array, but doesn't change the original array. Instead, this method returns a new array with the added elements.
- ❑ pop() — Deletes the last element of the array and returns its value.
- ❑ shift() — Deletes the first array element and returns its value. The indices of the other elements are decreased by one.

4.7.2. *The* MovieClip *Class*

MovieClip is the main class in Flash. To be more precise, it is a special data type, rather than a class. It doesn't have a constructor because clips are created in the development environment. You can create clip instances based on library symbols or by duplicating existing clips. Flash MX offers you a new feature that allows you to create and draw clips programmatically. Here are a few important properties of the MovieClip class, as well as of the main timeline, _root:

- ❑ _alpha — A transparency level: 0 — fully transparent, 100 — fully opaque.
- ❑ _currentframe — The number of the current frame, starting from one. This is a read-only property.
- ❑ _framesloaded — The number of loaded frames (e.g., when reading a document with a movie from a server). Read-only.
- ❑ _height — The clip height in pixels.
- ❑ _rotation — The angle of rotation counterclockwise, in degrees.
- ❑ _totalframes — The number of timeline frames. Read-only.
- ❑ _useHandCursor — A property used if a button event handler, such as onRollOut, is set for this clip. When the handler is set, the mouse pointer takes the shape of a hand when it is on this clip. To disable this feature, set the _useHandCursor property to false.
- ❑ _visible — The visibility. This is equal to true if the clip is visible and to false if it is not.
- ❑ _width — The clip width in pixels.

❑ _x — The X coordinate of the registration point, in pixels.

❑ _xmouse — The X coordinate of the mouse pointer relative to the registration point. Read-only.

❑ _xscale — The vertical scaling of the clip.

❑ _y — The Y coordinate of the registration point in pixels.

❑ _ymouse — The Y coordinate of the mouse pointer relative to the registration point. Read-only.

❑ _yscale — The horizontal scaling of the clip.

Here are a few methods of clips and of the main timeline, _root:

❑ attachMovie(*identifier, new_name, depth*) — Creates a new clip instance, with the *new_name* name, based on the library symbol with the *identifier* identifier. The *depth* parameter is an integer (zero, one, etc.) that specifies how the clip is positioned among the other clips. The higher the clip, the closer it is to the viewer. Each parent clip has its own hierarchy of levels. If the *new_name* argument is specified as a string literal, the attachMovie method creates a variable with the *new_name* name.

❑ getBytesLoaded() — Returns the number of bytes loaded to the Flash player. Use _root.getBytesLoaded() to detect whether the entire movie is loaded.

❑ getBytesTotal() — Returns the size of the clip in bytes. Use _root.getBytesTotal() to detect whether the entire movie is loaded.

❑ gotoAndPlay(*frame_number*) or gotoAndPlay(*frame_label*) — Makes the player continue playback from the frame with the specified number or label. You can assign string labels to frames.

❑ gotoAndStop(*frame_number*) or gotoAndStop(*frame_label*) — Makes the player stop playback in the frame with the specified number or label.

❑ nextFrame() — Goes to the next frame, and stops the playback.

❑ play() — Plays the clip, beginning with the current frame.

❑ prevFrame() — Goes to the previous frame, and stops the playback.

❑ removeMovieClip() — Removes the clip from the movie.

❑ startDrag(), startDrag(*center*), or startDrag(*center, left, up, right, down*) — Makes the clip follow the mouse pointer. The *center:* parameter is true if the registration point of the clip should be in the hot spot of the mouse pointer, and false if this is not the case. Use false to prevent the clip from jumping when it is clicked. The *left, up, right, down* parameters are the coordinates of a rectangle, within which the clip registration point should remain (you cannot drag the clip outside this rectangle). Only one clip can follow the mouse pointer after the startDrag command is given.

❏ stop() — Stops the playback of the clip.

❏ stopDrag() — Stops the clip following the mouse pointer. It is usually called when the mouse button is released.

4.7.3. The Sound Class

The Sound allows you to control sounds programmatically. You'll use it in your current project to control certain sounds on the main timeline. First, you need to create a Sound class object of the:

```
var sound1 = new Sound();
```

Now, attach a library sound to the object in the way you used attachMovie earlier:

```
sound1.attachSound('explodesnd');
```

Here, explodesnd is the name of the sound imported to the library. Then you can start the sound:

```
sound1.start();
```

or stop it when you like:

```
sound1.stop();
```

For setting the volume and panorama, see Flash online help.

4.8. Built-in Objects

Flash has the following built-in objects: Arguments, Key, Math, Mouse, and Selection. I'll describe objects that will be used in this project.

4.8.1. The Key Object

The Key object is used to find the status of a particular key, as well as which key was pressed last.

The Key object has the following properties, which are actually the names of keys (the numeric values are the decimal codes of the corresponding keys):

- BACKSPACE — 8
- CAPSLOCK — 20
- CONTROL — 17
- DELETEKEY — 46
- DOWN — 40
- END — 35
- ENTER —13
- INSERT — 45
- LEFT — 37
- PGDN — 34
- PGUP — 33
- RIGHT — 39
- SHIFT — 16
- SPACE — 32
- ESCAPE — 27
- HOME — 36
- TAB — 9
- UP — 38

Methods of the Key object are the following:

- addListener(*object_name*) — Adds a listener, which is a special object. When the user presses or releases the key, the listener catches these events using its methods onKeyDown and onKeyUp. When these events take place, certain funct-ions are called, and you can choose them during the playback of the movie. The use of this method is described later.
- getAscii() — Returns the ASCII value of the last key pressed.
- getCode() — Returns the decimal code of the last key pressed.
- isDown(*key_code*) — Returns true if the key with the specified decimal code is currently pressed. Otherwise, it returns false.
- isToggled(*key_code*) — Checks whether the <Caps Lock>, <Num Lock>, or <Scroll Lock> key is on, and returns true or false. For example: isToggled(Key.CAPSLOCK).
- removeListener(*object_name*) — Removes the listener that catches the KeyDown and KeyUp events.

4.8.2. The Mouse *Object*

The Mouse object is used only to hide or unhide the system mouse pointer. You need to hide it when a movie uses its own mouse pointer. To get the coordinates of the mouse pointer, use the _root._xmouse and _root._ymouse properties.

Methods of the Mouse object are the following:

❑ hide() — Hides the system mouse pointer.
❑ show() — Unhides the system mouse pointer.

4.8.3. The Selection *Object*

The Selection object is used to select a text fragment in the text field and read the selected text. You'll use the setFocus('*text_field_name*') method, which sets the keyboard input focus to the specified text field and places the cursor there. If the text field contains any text, it will be selected. To unselect, you can set the cursor to the end of the text field:

```
Selection.setSelection(text_field_name, text_field_name.length)
```

4.9. Event Handling

As you already know, the ActionScript code attached to a frame of a clip or the _root timeline is executed when the Flash player enters this frame. When the execution completes, the frame contents are displayed in the clip window. Then the player enters the next frames of the clips and the main timeline, unless a clip dispatches it to another frame using the gotoAndPlay() method or stops the playback using the stop() method. However, the code of certain special functions called *event handlers* is executed asynchronously, as soon as an appropriate event takes place.

Events are divided into user and playback events. User events are related to the mouse or the keyboard. A Flash movie without plug-ins cannot detect clicks with the right mouse button. So, by button, I'll mean the left mouse button.

4.9.1. User Events

Here are events of clips and buttons that are related to user activities. If an event is related only to a clip, but not to a button, I indicate this explicitly.

❑ MouseMove — The mouse pointer moves in the movie window.
❑ MouseDown — The mouse button is clicked.

❏ `MouseUp` — The mouse button is released.

❏ `RollOver` — The mouse pointer enters the hot area of a button (clip) when the mouse button isn't pressed.

❏ `RollOut` — The mouse pointer leaves the hot area of a button (clip) when the mouse button isn't pressed.

❏ `DragOver` — The user presses the mouse button when the mouse pointer is inside the hot area of a button (clip), and then moves the mouse pointer outside this area while keeping the mouse button pressed. If the user doesn't release the mouse button, this event will be triggered every time the mouse pointer leaves the hot area of the button (clip).

❏ `DragOut` — The mouse pointer leaves the hot area of a button (clip) when the mouse button isn't pressed.

❏ `Press` — The user presses the mouse button when the mouse pointer is inside the hot area of a button (clip).

❏ `Release` — The user presses the mouse button when the mouse pointer is inside the hot arca of a button (clip), and then releases the mouse button when the mouse pointer is inside the hot area of a button (clip).

❏ `ReleaseOutside` — The user presses the mouse button when the mouse pointer is inside the hot area of a button (clip). Then he or she moves the mouse pointer outside this area, while keeping the mouse button pressed, and releases it there. (In Windows, this indicates that the user wanted to perform an action, but then changed his or her mind).

❏ `KeyDown` — This is a clip event triggered when a key is pressed. If the user keeps on pressing the key, the event is triggered repeatedly with intervals depending on the keyboard settings. Not every key triggers a keyboard event in Flash. When a movie is played in the Flash environment, it recognizes as many keys as when it is played in a browser or the Flash player. For example, it doesn't respond to the <Enter> key.

❏ `KeyUp` — This is a clip event triggered when a key is released.

To see how it works, start a new movie, create a clip with the c name, and check the **Export for ActionScript** checkbox. Draw a rectangle, and the clip will be ready.

Then, enter the main scene and create an empty clip with the name `inner`. Just press the <Ctrl>+<F8> shortcut and name the clip. The `inner` clip is also ready. Select the first frame of the main timeline, press <F9>, and attach the code from Listing 4.4 to the frame.

Listing 4.4. Examining the mouse events

```
// Call the c clip to the movie work area.
attachMovie('c', 'c', 1);
c._x = 100; c._y = 100;
// Disable the "hand" mouse pointer.
c.useHandCursor = false;
c.onRollOver = function()
{ trace('RollOver');
}
c.onRollOut = function()
{ trace('RollOut');
}
c.onReleaseOutSide = function()
{ trace('ReleaseOutSide');
}
c.onRelease = function()
{ trace('Release');
}
c.onDragOver = function()
{ trace('DragOver');
}
c.onDragOut = function()
{ trace('DragOut');
}
c.onPress = function()
{ trace('Press');
}
c.onMouseDown = function()
{ trace('MouseDown');
}
c.onMouseUp = function()
{ trace('MouseUp');
}
// Uncomment to see the work of the event handler.
// It responds too often.
/*c.onMouseMove = function()
{ trace('MouseMove');
}
*/
```

You created the event handler for mouse events dynamically, that is, using ActionScript code. To do this, you assigned the clip a few properties with predefined names, such as onMouseMove. You then assigned these properties pointers to the functions that should handle the events. You defined the functions as literals. You could also define them in another fragment of the code and assign the names of the functions to the properties. For example:

```
function moMove()
   { trace('MouseMove');
   }
c.onMouseMove = moMove;
```

You can reassign such an event handler to another function, or even delete it, by deleting the corresponding property of the c clip. For example:

```
delete c.onMouseMove;
```

This is very convenient. You can have one set of event handlers in the menu and another in the game.

The onClipEvent(keyDown) and onClipEvent(keyUp) keyboard event handlers don't work in the timeline frames. You have to attach them to clip instances. To do this, enter the editing mode for the c clip by double-clicking on the clip in the symbol library, and drag the inner clip onto the work area. Click on this clip inside the work area to select it, and open the code editor window. In this window, type the code from Listing 4.5.

Listing 4.5. Examining the keyboard events

```
onClipEvent(keyDown)
{ // Getting the ASCII code of the key pressed last
  lastkey = String.fromCharCode(Key.getAscii());
  trace('KeyDown. Key = ' + lastkey + ', ' + Key.GetCode(lastkey));
}
onClipEvent(keyUp)
{ trace('KeyUp');
  // Deleting the onMouseUp event handler
  delete _root.c.onMouseUp;
}
```

Start playback of the movie (with the <Ctrl>+<Enter> shortcut) and watch how the handler works. After you release the key being detected, the `onMouseUp` will stop working, just as you would expect. You can find this example in the events.fla file.

When using this method for attaching event handlers to instances of child clips, you can delete the handlers by removing the parent clip: `c.removeMovieClip()`.

NOTE

When duplicating clips using the `duplicateMovieClip()` function, the event handlers inside these clips (including those inside the nested clips) and the attached event handlers are also duplicated. When an event takes place, all the handlers for this event in all of the clips in the movie's work area will gain control.

The buttons have the following events: `press`, `release`, `releaseOutside`, `rollOver`, `rollOut`, `dragOver`, and `dragOut`. In addition, there is a "pure" button event, `keyPress`, triggered when the specified key is pressed. However, ActionScript programmers prefer to use the `keyDown` event. Button event handlers have a different format: The `on` keyword is used. For example:

```
on (rollOver)
{ // Event handler code
}
```

The one button event handler can handle several mouse events separated with commas:

```
on (rollOver, rollOut)
{ // Event handler code
}
```

In the `keyPress` event handler, you should specify a particular key, so that the event handler responds to the pressing of that key:

```
on (keyPress 'y')
{ // Event handler code
}
```

For special keys, use the '<key_name>' format. For example:

```
on (keyPress '<Left>')
{ // Event handler code
}
```

The following key names are valid:

```
<Backspace> <Delete> <Down> <End> <Enter> <Home> <Insert>
<Left> <PgDn> <PgUp> <Right> <Space> <Tab> <Up>
```

Button event handlers can only be placed in button instances. To place an event handler, select a button instance in the work space, open the ActionScript editor window, and type all handlers for this button.

A new property for the Key object was introduced in Flash MX. It is addListener, which allows the object to listen to the keyboard. You can assign this property a reference to an object with the onKeyDown and onKeyUp methods. In the next paragraphs, I'll describe this feature in detail. Start a new project and attach the code from Listing 4.6. to its first frame.

Listing 4.6. Listening to the keyboard

```
l = new Object();
l.onKeyDown = function()
{ // Getting the ASCII code of the key pressed last
  lastkey = String.fromCharCode(Key.getAscii());
  trace('KeyDown. Key = ' + lastkey + ', ' + Key.GetCode(lastkey));
}
l.onKeyUp = function()
{ trace('KeyUp');
}
Key.addListener(l);
```

You obtained event handlers similar to those attached to the inner clip.

You can add several keyboard event handlers to the Key object. To remove them, use the Key.removeListener(l) command, like in the above example.

4.9.2. An Example: Creating Customized Mouse Pointer

Consider an example of the use of event handlers. You'll create your own mouse pointer with its coordinates displayed below it. The mouse pointer will be a common clip with an arrow image, the coordinates being displayed in a text field below the pointer.

Start a new project, and set a 18-pixel grid spacing (this is by default). To do this, use the **View | Grid | Edit Grid** menu command. Check the **Show Grid** and **View | Snapping | Snap to Grid** checkboxes. Leave the **View | Snapping | Snap to Objects** checkbox checked. Press the <Ctrl>+<F8> shortcut, give the clip the name fmouse, and check the **Export for ActionScript** checkbox. Set the zoom level to 400%, open the properties window (with the <Ctrl>+<F3> shortcut), and select the **Line** tool and the **hairline** line type. Set the pointer to the origin of the coordinates and draw an arrow as shown in Fig. 4.2. Fill it with yellow.

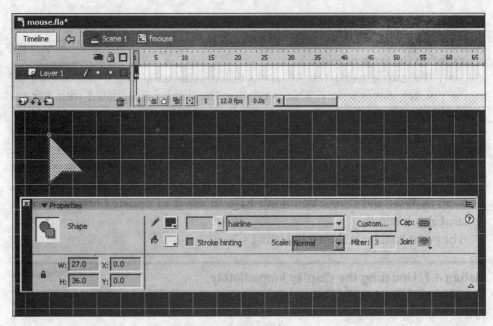

Fig. 4.2. The fmouse clip

Select the first frame on the main timeline, and press the <F9> key. In the code editor window, type the code from Listing 4.6.

Listing 4.6. Creating your own mouse pointer

```
// Hiding the system mouse pointer
Mouse.hide();
// Attaching the clip with your mouse pointer and assigning it level 100.
// The mouse clip should have the greatest level so that
// it is on top of the movie.
attachMovie('fmouse', 'fmouse', 100);
fmouse._x = _xmouse;
fmouse._y = _ymouse;
// Setting the mouse move event handler
fmouse.onMouseMove = mouseMove;
// The mouse move event handler
function mouseMove()
{ fmouse._x = _xmouse;
  fmouse._y = _ymouse;
}
stop();
```

Note that you don't need to write _root._xmouse and _root.mouse._x. Rather, you can write _xmouse and mouse._x, because the code and the objects that it accesses are on the same timeline.

Start the movie using the <Ctrl>+<Enter> shortcut. You'll notice that the mouse pointer moves jerkily. This is because the display is updated with a frame rate of 12 fps. If you specify 30 fps, the mouse pointer will move smoothly. However, there is a more elegant solution to this problem. This involves the use of the updateAfterEvent() global function, which makes the Flash player update the work area immediately, without waiting for the output of the next frame. This function is only available in the clip event handlers: mouseMove, mouseDown, mouseUp, keyDown, and keyUp. You don't have to use it to update buttons; they are updated automatically.

The event handler is shown in Listing 4.7.

Listing 4.7. Updating the display immediately

```
function mouseMove()
{ fmouse._x = _xmouse;
  fmouse._y = _ymouse;
  updateAfterEvent();
}
```

Now you can set any frame rate you like (for example, one frame per second), but the mouse pointer will move as smoothly as the Windows mouse pointer.

You might have noticed that when the mouse pointer leaves the movie window, the fmouse clip keeps on "hanging" on the window. How can you hide it? Could you create a _root.onRollOut event handler with the fmouse._visible = false command inside it? Unfortunately, this doesn't work. You cannot create such event handler for the entire movie. One solution to this problem is the following: Create a transparent clip, and place an instance of it onto the lowest layer in the development environment. Then create the on (rollOut) and on (rollOver) event handlers for this instance.

Create a button with the name out. Draw a rectangle without an outline (remember the **No Color** button of the **Line** tool?). The rectangle should be the size of the film, that is, 550 × 400 pixels. Position the upper left corner of the rectangle at the origin of coordinates. If your clip isn't transparent enough, open the **Color Mixer** panel, select the image, select the **Fill Color** tool, and set the **Alpha** parameter to 0%. Create a **Layer 2** under **Layer 1** on the main timeline, drag the clip onto the new layer, and set its coordinates to 0 and 0 in the **Info** window. Then, click on the clip instance to select it, and attach the code from Listing 4.8 to this instance in the ActionScript editor window.

Listing 4.8. Hiding and unhiding the mouse pointer

```
on (rollOut)
{ _root.fmouse._visible = 0;  // 0 is interpreted as false.
}
on (rollOver)
{ _root.fmouse._visible = 1;  // 1 is interpreted as true.
```

Make sure to restore the fmouse clip when the mouse pointer returns to the movie window. You can easily check that no event handlers are needed when you drag the mouse pointer beyond the window and back: It appears and disappears automatically.

As you can see, you can use the on (event) syntax of button event handlers in clip event handlers.

NOTE

You could create a button instead of the out clip. Everything would work the same as in this example. You can check this by changing the **Type** parameter of the out symbol from **Movie Clip** to **Button**. Change the behavior of the instance of the out symbol in the same way. However, save the code attached to it before doing so: You'll need to restore the code after the behavior changes. In event handlers of this instance, you can write fmouse._visible = ... without the _root prefix, because the scope of the button's event handlers is the main timeline.

Now you should carry out the display of the coordinates of the mouse pointer. You'll need to create a text field below the pointer in the fmouse clip. First, however, enter the editing mode of the fmouse symbol, open the properties panel with the <Ctrl>+<F3> shortcut, and select the **Text** tool. Draw a text field below the mouse pointer, specify the **Dynamic Text** property, and select the **_typewriter** font with a font size of 12 pts and a light-gray color. In the **Var:** input box, give the text field the name t. Set the width of the text field so that the "999,999" text fits into it as shown in Fig. 4.3.

Move to the first frame in the main scene, and open the ActionScript editor window. Add a line of code to the mouseMove function, so that it appears as shown in Listing 4.9.

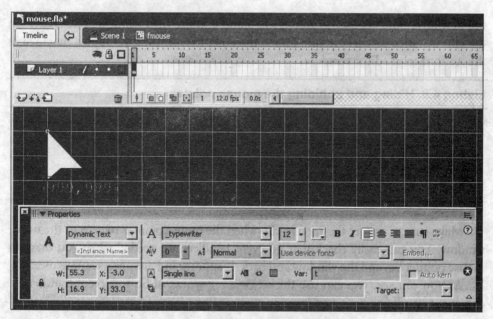

Fig. 4.3. The text field below the mouse pointer

Listing 4.9. A modification of the function that shows your mouse pointer

```
function mouseMove()
{ fmouse._x = _xmouse;
  fmouse._y = _ymouse;
  fmouse.t = Math.round(_xmouse) + ', ' + Math.round(_ymouse);
  updateAfterEvent();
}
```

Every time you move the mouse pointer, its coordinates are computed, and the text field is updated. The rounding off is necessary because Flash sometimes displays fractional coordinates, which is probably a bug.

The finished project is available in the mouse.fla file.

4.9.3. Clip Events Related to the Movie

When the Flash player is about to enter the next frame of a movie, the onEnterFrame event is triggered. This event takes place regardless of whether the playback is stopped (e.g., with the `stop()` command). Handlers of this event usually execute code implementing a certain routine action. For example, in an arcade game, this code moves the main characters and defines their subsequent activities. For this purpose, you can create an empty clip, and attach a handler like this to it. The code of this handler will be executed before any other code on the timeline of the clip that contains the `onEnterFrame` event handler.

The `load` event takes place when a clip appears on the movie work space, that is, when the key frame containing this clip is played first (assuming that the clip was put into the key frame in the Flash development environment). The `load` event also takes place when a clip is created programmatically using the `duplicateMovieClip()` or `attachMovie()` functions.

The `unload` event is triggered before a clip ceases to exist. This can happen when the playback reaches the last timeline frame containing this clip, or when the `removeMovieClip()` function is called.

The `data` event is triggered when the `loadVariables()` function loads data from the server to the clip. I'm not going to describe this event, because you'll use a more convenient method for detecting the completion of data loading.

4.9.4. Scopes of Event Handlers

You can define variables inside event handlers. In a clip, these variables belong to the timeline of the clip as if they were declared in a frame of its timeline. In a clip's event handler, you can access variables and functions defined on the timeline of this clip directly. The `this` keyword in a clip's event handlers refers to the instance of the clip. In Flash, there are a few global functions with names that are the same as the names of clip methods. To call a clip method from this clip's event handler, use the identifier of this clip or the `this` keyword. For example:

```
this.duplicateMovieClip()
```
`this.loadMovie()` — load an SWF file into the clip
```
this.loadVariables()
```
```
this.removeMovieClip()
```
```
this.startDrag()
```
`this.unloadMovie()` — unload the movie from the Flash player

For buttons, the scope of variables declared inside button event handlers is the timeline that contains the button. So you shouldn't declare too many variables in event handlers.

Chapter 5: Coding the Script of the Game

Now, having read the previous chapter, you can start to program the game. In this chapter, we'll programmatically control the clips created earlier. We will use the chapter4.1.fla project as a base for this, so open it in Flash.

5.1. Final Preparations

Move the first key frames to the fourth frame, as the first frames will be used as a loop waiting for the movie to be loaded, and for the parameters from the server. To move the frames in both layers, click on the first frame on one layer, and then click on the first frame on the other, all the while keeping the <Shift> key pressed. The frames will be selected. Then, click on one of the selected frames, and drag both frames to the fourth frame of these layers. Create the **Actions** layer above the other layers. As you already know, you can double-click on the layer's name to re-name it. To make the scene's name self-explanatory, rename it Game. To do this, open the **Scene** panel using the **Window | Other Panels | Scene** menu command or the <Shift>+<F2> shortcut, and double-click on the scene name. Rename the scene, and close the **Scene** panel. Compare your result with Fig. 5.1.

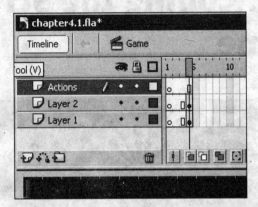

Fig. 5.1. Moving frames and adding a layer

Click on the fourth frame on the **Actions** layer, press the <F6> key to insert a key frame, open the code editor window, and enter the following code:

```
if (!_totalframes || _framesloaded != _totalframes) gotoAndPlay(2);
```

This means that, if the number of frames in the movie equal zero or isn't equal to the number of currently loaded frames, playback should continue from frame 2. As a result, a loop is created that waits for the SWF file to load into the player completely.

Your movie will consist of only five frames. When the playback reaches the fifth frame, it will stop, and the subsequent actions will be performed by event handlers. The main program will be attached to the fourth frame as an external file. To achieve this, create a key frame in the fourth frame of the **Actions** layer, and type the following directive in the code editor window:

```
#include "tet5.1.as"
```

This tells the code editor that the code for this frame is in the tet5.1.as file in the same folder as the project file. Create an empty file tet5.1.as.

NOTE

There will be an individual external file with the main program for each intermediate project file. For example, the tet5.2.3.as file corresponds to the chapter5.2.3.fla project. So, you'll have to edit the file name repeatedly in the `#include` directive in the fourth frame of the **Actions** layer.

You should stop the playback explicitly to prevent it from resuming after the last frame ends (at least, in Flash development environment). To do this, create a fifth frame in the **Actions** layer and attach the following code to it:

```
stop();
```

To make the objects survive until the fifth frame, select the fifth frames of **Layer 1** and **Layer 2**, and press the <F5> key. Test your movie by pressing the <Ctrl>+<Enter> shortcut. The pits and the control panel should appear.

You should then add actions to the square symbols. They will call the sound of an explosion. Import this sound to the movie.

Open the **File | Import | Import to Library** window, and select the Examples\ Chapter 5\explode.wav file. The sound will be imported to the library, and you'll be able to test this by clicking the appropriate button in the preview window. Right-click on the icon for the imported sound, and select the **Linkage** item in the pop-up menu. In the **Linkage Properties** window, check the **Export for ActionScript** checkbox, and give the sound the `explodesnd` identifier. Right-click on the icon again, and select the **Move to New Folder** item. Name the new folder "Sounds".

Enter the editing mode for the `k0` symbol. Attach the following code to its first frame in the **Actions** layer.

```
var t;
stop();
```

Make the third frame a key frame, and attach the following code to it:

```
if (--t > -1) gotoAndPlay(2);
```

Attach the following code to the fourth frame:

```
if (Math.random(3) < 1) _root.playSound(_root.explodesnd);
```

Finally, create the 11th key frame in the **Actions** layer, and attach the following code to it:

```
--_root.ctremove;
this.removeMovieClip();
```

This code will work as follows: In the first frame, the `t` variable is declared, and the playback stops. This is why common static squares will appear in the pits when the `attachMovie()` function creates square clips from library symbols. However, as soon as you set the playback of the third frame in some clips of squares, animation will start inside them. This animation will eventually destroy both the squares and their clips. The process will be controlled by the main program. In the program, random numbers will be assigned to the `t` variables in appropriate clips of the squares before deleting the filled lines from the pits. As a result, waiting loops will start in the third frame. These loops will run at various time intervals, determined by the `t` variables. After an interval expires, the playback will move to the third frame, in which the `explodesnd` sound will be played using the `playSound()`

function from the main program. However, the probability of playing the sound will be 1/3, to avoid situations where too many explosions are heard simultaneously. Then, the squares will fly off into bits until the tenth frame, finally vanishing in the 11th frame. The ctremove global variable first contains the number of squares in the filled lines. Each square clip will reduce this number by one before it destroys itself. This variable lets the main program know whether all of the clips have been removed.

You should duplicate this code in the **Actions** layer for the other symbols: k1, k2, k3, ..., and k8. To do this, click on the caption of the **Actions** layer for the k0 symbol to select all the frames in this layer. Then, select the **Edit | Copy Frames** menu command or press the <Ctrl>+<Alt>+<C> shortcut. Enter the editing mode for the k1 symbol, click on the caption of its **Actions** layer, and then select the **Edit | Paste Frames** menu command or press the <Ctrl>+<Alt>+<V> shortcut.

Now, import the other sounds just as you imported the explode.wav sound, and place them in the Sound folder. Refer to Table 5.1.

Table 5.1. Attributes of imported sounds

Sound file name	Identifier for export	Meaning of the sound
bleenk.wav	bleenksnd	A square falling in the splash screen
bleep3.wav	bleep3snd	Increasing game speed
cannon.wav	cannonsnd	The thunder sound
fall.wav	fallsnd	A piece falling during the game
gover.wav	goversnd	Game over
movelayer.wav	movelayersnd	The upper lines substituting for re-moved lines
scoreup.wav	scoreupsnd	Increasing the score

You should now create a few more empty clip symbols. You'll attach event handlers to them later. Create a symbol with the name emptyclip, but don't check the **Export for ActionScript** checkbox. Then, create an empty clip named gameact name and the gameact identifier, and check the **Export for ActionScript** checkbox. Finally, create two clip symbols with the names keydownact and keyupact and the same identifiers, and check the **Export for ActionScript** checkbox for each. Drag an instance of the emptyclip clip into each of these clips. In the keydownact clip, right-click on the emptyclip instance (shown as a white circle) and select the **Actions** item in the pop-up menu. In the code editor window, type the following code:

```
onClipEvent (keyDown)
 { if (_root.controlenabled)
   { _root.keyDown();
     updateAfterEvent();
   }
 }
```

Repeat this procedure with the emptyclip instance inside the keyupact clip, and enter the following code:

```
onClipEvent (keyUp)
 { _root.keyUp();
 }
```

When the keyDown event takes place, the keyDown() function from the main program will be called if the controlenabled variable is set. This variable indicates whether a piece is controlled using the keyboard. Similarly, when the keyUp event occurs, the keyUp() function will be called.

Compare the result of your work with mine, which is located in the chapter5.1.fla file.

5.2. Writing the Data Section of the Game Script

As you already know, each instance of a clip in a movie should have its own depth, or level, specified using the attachMovie() or duplicateMovieClip() function. If you place a new instance at a depth of another instance, the new instance will replace the old one. Of course, you don't want squares to disappear when a lightning bolt appears. Therefore, you should set a particular depth for every clip instance.

5.2.1. Specifying Depths for Clips

Let the initial (minimum) depth be depth0. It is equal to zero. This is the depth of the first square clip on the splash screen and of the square in the upper left corner of the left game pit. (All squares on the splash screen are destroyed before the game starts). The horizontal size of each pit measured in squares is xx = 12, while its vertical size in squares is yy = 24. Therefore, you need xx × yy = 288 depths for each pit.

The depth of the square clip in the upper left corner of the left pit is zero. The depth of its neighbor to the right is one, the depth of the rightmost square clip in the top line of the left pit is 11, and so on to the lower right square in the left pit, for which the depth is 277. The depths of the squares in the other pit start at 288 and are numbered in a similar manner. Note that fragments of broken squares in the filled lines fly upwards, so the fragments will be above the squares in the upper lines because those squares are at lower depths.

The next unused depth is depth1 = depth0 + xx*yy*2. This is the initial depth of the clips for digits on the panels (score, speed, etc.). There are 25 such clips. The next six depths are for lightning clips, the menu, and the Game Over! clip. These clips won't appear simultaneously. The top three levels are for the empty clips gameact, keydownact, and keyupact.

5.2.2. Creating Arrays for Pits and Filled Lines

You should now code arrays for the game pits. Each of these two arrays should contain 28 rows and 12 columns. The elements of the arrays are either references to square clips, when the corresponding cells of the pits contain squares, or the null values (undefined when the game starts), if the pit cells are empty.

In ActionScript, you cannot declare a multi-dimensional array without specifying values for all of its elements. This is why you first need to declare the same number of one-dimensional arrays, as there are lines in the pits. You'll then use a loop to declare an array of columns for each line. The required code is in Listing 5.1.

Listing 5.1. Creating arrays for the game pits

```
// Arrays for the left and right pit; each contains yy = 24 elements
 p1 = new Array(yy), p2 = new Array(yy),
...
// An array of xx = 12 columns for each line
for (i = 0; i < yy; i++)
 { p1[i] = new Array(xx);
   p2[i] = new Array(xx);
 }
```

As a result, the p1[0][0] element corresponds to the upper left cell of the left pit, the p1[0][1] element to the cell's neighbor to the right, and so on. The p1[23][11] element corresponds to the lower right cell. You'll manipulate these arrays in a loop. Because both arrays should be processed in similar ways, create another array, `pits`, containing two elements that refer to the `p1` and `p2` arrays. The required code is `pits = new Array(p1, p2)`. As a result, `pits[0][23][11]` corresponds to the lower right cell in the first pit, and `pits[1][23][11]` corresponds to the lower right cell in the second pit.

After two falling pieces stop, you'll look for filled lines in both pits. To remember the positions of these lines (i.e., the numbers of the rows in the `p1` and `p2` arrays), create a `layers` array containing two elements. In a loop, make each of these elements an array of 24 elements (Listing 5.2).

Listing 5.2. Creating arrays to remember filled lines

```
layers = new Array(2)
...
layers[0] = new Array(yy);
layers[1] = new Array(yy);
```

If, for example, `layers[0][23]` isn't empty, this indicates that the bottom line in the left pit is filled with squares, and you should remove it. You'll store the numbers of filled lines in each pit in the `numlayers` array containing two elements.

5.2.3. Coding Pieces, Check Arrays, and Piece Rotation Arrays

Because pieces in this game consist of no more than three squares, they can all be defined using arrays containing 3×3 elements (three rows and three columns). Code all nine pieces in arrays of this type. For example, an array `f0 = new Array([0,0,0], [0,1,0], [0,0,0])` codes a piece that consists of one square (located in the center of a 3×3 square). An array `f4 = new Array([0,1,0], [0,1,0], [0,1,0])` codes a vertical piece consisting of three squares. You'll use these arrays to detect the positions of the squares in the pieces currently controlled by the gamer and to detect the coordinates of these squares in the pits. You'll store the coordinates of the upper left squares in the 3×3 squares (named `f0`, `f1`, ..., and `f8`), in which the current pieces are contained. You'll use these coordinates as a reference to detect which squares in the pits belong to the current pieces. The `mf` array will contain references to all of the arrays that code the pieces.

```
mf = new Array(f0, f1, f2, f3, f4, f5, f6, f7, f8)
```

To check whether a piece can be rotated (counterclockwise), use the arrays that code the pieces. Based on these arrays, create check arrays for each piece. In the check arrays, elements containing ones will indicate the positions of squares that could hamper rotation. If there is a square in the pit in a position indicated by an element with one, rotation will be impossible. Here is an example of a check array for a particular piece:

```
f3 = new Array([0,0,0], [1,1,1], [0,0,0]) // Three squares horizontally
pf3 = new Array([1,1,1], [0,0,0], [1,1,1])
```

From the pf3 array, you can see that all of the squares within the 3×3 square that don't belong to the piece will hamper the rotation of the piece.

Create an array with references to the check arrays:

```
ppf = new Array(pf0, pf1, pf2, pf3, pf4, pf5, pf6, pf7, pf8)
```

For the sake of convenience, it would be best to use the array that codes a piece to find an array that codes this piece rotated through 90 degrees, rather than to compute rotation. For this purpose, create arrays that code the intermediate positions of each piece when it rotates. Here is an example for the same piece:

```
f3 = new Array([0,0,0], [1,1,1], [0,0,0]) // Three squares horizontally
ff3 = new Array(f3, f4, f3, f4)
```

The zero element of the ff3 array refers to the array that codes the piece in its initial position. The first element refers to the array that codes the piece when rotated through 90 degrees. For the f3 piece, this is actually the f4 piece (three squares in a column). The second element refers to an array that codes the piece rotated by another 90 degrees. This is, in fact, f3 - the piece's initial position. The third element of the ff3 array refers to an array that codes the piece rotated through yet another 90 degrees. This is f4 again. Gather the references to all these arrays in one array:

```
mff = new Array(ff0, ff1, ff2, ff3, ff4, ff5, ff6, ff7, ff8)
```

To find the coding for a piece rotated through 90 degrees, you need to store indices of elements in the arrays of the ff0, ff1, ..., and ff8 series for two current pieces. For example, if a current piece is coded with the f3 array, its index in the ff3 array is equal to zero. After each rotation, the index increases by one modulo four, thus iterating cyclically through all of the elements of the ff3 array. You'll store the numbers for the positions of two current pieces in an array: ffn = new Array(2). To find, which two arrays of the ff0, ff1, ..., and ff8 series code the current two pieces, you should store each current piece's index in the mff array.

To store these indices, create a new array: `mffn = new Array(2)`. Finally, to code the current pieces being rotated, create another array, `figs = new Array(2)`. Its elements will take the values `ff0`, `ff1`, ..., and `ff8`, extracted from the `mff` array as the pieces rotate.

The horizontal and vertical coordinates of the current pieces in the pits (i.e., the coordinates of the upper left squares of the 3×3 squares that code the pieces) will be stored in two arrays:

```
figsx = new Array(2)
figsy = new Array(2)
```

When moving the pieces to the left or right, you'll subtract one from or add one to the elements of the `figsx` array, respectively. When moving the pieces down, you'll change the Y coordinates in the `figsy` array.

You'll store the colors of the current pieces in an array:

```
colors = new Array(2)
```

The square in the `k0` clip will have a color value equal to zero, the color value of the square in the `k1` clip will be equal to one, and so on.

I'll explain the use of these data later, when describing the program. The other data will be also explained when programming the game. Now, open the chapter5.1.fla project, and insert the code from Listing 5.3 into the tet5.1.as file.

Listing 5.3. The data section

```
var
 // Game states
 // The menu
 menust = 1,
 // The game is going on.
 gamest = 2,
 // The variable to store the game states
 gamestate,
 // If not zero, the gamer paused the game. Otherwise, no pause.
 ispaused = 0,
// Sizes of the square and its half (in pixels)
 kv = 23,
 kv2 = 11.5,
// Coordinates of the upper right square in each pit (in pixels)
 pitx = new Array(10, 322),
 pity = new Array(3, 3),
```

```
// Sizes of the pits (in squares)
xx = 12,
yy = 24,
// The initial depth of the squares in the pits and on the splash screen
depth0 = 0,
// Depths of the squares in both pits
dp = new Array(depth0, depth0 + xx*yy),
// The initial depth after the last square in the right pit
depth1 = depth0 + xx*yy*2,
// The initial depth for digits on the panel and currscore,
// starting from speed (25 depths)
depth2 = depth1,
// The initial depth for lightnings (6 depths), the menu, and Game over!
depth3 = depth2 + 25,
// Depths gameact, keydownact, and keyupact (3 depths)
depth4 = depth3 + 6,
// Pit arrays
p1 = new Array(yy),
p2 = new Array(yy),
// References to the two pit arrays
pits = new Array(p1, p2),
// Flags for filled lines
layers = new Array(2),
// The number of filled lines
numlayers = new Array(2),
// Arrays that code pieces
f0 = new Array([0,0,0], [0,1,0], [0,0,0]), // 1 square
f1 = new Array([0,0,0], [1,1,0], [0,0,0]), // 2 squares
f2 = new Array([0,1,0], [0,1,0], [0,0,0]), // 2 squares
f3 = new Array([0,0,0], [1,1,1], [0,0,0]), // 3 squares horizontally
f4 = new Array([0,1,0], [0,1,0], [0,1,0]), // 3 squares vertically
f5 = new Array([1,0,0], [1,1,0], [0,0,0]), // 3 squares, "corner"
f6 = new Array([0,1,0], [1,1,0], [0,0,0]), // 3 squares, "corner"
f7 = new Array([1,1,0], [0,1,0], [0,0,0]), // 3 squares, "corner"
f8 = new Array([1,1,0], [1,0,0], [0,0,0]), // 3 squares, "corner"
// References to the coding arrays
mf = new Array(f0, f1, f2, f3, f4, f5, f6, f7, f8),
// Arrays that check for the possibility of rotation
pf0 = new Array([0,0,0], [0,0,0], [0,0,0]),
```

```
pf1 = new Array([0,1,0], [0,0,0], [0,0,0]),
pf2 = new Array([1,0,0], [1,0,0], [0,0,0]),
pf3 = new Array([1,1,1], [0,0,0], [1,1,1]),
pf4 = new Array([1,0,1], [1,0,1], [1,0,1]),
pf5 = new Array([0,1,0], [0,0,0], [0,0,0]),
pf6 = new Array([1,0,0], [0,0,0], [0,0,0]),
pf7 = new Array([0,0,0], [1,0,0], [0,0,0]),
pf8 = f0,
// References to the checking arrays
ppf = new Array(pf0, pf1, pf2, pf3, pf4, pf5, pf6, pf7, pf8),
// The positions of the pieces during rotation
ff0 = new Array(f0, f0, f0, f0), ff1 = new Array(f1, f2, f1, f2),
ff2 = new Array(f2, f1, f2, f1), ff3 = new Array(f3, f4, f3, f4),
ff4 = new Array(f4, f3, f4, f3), ff5 = new Array(f5, f6, f7, f8),
ff6 = new Array(f6, f7, f8, f5), ff7 = new Array(f7, f8, f5, f6),
ff8 = new Array(f8, f5, f6, f7),
// The array of rotation positions
mff = new Array(ff0, ff1, ff2, ff3, ff4, ff5, ff6, ff7, ff8),
// The numbers of the current pieces in the mff array
mffn = new Array(2),
// The numbers of the positions of the current pieces
// in the arrays ff0, ff1, ..., ff8
ffn = new Array(2),
// The array of two current pieces
figs = new Array(2),
// Coordinates of the 3*3 squares for both pieces (x can be < 0!)
figsx = new Array(2),
figsy = new Array(2),
// Colors of the squares of the two current pieces
colors = new Array(2),
// The Speed (from 0 to 9), the numbers of the pieces and the lines,
// and the score
// The initial speed
speed0,
// The current speed
speed,
// The number of the pieces spent
pieces,
```

```
// The number of the lines filled
lines,
// The current score
score,
// The score for the current pieces. It decreases if the gamer hesitates.
currscore,
// The indication of whether the gamer controls the pieces
// or they just fall
controlenabled,
// A move of the uncontrolled piece (in milliseconds)
timestep,
// Variables for a time delay
nexttime,
numact,
// Loop variables
i, j,
// The coordinates of the squares in the splash screen title
  kx - new Array(
  0, 2, 1, 1, 1,
  6, 8, 6, 7, 5, 7,
  10, 12, 14, 12, 12,
  17,
  22, 21, 23, 20, 24, 22, 24, 20, 24,
  27, 28,  31, 34, 32, 32,
  37, 39, 36, 38, 36, 37, 39,
  42, 45, 43, 43, 43,
  48, 49, 50, 47, 49, 47, 50, 51,
  53, 53, 53,
  57, 55, 59, 57, 59, 55, 56, 58
  ),
ky = new Array(
  -1, -1, 1, 4, 5,
  0, -1, 2, 2, 4, 5,
  -1, 0, -1, 2, 4,
  2,
  -1, 0, 0, 2, 1, 3, 3, 5, 5,
  2, 2,
  -1, -1, 1, 4,
```

```
      0, -1, 2, 2, 3, 5, 5,
      -1, -1, 0, 2, 5,
      0, -1, 1, 2, 3, 5, 4, 5,
      -1, 2, 4,
      -1, 1, 0, 2, 4, 4, 5, 5
    ),
  nk = new Array(
      1, 3, 4, 2, 0,
      8, 1, 5, 0, 4, 3,
      0, 7, 1, 2, 4,
      3,
      0, 0, 0, 4, 0, 1, 6, 2, 2,
      1, 0,
      3, 1, 4, 4,
      8, 1, 2, 1, 0, 5, 1,
      3, 1, 0, 4, 2,
      8, 0, 2, 4, 7, 2, 0, 0,
      0, 2, 4,
      3, 2, 0, 3, 2, 0, 0, 1
    ),
// Variables for the splash screen
dropind = 1,
lastind = nk.length - 1,
stepind = 134,
// The counter of the intact squares in the filled lines
ctremove,
// The indication of whether the key is pressed
keyisdown,
// Sound objects
explodesnd = new Sound(),
fallsnd = new Sound(),
movelayersnd = new Sound(),
cannonsnd = new Sound(),
goversnd = new Sound(),
bleenksnd = new Sound(),
scoreupsnd = new Sound(),
bleep3snd = new Sound();
```

Add a few empty lines, and then insert the code from Listing 5.4.

Listing 5.4. The beginning of the program

```
// *** The beginning of the program ***
// Load sounds from the library.    -
explodesnd.attachSound('explodesnd');
fallsnd.attachSound('fallsnd');
cannonsnd.attachSound('cannonsnd');
movelayersnd.attachSound('movelayersnd');
goversnd.attachSound('goversnd');
bleenksnd.attachSound('bleenksnd');
scoreupsnd.attachSound('scoreupsnd');
bleep3snd.attachSound('bleep3snd');
// Create arrays for the pits and lines.
for (i = 0; i < yy; i++)
 { p1[i] = new Array(xx);
   p2[i] - new Array(xx);
 }
layers[0] = new Array(yy);
layers[1] = new Array(yy);
// Call empty clips to listen to the game's actions.
attachMovie('gameact', 'gameact', depth4);
gameact.onMouseDown = function(){ keyisdown = 1 }
attachMovie('keyupact', 'keyupact', depth4 + 2);
```

I trust that you understand the code. An onMouseDown event handler is attached to the gameact clip to watch mouse clicks. Now, I'll take the opportunity to explain how the data from Listing 5.3 work, beginning with the appearance of a new pair of figures. I'll illustrate this using a left-pit piece as an example.

Jumping ahead of myself, I'll just mention that the newFigs function is responsible for the "birth" of a new pair of pieces. First, you need to choose a random value between zero and eight that will be the number of the piece and an indicator of its color. Let the value be three. It will be assigned to the mffn[0] element:

```
mffn[0] = Math.floor(Math.random()*9);
```

Copy this value to the colors array, because the mffn[0] value will change as the piece rotates.

```
colors[0] = mffn[0]
```

First, the number of the piece's position in the `ff3` array (the array for the third piece) is equal to zero, because the piece hasn't rotated yet:

```
ffn[0] = 0
```

`figs[0]` refers to the array that codes the left piece in its initial position:

```
figs[0] = mff[mffn[0]][0]
```

In other words, it refers to `f3`. Indeed, `mffn[0]` is equal to three, therefore, `mff[3]` refers to the `ff3` array (four positions of rotation), and `ff3[0]` refers to the `f3` array. It looks a little too sophisticated, doesn't it?

You need the coordinates of this piece in the left pit. By the coordinates of a piece in the pit, I mean the coordinates of the upper left square of the 3×3 square that contains the piece (this square is defined with the `f3` array). For all of the pieces and both pits, these coordinates are the same.

```
figsx[0] = 5
figsy[0] = 0
```

They correspond approximately to the central horizontal position of the pieces.

A new piece is created logically. Now, you need to check whether one of its squares overlaps a square in the pit. To do this, use the following dual loop, which iterates through the `figs[0]` array (in this example, it is the same as the `f3` array):

```
for (i = 0; i < 3; i++)
  for (j = 0; j < 3; j++)
    if (figs[0][i][j] && p1[figsy[0] + i][figsx[0] + j]) flag = 1;
```

Each loop iteration reads the contents of the element in the `i`th column and `j`th row of the `figs[0]` array. If it is a non-zero element, the code reads the elements of the `p1` pit array that is below this square of the piece. To find its X coordinate, add together the X coordinate of the 3×3 square (`figsx[0]`) and the X coordinate of the cell in this square, that is `j`. If there is a square (clip) on this place in the `p1` pit, the pieces overlap. Therefore, the **Game Over!** message should appear after the pieces are drawn. This fact is noted using the `flag` variable.

The current pieces will be displayed using the `paintFigs` function. It will contain the following loop:

```
for (i = 0; i < 3; i++)
  for (j = 0; j < 3; j++)
    if (figs[0][i][j] > 0) paintSq(0, colors[0], figsx[0] + j, figsy[0] + i);
```

The internal loop checks for a square in the ith column and the jth row of the figs[0] array. If there is one here, the paintSq function is called to draw the square, and the following parameters are passed to it:

- ❏   0 — The pit number (0 is the left pit, 1 is the right one)
- ❏   colors[0] — The number of the square among the clips k0, k1, …, and k8
- ❏   figsx[0]+j — The X coordinate of the square in the pit
- ❏   figsy[0]+i — The Y coordinate of the square in the pit

Consider the paintSq function. Clearly, it should call attachMovie for the symbol with the 'k' + colors[0] name. Depending on the colors[0] value, this will be k0, k1, …, or k8. It is then necessary to name the instance. There can be a large number of squares in the pits, and each should have a name. Remember that the depth of the upper left square in the left pit is depth0 (in fact, zero). The depth of the corresponding square in the right pit is greater than this by the number of squares in the pit. These initial depths are stored in the dp array. They are suitable for naming an instance of the square clip. Just append the depth of the square to the name of the symbol, and you'll obtain the name of the instance. In the left pit, the depth of the square clip with the (x, y) coordinates is

```
depth = dp[0] + y*xx + x
```

Here, the y line number multiplied by the number of the elements in the xx line (i.e., 12) is added to the depth of the first square in the left pit, dp[0], and the x coordinate is added to the result.

Create an instance on the work space at the depth depth:

```
attachMovie('k' + colors[0], 'k' + colors[0] + depth, depth)
```

Now you need to specify the coordinates in pixels for this instance. However, you know only its name 'k' + colors[0] + depth. You can get a reference to an instance object by its name using the eval function:

```
k = eval('k' + colors[0] + depth)
```

Now you can say that k is the instance of the square clip. You can access this instance's methods and properties using k. You are only interested in its coordinates in the movie window, which are its _x and _y properties. To compute the X coordinate of the square in the left pit in pixels, add the X coordinate of the left side of the pit (the pitx[0] value) to the X coordinate of the square (the x value), multiplied by the length of the square's side (the kv value, i.e., 23). For the Y coordinate, the formula is similar.

```
k._x = x*kv + pitx[0]
k._y = y*kv + pity[0]
```

Finally, assign the appropriate element of the left pit's array pits[0] (which is p1) the k reference to this clip instance, or in other words, the instance itself:

```
pits[0][y][x] = k
```

That's all. The square will be drawn in an appropriate place, and, therefore, two new pieces will be drawn. At this point, you might be thinking: "Too much theory, and still no results!" This is, indeed, the case. Even the simplest real-life program is much more complicated and larger than tasks in a tutorial such as printing the first N prime numbers. However, at this point on the long road we are travelling, we already can see how the pieces are drawn in their initial positions, that is, when they first appear in the pits. Insert functions that draw the square and the pieces from Listing 5.5 in the program code between the data section and the beginning of the program.

Listing 5.5. The function that displays the square and the pieces

```
// Display a square for the pit (0 or 1) with a particular color
// (from 0 to 8) and coordinates.
function paintSq(p, c, x, y)
{ var depth = dp[p] + y*xx + x, k;

  attachMovie('k' + c,'k' + c + depth, depth);
  k = eval('k' + c + depth);
  k._x = x*kv + pitx[p];
  k._y = y*kv + pity[p];
  pits[p][y][x] = k;
}


// Draw pieces in the pits.
function paintFigs()
{ var
    i, j, k,
    fx = new Array(),
    fy = new Array(),
    fig = new Array();
```

```
for (k = 0; k < 2; k++)
{ fx = figsx[k];
  fy = figsy[k];
  fig = figs[k];
  for (i = 0; i < 3; i++)
    for (j = 0; j < 3; j++)
      if (fig[i][j] > 0) paintSq(k, colors[k], fx + j, fy + i);
}
}
```

These are functions that you will use in the game. The external loop iterates k to draw figures in both pits. For k = 0, it draws them in the left pit, while for k = 1, it draws in the pit on the right. The local arrays fx, fy, and fig are used in the paintFigs function to avoid writing too many indexed variables inside the loop.

NOTE

In one fragment of code, you can put functions in any order. You can declare functions after calls to them. Scripting languages differ from languages such as Pascal.

To make these functions work, you need to initialize the figsx, figsy, figs, and colors arrays. This is done at the end of the main program, in the loop shown in Listing 5.6.

Listing 5.6. The Display of a pair of pieces in their initial positions

```
for (i = 0; i < 2; i++)
{ figsx[i] = 5;
  figsy[i] = 1;
  figs[i] = f5;
  colors[i] = 5;
  paintFigs();
}
```

By changing the values of figs[i] (or by assigning figs[0] and figs[1] various individual values), you can obtain various pairs of figures.

This stage of the project is fixed in the chapter5.2.3.fla and tet5.2.3.as files. After you view various pieces, be sure to remove the code of Listing 5.6 from the tet5.2.3.as file.

5.2.4. Coding the Splash Screen

The discussion in the previous section, covering the display of pieces, was a little premature, because the program begins with the splash screen and the menu. I didn't say a word about the **New**, **Sound**, and **Pause** buttons. Place them in the fifth frame of the movie, because the code attached to them accesses variables and calls functions declared in the main program attached to the fourth frame. (Generally speaking, accessed code should appear on the timeline before code that accesses it.)

Select the fifth frame on **Layer 2** of the movie, and press <F6>. Drag the btNew, btSound, and btPause clips from the library to the panel, and drop them to the right of the pits. Using the **Info** window, set the coordinates of the btNew instance to 618 and 378, the coordinates of the btSound instance to 692 and 378, and the coordinates of the btPause instance to 618 and 412. Using the properties window opened with the <Ctrl>+<F3> shortcut, assign the instances of these symbols the names btNew, btSound, and btPause. Select the btNew instance, open the code editor window, and type the code shown in Listing 5.7.

Listing 5.7. Code for the btNew clip

```
onClipEvent (load)
  { useHandCursor = 0;
  }
on (rollOver, dragOver)
  { if (_root.gamestate == _root.gamest && !_root.ispaused)
    this.gotoAndStop(2);
  }
on (rollOut, dragOut)
  { this.gotoAndStop(1);
  }
on (release)
  { if (_root.gamestate == _root.gamest && !_root.ispaused)
    _root.startGame(1);
  }
```

The load event handler starts as soon as the btNew instance appears. It disables the mouse pointer that looks like a hand. The hand mouse pointer will appear only over active button clips. The handler of the rollOver and dragOver events checks the state of the game. If the current state allows you to start the game, and the game hasn't been paused, the playback goes to the second frame, where this clip is high-lighted. The handler of the rollOut and dragOut events returns the playback to the first frame. When the mouse button is released, the appropriate event handler checks the state of the game. If it allows you to start the game, and the game isn't paused, the startGame function is called. The argument equal to one indicates that the new game starts when no other game is running.

Select the btSound clip instance, and attach the code from Listing 5.8 to it.

Listing 5.8. The code for the btSound clip

```
onClipEvent (load)
  { s._visible = _root.snd;
  }
on (rollOver, dragOver)
  { this.gotoAndStop(2);
    s.gotoAndStop(2);
  }
on (rollOut, dragOut)
  { this.gotoAndStop(1);
    s.gotoAndStop(1);
  }
on (release)
  { s._visible = _root.snd ^= 1;
  }
```

When an instance of the btSound clip appears in the movie (the load event takes place), the event handler hides the check (with the name s) if the snd variable declared on the main timeline is equal to zero. This variable indicates whether the sound is enabled in the game. The movie can receive it from the server from a data array related to a registered gamer. Alternatively, this variable can be stored in a cookie on the user's computer.

The next two mouse event handlers don't need explanations. They move the playback to the second and first frames of the btSound clip and of the attached clip with checks. As a result, the clip becomes highlighted or ceases to be highlighted. When the mouse button is released, the appropriate event handler uses the ^ op-erator (addition modulo 2) to change the value of the snd variable from zero to one or from one to zero, and assigns the result to the check's _visible property. If the sound is disabled, the check will disappear. Otherwise, it will appear.

Attach the code from Listing 5.9 to the `btPause` clip instance.

Listing 5.9. The code for the `btPause` clip

```
onClipEvent (load)
  { s._visible = 0;
    useHandCursor = 0;
  }
on (rollOver, dragOver)
  { if (_root.gamestate == _root.gamest)
      { this.gotoAndStop(2);
        s.gotoAndStop(2);
      }
  }
on (rollOut, dragOut)
  { this.gotoAndStop(1);
    s.gotoAndStop(1);
  }
on (release)
  { _root.togglePause();
  }
```

When an instance appears, the event handler hides the check and disables the hand mouse pointer, because there cannot be a pause at the beginning. The next two event handlers were explained earlier. When the mouse button is released, the state of the game is checked. If the state allows the user to click on the pause button, the value for the `ispaused` variable changes from zero to one, or from one to zero. If the pause is off, the mouse pointer is allowed to take the hand shape when it is over the `btNew` clip. This permission is given with the `togglePause` function in the main program. This function is also called when the <P> key is pressed, so it wouldn't be particularly wise to repeat this code twice.

If you start the movie right now (using the <Ctrl>+<Enter> shortcut), the `btSound` clip will not work correctly, because the check is displayed at the beginning, but the `snd` variable doesn't exist. This is the equivalent to disabling the sound. You'll create the variable later. To be able to hear the sound, add the following code to the third frame of the movie (you should delete this code later):

```
snd = 1;
```

For the splash screen, you need the code shown in Listing 5.10.

Listing 5.10. The code for the splash screen

```
// Output squares for the splash screen.
function spl()
{ var
    x0 = 35, y0 = 100,
    i, j, k,
    k1 = nk.length,
    name,
    depth = depth0;

  // Make the header from pieces, and place it above the window.
  for (k = 0; k < k1; k++)
    { for (i = 0; i < 3; i++)
      for (j = 0; j < 3; j++)
        if (mf[nk[k]][i][j])
          { attachMovie('k' + nk[k], 'kk' + depth, depth);
            name = eval('kk' + depth++);
            name._x = x0 + (kx[k] + j)*kv2;
            name._y = y0 + (ky[k] + i)*kv2 - 185;
            name._xscale = 50;
            name._yscale = 50;
            name.t = 80 + Math.random()*65;
          }
      depth = (k+1)*3;
    }
  keyisdown = 0;
  gameact.onEnterFrame = dropHeader;
}

// Drop the squares.
function dropHeader()
{ var
    i, j, k, k1,
    depth = lastind*3;

  // Move the piece down one step.
  for (i = 0; i < 3; i++)
    for (j = 0; j < 3; j++)
      if (mf[nk[lastind]][i][j])
```

```
      { name = eval('kk' + depth++);
        name._y += stepind;
        playSound(bleenksnd);
      }
  if (--dropind > -1) return;
  dropind = 1;
  if (keyisdown)
   { // Remove the squares.
     for (i = 0; i < 188;) eval('kk' + i++).removeMovieClip();
     menuorOver.name = 'menu';
     menuorOver();
     return;
   }
  if (--lastind > -1) return;
  // Start exploding the squares.
  k1 = nk.length;
  depth = 0;
  ctremove = 0;
  for (k = 0; k < k1; k++)
   { for (i = 0; i < 3; i++)
       for (j = 0; j < 3; j++)
         if (mf[nk[k]][i][j])
          { eval('kk' + depth++).gotoAndPlay(3);
            ++ctremove;
          }
     depth = (k + 1)*3;
   }
  gameact.onEnterFrame = wait;
  nexttime = getTimer() + 2400;
}


// Wait for lightning on the splash screen.
function wait()
{ if (getTimer() < nexttime) return;
  if (!wait.islight)
   { attachMovie('lightning', 'l1', depth3);
     l1._x = 10;
     l1._y = 225;
     attachMovie('lightning', 'l2', depth3+1);
     l2._x = 750;
     l2._y = 225;
```

```
     12._xscale = -100;
     playSound(cannonsnd);
     wait.islight = 1;
  }
  if (!ctremove)
  { menuorOver.name = 'menu';
    menuorOver(0);
  }
}


// Play the specified sound s if the snd variable isn't empty.
function playSound(s)
{ if (snd) s.start();
}
```

Insert this code after the `paintFigs` function, and insert the following call to the splash screen at the end of the main program file:

```
spl();
```

Test how the splash screen works. On my computer, it works fine.

The inserted code works as follows. The `spl()` function places the pieces, scaled by 50%, above the movie window. (Their Y coordinates are negative, and the pieces are placed 185 pixels higher than their final positions). There are 63 pieces. The function uses the `nk` array, which contains the numbers of the squares for each piece. The `kx` and `ky` variables contain the coordinates of the upper left cell of the 3×3 square. You might be wondering how these arrays appeared. I created them manually using a sheet of graph paper.

In addition, the `spl` function sets the `t` variable in each square instance to a pseudo-random value:

```
name.t = 80+Math.random()*65;
```

This is done to prevent the squares from exploding simultaneously. I found the formula by experimentation. After each piece is output, the following statement is executed:

```
depth = (k + 1)*3;
```

It assigns the initial depth of the next piece's squares a value that is a multiple of three. This will allow the program to compute the names of clip instances for this piece. Pieces can contain various numbers of squares, and you need to use the names of their instances.

After all of the pieces are placed, the function resets a flag to indicate that no key is pressed:

```
keyisdown = 0;
```

Then the dropHeader function is called. It will drop the pieces so that they make up the name of the game 185 pixels below their current positions:

```
gameact.onEnterFrame = dropHeader;
```

You need the keyisdown flag to enable skipping over the remainder of the splash screen code if the gamer presses a key or clicks the mouse button. However, you haven't written an onkeyDown event handler; so the code can handle only the mouse click. Control is passed using an empty clip, gameact, that was placed in the movie in the main program. You just assign its onEnterFrame property the name of a function (more precisely, its address), which will be called when the next onEnterFrame event is triggered. You need to take care to prevent this function from being called over and over again, infinitely, in response to each onEnterFrame event. In this project, the dropHeader is called 126 times for onEnterFrame events, because each of 63 pieces falls in two steps. If the gamer clicks the mouse button, the gameact.onMouseDown event handler will set the keyisdown variable to one. The dropHeader function then starts the loop that destroys all of the squares on the splash screen:

```
if (keyisdown)
   { // Remove the squares.
     for (i = 0; i < 188;) eval('kk' + i++).removeMovieClip();
   menuorOver.name = 'menu';
   menuorOver();
   return;
   }
```

Because there are 63 pieces, there are no more than 189 squares. During deletion, the removeMovieClip methods of non-existent clips will be called. Don't worry, the interpreter will ignore them. After the squares are removed, the menuorOver() function should output the menu. However, you haven't written this function yet. This is why, if you click on the mouse button while the splash screen is on, the squares will disappear, but you will still hear the sounds of falling squares for a while, because the program will be calling the dropHeader function 15 times per second. To cope with this problem, you could insert the following code:

```
delete gameact.onEnterFrame;
```

after the loop that removes the squares:

```
for (i = 0; i < 188;) eval('kk' + i++).removeMovieClip();
```

However, this code would be redundant in the actual project, because it is present at the beginning of the menuorOver() function.

After the dropHeader function drops the pieces, it starts to explode them in a loop:

```
for (k = 0; k < kl; k++)
  { for (i = 0; i < 3; i++)
     for (j = 0; j < 3; j++)
      if (mf[nk[k]][i][j])
       { eval('kk' + depth++).gotoAndPlay(3);
          ++ctremove;
       }
    depth = (k + 1)*3;
  }
```

During the process, the ctremove counter gets the number of the squares on the splash screen. Each square clip instance reduces this variable by one before it is destroyed. This will allow you to know that all of the the squares have ceased to exist when the ctremove variable becomes equal to zero. After that, the dropHeader function calls the wait function, which waits for 2,400 ms before the squares break into fragments and starts firing lightning bolts. The wait is implemented in the following code:

```
if (getTimer() < nexttime) return;
```

The wait function is called by the onEnterFrame event handler repeatedly until its timeout elapses. The lightning is then retrieved from the symbol library, and two instances of this are created. Note that the lightning on the right is a mirror image of that on the left, but you don't need a special symbol for it. Just scale it along the X axis using a factor of –100, and you'll get an instance that is a mirror image along the X axis. Also note how a function property is used: After the lightning bolts are fired, you create the islight property of the wait function and assign it the number one. This indicates that the lightning bolts have been fired, and there is no need for the program to fire again. The fragment of code at the end of the wait function's body checks whether all the squares have been destroyed. If this is the case, the menuorOver function that displays the menu is called.

The playSound function is simple, so it doesn't require any special comments. It checks whether sound is enabled. If it is, the function plays the sound instance it received as a parameter.

Now, I'll describe the menuorOver function. It calls either the menu clip or the gover clip. The name of the required clip is passed to the function using its name property. The function takes the parameter, arg. When it is equal to zero, the function shouldn't display the infoPanel clip. Otherwise, it should. (The latter situation occurs when the game is forced to terminate after five minutes). The clip contains some text for a gamer who hasn't registered yet. In the message, the producer of the game asks for payment in order to play full-featured versions of online games. The rules are the following: After a gamer pays a certain amount of money, he or she obtains a certain number of points and receives a password that allowing the user to play full-featured versions of online games on our site. Every time the gamer downloads a Flash game, the number of points is reduced by one. When all of the points have been exhausted, the gamer can only play "lightweight" versions of the games. For example, the gamer can only play Tetris for five minutes. A Flash game gets information about a gamer from the Web server. I believe you can create the infoPanel on your own: It's easy. Just create a green rectangle with rounded corners and with the **Alpha** parameter set to 70%, and put **Multiline** text inside it.

The code shown in Listing 5.11 contains the menuorOver function and auxiliary functions. Insert it after the playSound function.

Listing 5.11. Displaying and processing the menu

```
// Highlight the d0, d1, ..., or d9 clip when the gamer points to it
// with the mouse pointer when selecting the game speed.
function go2()
{ this.gotoAndStop(2)
}


// Remove highlight from the d0, d1, ..., or d9 clip when
// the mouse pointer leaves it.
function go1()
{ if (speed != parseInt(this._name.substr(1))) this.gotoAndStop(1);
}


// Set the speed when the mouse button is released.
// on the d0, d1, ..., or d9 clip.
function rel()
{ name = rel.name;

   eval(name + '.is.d' + speed).gotoAndStop(1);
```

```
    speed = parseInt(this._name.substr(1));
    eval(name + '.is.d' + speed).gotoAndStop(2);
}


// Display the menu or the GameOver panel. If arg is non-zero,
// display the panel for a non-registered gamer.
function menuorOver(arg)
{ var i, name,
    name1 = menuorOver.name;

    delete gameact.onEnterFrame;
    attachMovie(name1, name1, depth3);
    name = eval(name1);
    name._x = 303;
    name._y = 197;
    speed = 0;
    gamestate = menust;
    if (arg)
     { attachMovie('infoPanel', 'infoPanel', depth3 + 1);
       infoPanel._x = 303;
       infoPanel._y = 447;
     }
// Write the game speed values on the d0, d1, ..., and d9 clips.
    for (i = 0; i < 10; i++)
     { name = eval(name1 + '.is.d' + i);
       name.t = i;
       // Highlight the clip with the current game speed.
       if (i == speed) name.gotoAndStop(2);
       // Create mouse event handlers for
       // ten game speed selection clips.
       name.onRollOver = name.onDragOver = go2;
       name.onRollOut = name.onDragOut = go1;
       rel.name = name1;
       name.onRelease = rel;
     }
}
```

So the wait function calls the menuorOver function after it assigns the name property the 'menu' string. When the game is over, the name property will be assigned the 'gover' string. Menu and gover are identifiers of clips that display the menu when the program starts, and after the end of each game. These clips have a common component, which is the game speed-selection panel. This is why they are processed by one function, which receives the identifier of the clip it should display. This identifier is also used to access text fields in clips d0, d1, ..., and d9 to write the game speeds on them and to highlight them. For example, a path to the d0 clip when the speed is zero is either menu.is.d0.t or gover.is.d0.t (here is is the identifier for the **Initial Speed** clip).

The menuorOver function stores the name of the clip (menu or gover) in the name1 variable, and stores the reference to the clip in the name variable. It then deletes the gameact.onEnterFrame event handler, calls the clip with the name name1 from the library, sets the current speed (the speed variable) to zero, and assigns the gamestate variable the menust value (indicating that the game should show the menu) if arg isn't empty. After that, the function displays the clip with a message addressed to a non-registered gamer. It then starts a loop iterating through all ten clips. In the loop, the speed values (from 0 to 9) are written on the clips, the clip with the current speed is highlighted, and event handlers are set. The event handlers should work as follows: When the mouse pointer is on a button clip, the button should be highlighted. When the pointer moves away from the button clip, the button should become not highlighted unless it reads the current speed. When the gamer releases the mouse button, the current speed should be set, and the button that reads it should be highlighted. Remember that each speed-selection clip has two frames: In one it is highlighted, while in the other it isn't. To check this, you can insert the following code in the go2 function:

```
trace(this);
```

When you move the mouse pointer onto the d0 clip, the output window will display:

```
_level0.menu.is.d0
```

That is, the this property of the go2 function contains the reference to the clip, in which the handled event took place. Here, _level0 is the level (depth) of the current movie. The Flash player allows you to load several SWF files on different layers, which are similar to timeline layers. You can use ActionScript to load, unload, and control movies.

At this point, I'd like to explain the following fragment of code in the go1 function:

```
if (speed != parseInt(this._name.substr(1))) this.gotoAndStop(1);
```

It is called when the mouse pointer moves away from a speed-selection clip. Here, this._name is the name of this clip, that is, d0, d1, ..., or d9, and `this._name.substr(1)` is the character of the name whose index is 1 (i.e., a digit from 0 to 9). The `parseInt` function converts the string containing this digit into an appropriate number. The number is compared to the `speed` value, which is the current speed. If they aren't equal, highlight is removed from the clip.

The `name` property of the `rel` function also contains the `'menu'` or `'gover'` name. The following code

```
eval(name + '.is.d' + speed).gotoAndStop(1);
```

removes the highlight from the clip that reads the `speed` value, after the `speed` variable is given a new value determined by the name of the clip, on which the gamer released the mouse button. Finally, this clip is highlighted.

Now you understand how the menu works. However, if you click on the **Play!** button, the game won't start. This is because you haven't inserted the `startGame` function called by this button into the main program. Before you insert it, you should understand how the pieces appear and move, how they fall, and how filled lines are removed. I'll explain this later. The next section describes how the score and points given for pieces are displayed.

The project in its current state is saved in the chapter5.2.4.fla and let5.2.4.as.

5.2.5. Coding Score Display and Auxiliary Functions

To display numeric information (e.g., the score), you created the `d0`, `d1`, …, and `d9` symbols, and stored them in the Digits folder. You allocated 25 levels for their instances, starting with `depth2`. The **Speed** control uses one digit, while **Score** uses five digits, and **Pieces**, **Lines**, and the points given for the current pair of pieces use three. In other words, there are five lines of digits, each containing up to five digits. This is why you allocated 25 depths for instances of the digit symbols. Each line of digits will take up five depths: Depths from `depth2` to `depth2 + 4` are allocated for **Speed**, those from `depth2 + 5` to `depth2 + 9` are allocated for **Score**, and so on. The points for the current pair take up the depths from `depth2 + 20` to `depth2 + 24`. Some depths won't be used, but this arrangement will make it easy to determine, at which depth each digit should be. In each line, the further a digit is to the right, the lower the depth of the instance of the corresponding clip. In other words, you'll output digits starting from the least significant characters.

The `showNum` function will be responsible for the output of numbers. It takes two parameters: the number to display and its index (position). The index for the speed is equal to zero, the index for the score is equal to one, and so on, until the points for the current pair of pieces, for which the index is four.

The function is shown in Listing 5.12.

Listing 5.12. Displaying numbers on the indicators

```
// Display the num value for speed, score, pieces, lines, and currscore
// depending on the ind value (from 0 to 4).
function showNum(num,ind)
{ var
    i, x, y,
    digit,
    depth,
    name,
    cl,
    oldnum;
  x = 750;
  y = ind*35 + 28;
  depth = depth2 + ind*5 - 1;
  for (i = 0; i < 5; i++)
    { digit = num%10;
      oldnum = num;
      num = Math.floor(num/10);
      cl = eval(name = 'dig' + ++depth);
      cl.removeMovieClip();
      if (!i || oldnum)
        { attachMovie('d' + digit, name, depth);
          cl = eval(name);
          cl._x = x;
          cl._y = y;
          x -= 15;
        }
    }
}
```

Place this function after the menuorOver function. In this code, x is first assigned 750, which is the X coordinate of the rightmost digit. The value of the Y coordinate is computed from the topmost coordinate (28), the vertical step (35), and the index of this number. The starting depth, depth, which is the depth of the rightmost digit, is also computed from the ind index. Then, a loop from zero to four starts to iterate through five positions of the digits in a number. Each iteration of the loop computes the next digit from right to left, removes the old clip from the current position, and displays an appropriate clip if the computed digit is significant. It is easy to compute the name of this clip from the digit. Then, x is decreased by 15, which is the horizontal step. The code tries to remove five old clips. (Don't worry, the interpreter will ignore "excessive" calls to removeMovieClip). This is done because the new number can be shorter than the previous (e.g., at the beginning of the next game), and you need to throw away the old garbage.

You obtain the next digits (from right to left) as a remainder of the division of the num number by 10. You then update num by dividing it by 10 to obtain the next digit in the next iteration. The previous value of the num variable is stored in the oldnum variable to determine whether the next digit is significant (you don't want to display leading zeroes). The condition that allows you to determine this is the following: !i || oldnum. This means either that this is the first iteration or that the num value updated in the previous iteration isn't equal to zero.

Note how the names are given to clips. For the speed, this is dig576 (depth2 is equal to 576). The clip of the rightmost digit of the score is dig581 (its depth is greater by five than that of the speed's rightmost digit). The name of the clip to the left is dig582, and so on.

Now, test how the numbers are outputted. To do this, temporarily insert the following code after showNum.

```
function startGame()
{ var i;
  showNum(9, 0);
  showNum(99999, 1);
  showNum(999, 2);
  showNum(999, 3);
  showNum(999, 4);
}
```

Start the game, and click on the **Play!** button. Each line will contain as many nines as necessary.

After you have admired the view, delete the startGame function.

You need a function to toggle the pause mode on or off. The togglePause function will be called after the gamer releases the mouse button when the pointer is on the **Pause** button, or after he or she presses the <P> key. Its code is in Listing 5.13.

Listing 5.13. The `togglePause` function

```
function togglePause()
{ if (gamestate == gamest)
  { btPause.s._visible = ispaused ^= 1;
    btNew.useHandCursor = ispaused ^ 1;
    btNew.gotoAndStop(ispaused);
  }
}
```

Insert it after `showNum`.

If the game isn't in progress, calls to the `togglePause` function are ignored. Otherwise, the `^=` operator toggles the value of the `ispaused` variable from zero to one, or vice versa, and assigns it to the `_visible` property of the check clip contained in the button. This hides it when the game isn't paused, and shows it when it is.

If the game isn't paused, the hand mouse pointer over the `btNew` button clip should be enabled. Otherwise, it should be disabled. The following statement

```
btNew.gotoAndStop(ispaused);
```

is necessary when the gamer pauses the game using the <P> key, and the mouse pointer is on the `btNew` clip that is highlighted. This statement removes the highlight.

Before you move a piece in the game, you should delete it from its previous place. This is done using the `wipeFigs` function (Listing 5.14).

Listing 5.14. The `wipeFigs` function

```
// Remove the pieces from the pit.
function wipeFigs()
{ var i, j, k,
    fx = new Array(),
    fy = new Array(),
    f = new Array(),
    p = new Array();

  for (k = 0; k < 2; k++)
  { fx = figsx[k];
    fy = figsy[k];
    f = figs[k];
```

```
    p = pits[k];
    for (i = 0; i < 3; i++)
     for (j = 0; j < 3; j++)
      if (f[i][j] > 0)
        { p[fy + i][fx + j].removeMovieClip();
          p[fy + i][fx + j] = null;
        }
   }
}
```

This function is similar to the paintFigs function. Insert it after togglePause.

In this function, you create local references to the arrays of the coordinates of the pieces, to the arrays of the pieces themselves, and to the array of the current pit (although the latter isn't necessary). The loop for k iterates the pits. Its internal loops iterate through the array that codes the piece, to which the f variable currently refers. When a one is found in this array, the clip of the corresponding square is removed from the pit, and null is written into the element of the pit array to replace the reference to the clip. As a result, the pieces are deleted both visually and logically.

When you created the keydownact and keyupact clips, you inserted calls to the keyDown and keyUp functions into the instances of the emptyclip clip. It's time to discuss these functions. The keyDown function is shown in Listing 5.15.

Listing 5.15. The keyDown function

```
// Handle pressing a key during the game.
function keyDown()
{ switch (Key.getCode())
   { case Key.LEFT:   moveLeft();
     break;
     case Key.RIGHT: moveRight();
     break;
     case Key.UP:     rotateFigs();
     break;
     case Key.DOWN:
     case Key.SPACE: dropFigs();
   }
}
```

This function is straightforward. It catches the pressing of the arrow keys or the spacebar. When the gamer presses the left arrow key, the `moveLeft` function will be called, which will move the pieces to the left, if this is possible. In a similar manner, the gamer can move the pieces to the right, rotate them, or drop them. The latter action can also be carried out using the spacebar. After control returns to the code attached to the instance of the `emptyclip` clip, the `updateAfterEvent` function will be called so that the response to the key is instantaneous.

Insert this code after the `wipeFigs` function.

The `keyUp` function is more complicated (Listing 5.16). It responds to a larger number of keys.

Listing 5.16. The keyUp function

```
// To handle releasing a key in the menu and during the game
// (during the game, this is only for the Sound, Pause, and New clips)
function keyUp()
{ var key1, name;

  // Indication that the key is pressed
  // This is necessary to exit the splash screen using a key.
  keyisdown = 1;
  switch (key1 = Key.getCode())
    // The S (s) key was released. This is for the Sound button.
  { case 83: btsound.s._visible = snd ^= 1;
    break;
    // The P (p) key was released. This is for the Pause and Play! buttons.
    case 80: if (typeof(menu) == 'movieclip') startGame();
    else togglePause();
    break;
    // The Y (y) key was released. This is for the Yes button.
    case 89: if (typeof(gover) == 'movieclip') startGame();
    break;
    // The N (n) key was released. This is for the New button.
    case 78: if (gamestate == gamest && !ispaused) startGame(1);
  }
  // If the game isn't in the menu, the function can return.
  if (gamestate != menust) return;
  // In the menu, <Enter> can start the game.
  if (key1 == Key.ENTER) startGame();
```

```
// Assign the name variable the id of the clip ('menu' or 'gover').
name = rel.name;
if (key1 == Key.LEFT && speed > 0)
  { // Skim over the speed selection buttons from right to left.
    eval(name + '.is.d' + speed).gotoAndStop(1);
    eval(name + '.is.d' + --speed).gotoAndStop(2);
  }
if (key1 == Key.RIGHT && speed < 9)
  { // Skim over the speed selection buttons from left to right.
    eval(name + '.is.d' + speed).gotoAndStop(1);
    eval(name + '.is.d' + ++speed).gotoAndStop(2);
  }
if (key1 > 47 && key1 < 58)
  { // Select the game speed using the keys from <0> to <9>.
    eval(name + '.is.d' + speed).gotoAndStop(1);
    eval(name + '.is.d' + (speed = key1 - 48)).gotoAndStop(2);
  }
}
```

Insert this code after the keyDown function.

First, the keyUp function sets the keyisdown flag. As a result, when a key is pressed in the menu, the dropHeader function destroys all of the squares, and the splash screen closes prematurely (as with a mouse click).

When the gamer releases the <S> key, for which the decimal code is 83, the following code executes:

```
btsound.s._visible = snd ^= 1;
```

You are already familiar with this. It toggles the value of the snd variable and the visibility of the check on the **Sound** button.

When the <P> key is released, you should distinguish between the cases where the menu is displayed and where the game is in progress. The "P" letter is underlined both on the **Pause** button and on the **Play!** button. To find out if this is the menu, the code checks whether the menu clip is present in the movie. This is done using the following condition:

```
if (typeof(menu) == 'movieclip')
```

If the menu clip is present, the **Play!** button is active and the **Pause** button is disabled. Thus, the game starts. Otherwise, the pause is toggled using the togglePause function.

When the <Y> key is released, and the menu is displayed after the game has ended (i.e., the `gover` clip is present in the movie), you should start a new game.

When the <N> key is released, you should check whether the game is paused. This is done using the following condition:

```
if (gamestate == gamest && !ispaused)
```

If the condition is met, you should start a new game before the current game terminates. Pass the `startGame` function the `1` parameter, so that it selects the same game speed as in the previous game.

After these cases are handled, you can exit the function if the menu isn't displayed.

As was the case with the <P> key, when the <Enter> key is released, you should start the game.

Now let's discuss how the speed selection buttons are skimmed over using the left and right arrow keys. To know the paths to the button clips and their text fields, the `name` variable is assigned the name of the clip (`menu` or `gover`).

When the left arrow key is released, and if a button with a speed value greater than zero is highlighted, you should move the highlight to this button's left neighbor and reduce the `speed` value by one. This is done in the following statements:

```
eval(name + '.is.d' + speed).gotoAndStop(1);
eval(name + '.is.d' + --speed).gotoAndStop(2);
```

Skimming over the buttons from left to right is done in a similar way.

In addition, it is possible to select the game speed using the numeric keys from <0> (its decimal code is 48) to <9> (the code is 57). This is done in the following statements:

```
eval(name + '.is.d' + speed).gotoAndStop(1);
eval(name + '.is.d' + (speed = key1 - 48)).gotoAndStop(2);
```

Now, consider the `startGame` function, which starts a new game when it is called from the menu after the splash screen, when the current game completes, or when the gamer gives up the current game and clicks the **New** button. The code for this function is shown in Listing 5.17.

Listing 5.17. The `startGame` function

```
// Start a new game. If arg = 1, the function is called with the New button
// before the current game is completed.
function startGame(arg)
{ var i, j, k, p,
```

```
 pit = new Array();

// Remove all clips that could be in the menu.
gover.removeMovieClip();
menu.removeMovieClip();
infoPanel.removeMovieClip();
// Set the initial game speed.
if (arg == 1) speed = speed0;
 else speed0 = speed;
// Reset the score and the numbers of pieces and filled lines to zero.
score = pieces = lines = 0;
// Set the interval (in ms) for one move down that a piece makes on its own.
timestep = 2000 - speed*200;
// Display the speed, the score, pieces, and filled rows.
showNum(speed, 0);
showNum(score, 1);
showNum(pieces, 2);
showNum(lines, 3);
// Clear the game pits.
for (k = 0; k < 2; k++)
 { pit = pits[k];
   for (i = 0; i < yy; i++)
    for (j = 0; j < xx; j++)
     if (p = pit[i][j])
       { p.removeMovieClip();
          pit[i][j] = null;
       }
 }
// Set the event handler.
attachMovie('keydownact', 'keydownact', depth4 + 1);
// Set the game state.
gamestate = gamest;
// Activate the Pause and New buttons.
btPause.useHandCursor = 1;
btNew.useHandCursor = 1;
// Set the nexttime variable to the current time
// to start newFigs() instantly.
nexttime = getTimer();
newFigs();
}
```

Insert this code after the `keyUp` function.

This function is straightforward. First, it removes all clips that could be in the menu. It then sets the initial game speed:

```
if (arg == 1) speed = speed0;
 else speed0 = speed;
```

If `arg` is equal to one, this indicates that the function was called with a click on the `btNew` button. In turn, this means that the gamer didn't select the game speed because he or she didn't enter the menu. Therefore, you should set the `speed` variable to the value of the `speed0` variable, which is the initial speed of the previous game. Otherwise, meaning that the gamer selected the speed in the menu, you should store the initial game speed in the `speed0` variable.

The `startGame` function then resets the numbers on the panel to zeroes, and displays them. It should also set the `timestep` variable, which determines the number of milliseconds it takes a piece to move one step down on its own. The value depends on the game speed, and is computed using the following formula: `2000 - speed*200`. As you can see, when the speed is zero, pieces move down every 2 s, and when the speed is equal to nine, they move every 0.2 s. These values were found through experimentation to make it possible, but very difficult, to play at the maximum speed.

The function then starts a loop to clear the pits of squares remaining from the previous game. This fragment of code is already familiar to you. It will be necessary if a new game started while the previous one was still in progress. The `keydownact` handler only works during a game and calls the `keyDown` function. This is why it is set at the beginning of a game and removed when the game completes. The `startGame` function then sets an indication that the game is in progress, and activates the `btPause` and `btNew` buttons.

I'll provide a few comments on the following line of code:

```
nexttime = getTimer();
```

The `newFigs` function, which displays a new pair of pieces and checks whether the game time is over, is called at the beginning of a game and every time the pair of pieces stops and points are given. When the score is updated, the game should pause for a while to prevent a new pair of pieces from appearing instantly. This is why the `onEnterFrame` event handler calls the `newFigs` function only after the

```
nexttime = getTimer() + 100;
```

statement sets a delay of 0.1 s. The `newFigs` function begins with an empty loop that waits until the `nexttime` value becomes lower than the age of the movie returned by the `getTimer` function, and until the `ispaused` variable is equal to zero, indicating that the game isn't paused. New pieces appear only if these conditions are satisfied. This is why the `startGame` function sets the `nexttime` value to the current time, so that the `newFigs` starts without a delay. Alternatively, you could simply assign zero the `nexttime`.

Now consider the `newFigs` function (Listing 5.18). Insert its code after the `startGame` function.

Listing 5.18. The `newFigs` function

```
// Create and output a pair of pieces.
function newFigs()
{ var i, j, k, t, flag, corr,
  f = new Array(),
  fx,
  fy,
  p = new Array();

  if ((t = getTimer()) < nexttime || ispaused) return;
// Decrease the probability of an inconvenient pair of pieces No.3 and No.4.
  do
    for (k = 0; k < 2; k++)
    { mffn[k] = Math.floor(Math.random()*9);
      ffn[k] = 0;
      colors[k] = mffn[k];
      figs[k] = mff[mffn[k]][0];
      figsx[k] = 5;
      figsy[k] = 0;
    }
  while (mffn[0] + mffn[1] == 7 && mffn[0]*mffn[1] == 12 && ++corr == 1);
// Check whether the pieces overlap.
  for (k = 0; k < 2; k++)
  { fx = figsx[k];
    fy = figsy[k];
    f = figs[k];
    p = pits[k];
    for (i = 0; i < 3; i++)
      for (j = 0; j < 3; j++)
        if (f[i][j] && p[fy + i][fx + j]) flag = 1;
```

```
        }
    paintFigs();
    showNum(pieces += 2,2);
    if (flag)
      { playSound(goversnd);
        keydownact.removeMovieClip();
        btPause.gotoAndStop(1);
        btPause.useHandCursor = 0;
        btNew.gotoAndStop(1);
        btNew.useHandCursor = 0;
        menuorOver.name = 'gover';
        menuorOver();
        return;
      }
    // Enable control from the keyboard.
    controlenabled = 1;
    // The gamer can move a piece three times until it moves down.
    numact = 3;
    // Should the speed be increased?
    if (!(pieces%40) && speed < 9)
      { ++speed;
        timestep -= 200;
        showNum(speed, 0);
        playSound(bleep3snd);
      }
    showNum(currscore = (speed + 1)*20, 4);
    downOrWaitAction();
}
```

The waiting loop

```
if ((t = getTimer()) < nexttime || ispaused) return;
```

was described earlier. In *Chapter 1*, I mentioned that you would decrease the probability of inconvenient pairs of pieces. It's time to do this. A pair involving piece No. 3 and piece No. 4 (three squares vertically and three horizontally) is very inconvenient, and can quickly terminate a game. So the do-while loop makes the appearance of this combination less likely.

Inside the do-while loop, there is another loop for k with two iterations. It creates a new pair of pieces. You should be familiar with this loop, as you already tried to create pieces and looked at them. I'd like to provide some comments about the condition of the external loop:

```
while (mffn[0] + mffn[1] == 7 && mffn[0]*mffn[1] == 12 && ++corr == 1);
```

Here, the logical expression

```
mffn[0] + mffn[1] == 7 && mffn[0]*mffn[1] == 12
```

can be translated into English as "the total of the piece numbers is equal to seven, and their product is equal to 12". In other words, one piece is No. 3, and the other is No. 4. In this case, the phrases are equivalent. Another condition is necessary for the external loop to repeat:

```
++corr == 1
```

That is, first you increment `corr`, and then it should become equal to one. You have probably guessed that the `corr` variable should be equal to zero before these manipulations. When you created `corr`, you didn't assign it a value, so the interpreter assigned it the value `undefined`. In ActionScript, this value is considered to be zero in arithmetic operations.

You can probabloy guess how the loop works: It keeps on creating new pairs of pieces until one of the pieces is No. 3, the other is No. 4, and the `++corr` expression is equal to one. The latter condition can be satisfied only in the first iteration. If the pair appears in the second iteration, the loop will terminate, and the gamer will have to play with these pieces. After all, a game is a game.

After you created two pieces logically, you should check whether any of them overlaps a square in a pit. If it does, the game is over. To check this, loops for `i` and `j` start for each piece. The loops look for ones in the array that codes the piece to see whether there are squares on the corresponding positions in the pit. If the corresponding cell contains a value other than `null` (i.e., it contains a reference to a square clip), the `flag` variable is set to one.

After these check loops complete, the new pieces are displayed, the number of the pieces is increased by two, and the resulting value is outputted.

A conditional statement then follows. It is executed if the game is over. It plays the `goversnd` sound, removes the `keydownact` event handler, deactivates the **Pause** and **New** buttons, and calls the `menuorOver` function, passing it the `gover` clip name, because the starting menu and the game-over menu differ. After you call this function, you have to exit the `newFigs` function. Otherwise, its remainder will be executed after the gamer exits the menu. Behavior of this type by the program is bound to cause some puzzlement.

If the game isn't over yet, this conditional statement will be ignored, and the flow of execution will jump to the statement that sets the `controlenabled` variable to one to allow the `keydownact` event handler to call the `keyDown` function. Remember, this event handler is contained in an instance of the `emptyclip` symbol that, in turn, is contained in the `keydownact` clip.

Do you remember my promise that the gamer will be able to move the pieces after they encounter an obstacle? This is carried out in the next piece of code. It allows the gamer to move and/or rotate the pieces three times, and the permission is fixed in the `numact` variable.

What follows is a seemingly confusing condition:

```
if (!(pieces%40) && speed < 9)
```

This checks whether the game should increase its speed. The condition consists of two relatively simple sub-conditions, and the speed increases only if both are true:

❏ The number of pieces used is a multiple of 40.
❏ The current game speed is less than nine.

If `pieces` is a multiple of 40, the `pieces%40` expression is equal to zero, and its logical negation is `true`. The parentheses are necessary because the `!` operator has a priority higher than that of the `%` operator. In other words, the speed will increase every 20 pairs of pieces until it reaches the maximum value. Not only does the speed increase, but the time, during which pieces move down on their own, is decreased by 200 ms. The `bleep3snd` sound effect is played to celebrate this event.

After a new pair of pieces appears, the `currscore` variable should receive a new value, which is the "cost" of the new pair. The value decreases as the pieces move down until they stop, or until it becomes zero. Then, `currscore` is added to `score`, which is the total of the points the user received for each pair of pieces. The initial value of the `currscore` variable is in proportion to the `speed` value with a factor of 20. You'll see later that `currscore` decreases by `speed + 1` every time the pieces move down one step.

5.2.6. Coding the Moving down of Pieces

After the `newFigs` function completes its task, it passes control to the `downOrWaitAction` function. You might have guessed from its name that it waits for the gamer's actions and moves the pieces one step down if the gamer delays for a certain amount of time (only, of course, if the move is possible). Before you implement an action in a program, you should always check whether the program's logic allows this. Consider a small function, `isDown`, from Listing 5.19, that checks whether the pieces can be moved one step down (a step is equal to one square), and returns one if this is possible. Otherwise, it returns zero. The `downOrWaitAction` function calls this function. Insert its code after `newFigs`.

Listing 5.19. The `isDown` function

```
// Check whether both pieces can move one step down.
function isDown()
{ var i, j, k, fx, fy,
  f = new Array(),
  p = new Array();

  for (k = 0; k < 2; k++)
  { fx = figsx[k];
    fy = figsy[k];
    f = figs[k];
    p = pits[k];
    for (i = 0; i < 3; i++)
     for (j = 0; j < 3; j++)
      if (f[i][j] && (i + fy > yy - 2 || p[fy + i + 1][fx + j] &&
       (i == 3 || !f[i + 1][j]))) return 0;
  }
  return 1;
}
```

First, we'll phrase this condition in plain English, and then rewrite it in Action-Script. You want to move the pieces one step down, but you are checking for the opposite condition - where the pieces cannot be moved down. When this condition is satisfied, the function exits and returns zero. If all the loops have completed, the pieces can be moved down, and the function returns one. So, the pieces cannot be moved if there is another piece's square or the pit bottom below at least one square of at least one piece. You probably noticed in the previous functions that nested loops are preceded by the creation of temporal variables, `fx` and `fy`, that contain the coordinates of the upper left corner of the 3×3 square that contains the piece being analyzed in the loop for `k`. In addition, the `f` and `p` variables are created, which contain references to the array that codes this piece and the array of the pit containing the piece. Consider the body of the innermost loop:

```
if (f[i][j] && (i + fy > yy - 2 || p[fy + i + 1][fx + j] &&
 (i == 3 || !f[i + 1][j]))) return 0;
```

It checks whether there is a square in the ith row and the jth column in the array that codes the kth piece. If there is, the code checks whether there is an obstacle below. This complex condition consists of two components that are combined using the && operator, which is logical AND:

```
f[i][j]
  &&
(i + fy > yy - 2 || p[fy + i + 1][fx + j] && (i == 3 || !f[i + 1][j]))
```

The second condition is also complex, so I'll break it into simple conditions and run through them:

```
1) f[i][j]
     &&
2) (i + fy > yy-2
       ||
3)   p[fy + i + 1][fx + j]
       &&
4)   (i == 3
         ||
5)     !f[i + 1][j]))
```

Substitute the sub-conditions with their numbers and rewrite their combination in the following form:

1 AND (2 OR 3 AND (4 OR 5))

Now I'll explain the sub-conditions:

❏ 1 — The array that codes the kth piece has a square in the ith row and the jth column.

❏ 2 — If you add up i (the row number) and the Y coordinate of the 3 × 3 square, the result should be greater than 22. (Remember that the yy variable stores the depth of the pit, 24 squares, and the squares are numbered from zero). Seems too sophisticated? Look, the i + fy expression means the number of a pit line that contains the square, which is in the ith row of the piece. Therefore, sub-condition 2 means that this square is in, or even below, the 23rd pit line.

❏ 3 — This sub-condition means that there is a square (a clip) in the appropriate pit immediately below the square in question. However, it is still unclear whether that square in the pit belongs to the piece being analyzed or to another piece. To determine this, you should check two more sub-conditions.

❏ 4 — The square belongs to the bottom row in the array that codes the piece.

❏ 5 — There is no square below this one in the array that codes the piece.

In other words, the condition "4 OR 5" means that the array, which codes the piece doesn't contain a square below the (i, j)th square.

The condition in the conditional statement is true if condition 1 is true (the (i, j)th square exists). In addition, condition 2 or the complex condition "3 AND (4 OR 5)" should be true. In other words, this square is either at the pit bottom, or there is a square in the pit below it (condition 3), and that square belongs to another piece (condition "4 OR 5").

You had to expect that you would encounter complicated conditions like this when programming! Note that you check the condition

```
i + fy > yy - 2,
```

first, and only then do you examine the contents of the element

```
p[fy + i + 1][fx + j]
```

of the pit array. This is because you shouldn't examine the contents of the cell in the row

```
fy + i + 1,
```

until you make sure that this value doesn't overrun the array boundary (which is 23). If it does, the evaluation of the main condition will stop after evaluating the following condition:

```
i + fy > yy - 2.
```

In ActionScript, logical operations are carried out sparingly: If the result of a logical expression is known in advance, the rest of the expression isn't evaluated. In particular, functions that might be in that part of the expression aren't called. A similar situation exists for the condition "4 OR 5". First, you check the condition

```
i == 3
```

and examine the contents of the (i+1) th row of the piece-coding array only if the condition is false.

Now, consider the downOrWaitAction function (Listing 5.20). Add its code after the isDown function.

Listing 5.20. The downOrWaitAction function

```
// Move the pieces down one step. If this is impossible, wait for the gamer's
// actions (he or she might want to move the pieces to the left or right).
function downOrWaitAction(arg)
{  if (isDown())
```

```
{ gameact.onEnterFrame = downFigs;
  if (!arg) nexttime = getTimer() + timestep;
} else
{ nexttime = (--numact > 0) ? getTimer() + 400 : 0;
  gameact.onEnterFrame = waitForAction;
}
}
```

This function is called from the following functions: moveLeft, moveRight, rotateFigs, newFigs, and downFigs. The first three functions call it after the gamer moves the pieces, but this is not the case for the last two. Therefore, there are two different situations, in which the function is called. To distinguish between these situations, the downOrWaitAction function takes an argument, arg. The first situation is when it is equal to one. The other occurs when arg is undefined (or empty, or zero).

If it is possible to move the pieces down, the following branch is executed:

```
gameact.onEnterFrame = downFigs;
if (!arg) nexttime = getTimer() + timestep;
```

This means that when Flash player enters the frame, the downFigs function that moves the pieces down is put in the next frame. In addition, if the downOrWaitAction function was called from the newFigs or downFigs function (the arg argument is equal to zero), a delay of timestep milliseconds is set before the pieces move down. (The downFigs function begins with the loop, already familiar to you, that waits until the age of the movie becomes equal to the nexttime variable). The delay is necessary in this case to prevent the new pieces from moving down as soon as they appear, and to make the next move down precisely after timestep milliseconds elapse. If this isn't the case, the delay isn't required, because the pieces' movement down shouldn't depend on the gamer's actions.

If the pieces cannot move down, the following branch is executed:

```
nexttime = (--numact > 0) ? getTimer() + 400 : 0;
gameact.onEnterFrame = waitForAction;
```

Here, you see a ternary statement. It subtracts one from numact (which is initially equal to three), and compares the result to zero. If the result is greater than zero, the nexttime variable is assigned the getTimer() + 400 value. Otherwise, it is assigned zero. In the next line of code, the waitForAction function is set as a handler of the onEnterFrame event. This function waits for the gamer's actions until the age of the movie is equal to nexttime. In other words, it waits 400 ms for a key to be pressed, then for another 400 ms, and then 0 ms. This, in fact, means that the gamer can move the dropped pieces three times, and the game waits 0.4 s for each move. If the gamer doesn't move the pieces during this interval, the program will try to move them down. If it fails, a new pair of figures will be created.

You can see that one function is linked to another, and this chain might seem to be endless. Don't mind, as this is not actually the case. For now, consider the waitForAction function (Listing 5.21). Add its code to the main program after the downOrWaitAction function.

Listing 5.21. The waitForAction function

```
// Wait for the gamer's actions after at least one piece
// cannot move down.
function waitForAction()
{ var i;

  if (getTimer() < nexttime) return;
  controlenabled = 0;
  dropFigs();
  if (numlayers[0] + numlayers[1])
   { nexttime = getTimer() + 100;
     gameact.onEnterFrame = lightning1;
     return;
   }
  // Move currscore up to score.
  for (i = depth2 + 20; i < depth2 + 23; i++) eval('dig' + i).play();
  playSound(scoreupsnd);
  nexttime = getTimer() + 400;
  gameact.onEnterFrame = updateScore;
}
```

First, this function starts a loop and waits for the specified time:

```
if (getTimer() < nexttime) return;
```

If the gamer presses the control keys during this interval, the pieces will move (if possible), but they will move no more than three times (this is controlled by the numact variable). After this, the downFigs function will become an onEnterFrame event handler, instead of the waitForAction function. The downFigs function moves the pieces down one step. After the loop completes, the `waitForAction` function disables control from the keyboard by assigning zero to the `controlenabled` variable, and calls the `dropFigs` function, which will drop the pieces. If a line in the pit becomes filled with squares, the `lightning1` function will be called to display lightning bolts after 100 ms have elapsed. Having completed, it will call functions that break the squares and update the score. If there are no filled lines, the conditional statement

```
if (numlayers[0] + numlayers[1])
```

will be ignored. The `updateScore` function is called after the points given for the current pair of pieces fly up to the score display. This process is carried out in the following loop:

```
for (i = depth2 + 20; i < depth2 + 23; i++) eval('dig' + i).play();
```

Clips, which contain digits that make up the value of the current pair of pieces, will start their work and destroy themselves at the end.

Consider the `downFigs` function (Listing 5.22). Insert it after the `waitForAction` function.

Listing 5.22. The `downFigs` function

```
// Decrease and display currscore. Move the pieces one step down.
function downFigs()
{ if (getTimer() < nexttime) return;
  if (currscore)
  { currscore -= speed + 1;
    showNum(currscore, 4);
  }
  wipeFigs();
  ++figsy[0];
  ++figsy[1];
  paintFigs();
  downOrWaitAction();
}
```

This is a very simple function. It starts a loop, for which the wait time is set in the caller function. After the loop completes, the `waitForAction` function checks whether the `currscore` value is equal to zero. If it isn't, it is decreased by the `speed + 1` value, and displayed. The pieces are then erased from their current positions, their Y coordinates are incremented, the pieces are displayed on new positions, and the `downOrWaitAction` function is called. It starts the loop that waits for the gamer's actions.

Now, consider the `dropFigs` function (Listing 5.23). Insert its code after the previous function.

Listing 5.23. The `dropFigs` function

```
// Drop pieces when possible.
function dropFigs()
{ var i, j, k, l,
  h = new Array(yy, yy),
  fx, fy, klx, kly,
  fig = new Array(),
  pit = new Array();

  // Compute the number of moves to drop each piece.
  for (k = 0; k < 2; k++)
  { fig = figs[k];
    pit = pits[k];
    fx = figsx[k];
    fy = figsy[k];
    for (j = 0; j < 3; j++)
     for (i = 2; i >= 0; i--)
      if (fig[i][j] > 0)
      { l = 0;
        klx = fx + j;
        kly = fy + i;
        while (kly + l + 1 < yy && !pit[kly + l + 1][klx]) ++l;
        if (h[k] > l) h[k] = l;
        break;
      }
  }
  if (h[0] + h[1] == 0)
  { controlenabled = 0;
    if (isLayer())
    { nexttime = getTimer() + 100;
      gameact.onEnterFrame = lightning1;
    } else
```

```
            { nexttime = getTimer() + 330;
                gameact.onEnterFrame = updateScore;
            }
        return;
    }
    // Drop the pieces.
    wipeFigs();
    figsy[0] += h[0];
    figsy[1] += h[1];
    paintFigs();
    playSound(fallsnd);
    isLayer();
    nexttime = getTimer() + 400;
    gameact.onEnterFrame = waitForAction;
}
```

Before dropping the pieces, the function has to know how many moves down each piece can make. For this purpose, a new array is created. It is named h and contains two elements, each of which is assigned the yy value of 24, which is the depth of the pits. You can assign any value greater than 24. After the loop for k completes, h[0] will contain the number of moves necessary to drop the piece in the left pit, and h[1] will contain the required number for the piece in the right pit. These numbers are the smallest distances from the lowest squares of the pieces to squares in the pits below them or to the bottoms of the pits. In the external loop for k (i.e., for each piece), local references are created to the arrays that code the pieces, to the pits, and to the coordinates of the pieces in the pits. Inside the loop for k, you will see two other loops: one for j, which iterates through the columns in the array that codes the piece, and the other for i, which iterates through its rows. Note the header of the second loop:

```
for (i = 2; i >= 0; i--)
```

It differs from the headers you saw earlier. The loop iterates from the bottom row of the array that codes the piece to its top row when looking for a square. If it finds a square, it doesn't iterate any more, and returns control to the loop for j using the break statement. In other words, you need only the lowest squares in the pieces to compute the shortest distances from a piece to the squares below it or to the pit bottom.

Inside the loop for i, after the (i, j)th square is found, the l variable, which is the distance from the square to the object below it, is assigned zero. Then, the klx and `kly` variables are assigned the coordinates of this square in the pit to avoid using indexed variables inside the next loop. A `while` loop then follows:

```
while (kly + l + 1 < yy && !pit[kly + l + 1][klx]) ++l;
```

It moves this square down by incrementing `l` until the square encounters the bottom of the pit:

```
kly + l + 1 < yy
```

or, for the other square:

```
!pit[kly + l + 1][klx]
```

As a result, when the `while` loop completes, the `l` variable will contain the number of moves that the square in the `i`th row and the `j`th column of the `k`th piece can make. Your goal is to find the minimum of this value for all squares of the piece and assign it to the `h[k]` array element. This is done using the following conditional statement:

```
if (h[k] > l) h[k] = l;
```

Currently, the `h[k]` element contains the minimum number of moves for the `j`th column. The `break` statement then interrupts the loop for `i`, so that the next column of the piece is processed. When the loop for `j` completes, the `h[k]` element will contain the sought value for the `k`th piece.

The pieces have likely already encountered an obstacle, so you shouldn't drop them. This fact is checked using the following condition:

```
if (h[0] + h[1] == 0)
```

If this is the case, the `dropFigs` function disables keyboard control and calls the `isLayer` function, which checks whether there are any filled lines, and returns a non-empty value if there are. In this case, the `lightning1` function is called, which starts in 100 ms. Otherwise, the `updateScore` function is called to start in 330 ms to update the score, and start the procedure to create a new pair of pieces. If there is a free space below the pieces, they are dropped. This is similar to moving them down, but now their Y coordinates aren't incremented. Rather, they are increased by an appropriate value, and the appropriate sound is played. The `dropFigs` function then calls the `isLayer` function to check for the filled lines, and the control is passed to the `waitForAction` loop, because the gamer can move the pieces after they are dropped.

Next is the `isLayer` function (Listing 5.24). Add its code to the main program.

Listing 5.24. The `isLayer` function

```
// Check for filled lines. If there are any, mark the lines
// that should be deleted and stored their number.
function isLayer()
{ var i, j, k, flag, fy,
    flag1 = 0,
    pit = new Array();

  for (k = 0; k < 2; k++)
  { pit = pits[k];
    fy = figsy[k];
// Clear layers[k].
    for (i = 0; i < yy; i++) layers[k][i] = 0;
    numlayers[k] = 0;
    for (i = fy + 2; i >= fy; i--)
    { if (i >= yy) continue;
      flag = 1;
      for (j = 0; j < xx; j++)
       if (!pit[i][j])
        { flag = 0;
          break;
        }
      if (flag)
      { layers[k][i] = 1;
        ++numlayers[k];
        flag1 = 1;
      }
    }
  }
return flag1;
}
```

The task of this function is to mark the filled lines and store the number of these lines in the `layers` and `numlayers` global arrays, respectively. The function returns one or zero, depending on whether there is at least one filled line. The structure of the arrays is the following. The `numlayers` array contains two numbers: `numlayers[0]` is equal to the number of the filled lines in the left pit, and `numlayers[1]` is equal to the number of the filled lines in the right pit. The `layers` array is two-dimensional. You will remember that it was created at the beginning of the program. It consists of two one-dimensional arrays, each of which has yy elements (yy is equal to 24). The layers[0] array contains those in positions corresponding to the filled lines and zeroes in the other positions. For example, if lines No. 21 and No. 23 are filled in the right pit, the layers[1][21] and layers[1][23] elements are equal to one. In other words, the bottom line and the third line from bottom are filled with squares.

You could write such a function easily, but it has already been written. So let's look at it closely.

It begins with a loop for k that iterates the pits. The loop resets the layers[k] sub-array and the numlayers[k] element to zeroes, and stores the Y coordinate of the kth piece (i.e., the coordinate of the upper row of the array that codes the piece) in the fy variable. Then a loop follows that iterates through three lines in the pit that can contain the squares of the current piece. The lines are iterated from the bottom up. Note the following conditional statement:

```
if (i >= yy) continue;
```

It passes control to the next loop iteration if a square of the piece-coding array appears outside the pit. Although the piece itself cannot cross the boundaries of a pit, some of the squares of the 3 × 3 square containing the piece can.

If the ith row is inside the pit, the following statement is executed:

```
flag = 1;
```

This means: "The ith line in the pit is likely to be filled". A loop then iterates through all of the squares in the ith line from 0 to xx − 1 (i.e., to 11). If one of these doesn't contain a clip, the following condition is true:

```
!pit[i][j]
```

This means that the ith line isn't filled. The loop terminates prematurely, and the flag variable is reset to zero. If the flag variable remains equal to one after the loop for j, the following conditional statement will be executed:

```
if (flag)
  { layers[k][i] = 1;
    ++numlayers[k];
    flag1 = 1;
  }
```

In other words, the filled line is marked in the layers[k][i] array, the number of the filled layers of the kth pit (i.e., numlayers[k]) is incremented, and the flag1 flag is set to indicate that there is at least one filled line in the pits. Finally, the function returns flag1, that is, either one or zero.

Consider the updateScore function (Listing 5.25). Insert it into the main program.

Listing 5.25. The updateScore function

```
// Update the score and display it.
function updateScore()
{ if (getTimer() < nexttime) return;
  showNum(score += currscore, 1);
  nexttime = getTimer() + 100;
  gameact.onEnterFrame = newFigs;
}
```

This function isn't called directly. Instead, it is set as an onEnterFrame event handler, because it has a waiting loop. It is executed when the age of the movie reaches or exceeds the nexttime value specified when the function is set.

In the function body, the score variable is increased by the currscore value (the points given for the current pair of pieces), and the updated value is displayed immediately. Here, you use the fact that the += operation returns a result: the new value of the variable that precedes the operator. Because the updateScore function is the last function called before a new pair of pieces appears, it calls the newFigs function, with which you are already familiar, and sets that function as an event handler instead of itself. In 0.1 s, the life cycle of a new pair of pieces will resume.

Now let's return to lightnings bolts and exploding squares, that is, to the destruction of filled lines. Consider the following function (Listing 5.26) and add its code to the program.

Listing 5.26. The lightning1 function

```
// Display lightnings bolts.
function lightning1()
{ if (getTimer() < nexttime) return;
  var i, j, k, l,
  depth = depth3;

  for (k = 0; k < 2; k++)
  for (i = 0; i < yy; i++)
   if (layers[k][i])
     { attachMovie('lightning', 'l' + depth, depth);
       l = eval('l' + depth++);
```

```
        l._x = pitx[k];
        l._y = i*kv + pity[k];
      }
  playSound(cannonsnd);
  nexttime = getTimer() + 300;
  gameact.onEnterFrame = explode;
}
```

Like the previous function, this one isn't called directly. It is an onEnterFrame event handler, and starts after a delay. This is done because you don't want the pieces to fall, the lines to be filled, the lightning bolts to strike, the squares to explode, and the score to be updated simultaneously. Unfortunately, there are a few Tetris programs that behave in such a way (and respond slowly to keys).

This function uses the layers array to determine, which lines in the pits are filled. A loop for k iterates the pits, and a loop for i looks for filled lines (the top line is No. 0, and the bottom line is No. 23). If the ith line in the kth pit is filled, a conditional statement is executed. It creates an instance of lightning with a name made up by the l character and a number equal to the depth of the clip for this lightning bolt (the depths start with depth3). Because only one clip can be at a certain depth, the names differ. Alternatively, you could create names using the k and i values. The X coordinate of a lightning bolt is equal to pitx[k], which is the coordinate of the left side of the pit. The Y coordinate is computed from the coordinate of the top of the pit (pity[k]), to which the number of the filled line (i), multiplied by the size of a square in pixels (kv), is added. Lightning bolts are animated in eight frames. This is why you can explode the squares and play the cannonsnd sound 300 ms after the lightning appears. This is implemented by setting the explode function (Listing 5.27) as an event handler at the end of the lightning1 function. Copy the code of the explode function to the main program.

Listing 5.27. The explode function

```
// Explode squares.
function explode()
{ if (getTimer() < nexttime) return;
  var i, j, k,
  pit = new Array();

  for (k = 0; k < 2; k++)
  { pit = pits[k];
```

```
    for (i = 0; i < yy; i++)
     if (layers[k][i])
      for (j = 0; j < xx; j++)
       { name = pit[i][j];
         name.t = Math.random()*10;
         name.gotoAndPlay(3);
       }
   }
  scoreupdated = 0;
  nexttime = getTimer() + 1000;
  gameact.onEnterFrame = removeLayers;
}
```

This function also uses the `layers` array to determine, which lines in the pits are filled. For each filled line, a loop for `j` iterates through the square clips in this line. The references to the clips are stored in the pit array. The function computes the `name` reference to the clip of the current square during each iteration of the loop for `j`. The `t` variable of this clip is assigned a pseudo-random value, from zero to nine, so that the clips run their own code and explode after different delays. Note that delays here are measured in frames, rather than in milliseconds. Examine the fragment of code in a square clip's third frame:

```
if (--t > -1) gotoAndPlay(2);
```

Now you should understand what I told you when you started programming the game. During each iteration of this loop that takes place between frames, the `t` local variable is decremented, and an empty loop that moves the player to the previous and next frames is executed. After this loop completes (remember, its duration is different for different squares), animation that plays the sound of explosion in the third frame starts. However, only every third square explodes with the sound. If all of the squares exploded simultaneously, it would be too much. Up to six filled lines can explode at a time, and they contain 72 squares.

After the squares fly away, the `scoreupdated` global variable is reset to zero. This indicates that the clips of points given for the current pair of pieces haven't lifted to the total score yet. This indication is required because lifting the clips is implemented in two parts of the program, so you have to prevent it from being executed twice. Explosions of the squares last for one second, after which the clips of the exploded squares will cease to exist. The `removeLayers` function is then set. It moves the upper lines down to close the gaps that appeared after the squares exploded (Listing 5.28). Insert its code into the program.

Listing 5.28. The removeLayers function

```
// Remove the filled lines that are definitely present in the pit and
// increase the lines variable.
function removeLayers()
{ var i, j, iz, inz, ctl,
    pit = new Array();

  if (!scoreupdated && getTimer() > nexttime - 500)
    { // currscore lifts to score.
      for (i = depth2 + 20; i < depth2 + 23; i++) eval('dig' + i).play();
      playSound(scoreupsnd);
      scoreupdated = 1;
    }
  if (getTimer() < nexttime) return;
  for (k = 0; k < 2; k++)
    { if (!numlayers[k]) continue;
      lines += numlayers[k];
      // Look for the filled line that is 1st from bottom; its number is iz.
      // Look for the 1st incomplete line above it; its number is inz.
      iz = -1;
      inz = -1;
      for (i = yy - 1; i >= 0; i--)
        if (layers[k][i])
          { if (iz == -1) iz = i;
          } else
          if (iz > -1)
            { inz = i;
              break;
            }
// In the pit No. k, move the line No. inz to the position of the line No. iz.
      do
        { if (inz >= 0) moveLayer(k, inz--, iz--);
          while (inz >= 0 && layers[k][inz]) --inz;
        }
      while (inz >= 0);
      // Remove the upper lines.
      pit = pits[k];
      ctl = numlayers[k];
      for (i = 0; i < ctl; i++)
```

```
    for (j = 0; j < xx; j++)
      { pit[i][j].removeMovieClip();
        pit[i][j] = null;
      }
    }
  showNum(lines,3);
  playSound(movelayersnd);
  nexttime = 0;
  gameact.onEnterFrame = updateScore;
}
```

The `removeLayers` function represents an interesting solution: it implements a two-stage delay. As a result, the points for the current pair of pieces are animated and fly up to the score at the appropriate moment. This happens in the middle of the delay set for the explosion of the squares. The digits of the points start their flight while the squares are exploding, and reach the destination point simultaneously with the disappearance of the squares.

Now, examine the body of the function. Look at the following condition:

```
    if (!scoreupdated && getTimer() > nexttime - 500)
```

If the score hasn't been updated yet, and if the first half of the explosion interval has elapsed, the animation of points starts, and the accompanying sound is played. The `scoreupdated` flag is then set to one, so that this code is skipped, and the second stage of the waiting loop is executed when the subsequent `onEnterFrame` events take place:

```
    if (getTimer() < nexttime) return;
```

The next fragment of the code contains a complicated loop that moves the upper lines down to close the gaps that appeared after the filled lines had been removed. I'll explain this loop in the following paragraphs.

The procedure starts with a loop for k that iterates through both pits. If the kth pit misses filled lines, the next iteration starts at once:

```
    if (!numlayers[k]) continue;
```

Otherwise, the number of filled lines is added to the `lines` variable, which will be displayed later.

```
    lines += numlayers[k];
```

It is then necessary to iterate through the lines from bottom to top to look for the first filled line. When it is found, its number (from 23 to 0) is assigned to the iz variable. At the same time, the first line above the one that is not filled is sought. If it is found, the inz variable will take its number. Generally speaking, there can be no such lines when only the topmost layer or two or three top neighboring layers are filled. This is unlikely, and the inz variable is equal to -1 in such a case. The iz variable is always greater than -1, because the loop for k begins with a check for a filled line in the current pit.

Before the loop for i starts, the iz and inz variables are assigned the value -1, so that they are assigned new values only once inside the loop. The loop iterates through the lines from bottom to top, and consists of two branches that are executed depending on whether the ith line is filled. If the ith line is filled, the iz variable is assigned the value i. This, however, is done only once, because the iz variable is checked to see if it is equal to -1 before the assignment. If the ith line isn't filled, a check is carried out to determine whether a value has been assigned to iz:

```
if (iz > -1)
```

If it has, the inz variable is assigned the i value, and the loop for i terminates prematurely, because the sought lines are found.

This code is followed by a do-while loop, which moves down all the remaining lines. Another solution is sometimes used. It involves moving down all the lines above the filled line, looking for the next filled line, moving down the lines that are above it, and so on. This solution is easier to implement. However, I would like to offer a solution that is quick and thrifty.

The essence of this loop is that the inzth line is moved to the place of the izth line. Then, iz and inz are reduced by one. A while loop then keeps on decrementing the inz variable while it points to a filled line and is greater than -1. In such a way, you obtain the next upper line that isn't filled with squares. It will be moved to the place of the izth line. In other words, you don't do the extra work involved in moving the filled lines down. The do-while loop keeps on running until inz becomes equal to -1, that is, until the lines that can be moved down are exhausted. Note that the situation can arise, in which the do-while loop doesn't move a line. This can happen if inz is equal to -1 before the loop starts. (This indicates that there is no line that isn't filled above the filled one). In another case, when the first and second lines are filled, the zero line is moved to the place of the second line, and nothing is left to move to the place of the first line. Yet another case is common: The zero and second lines are filled. The do-while loop can fail to remove all of the filled lines, so additional actions are required to remove them. In particular, you should clean as many top lines as there were filled lines in the pit. This should be done for general reasons. The loops for i and j are included for this purpose. A line is cleaned in two steps: All the square clips are removed, and the corresponding elements of the pit array are assigned the null value.

When this task has been completed, the function updates the number of filled lines, plays the sound accompanying the movement down of the lines, and sets the updateScore function without a waiting loop, because one second was enough for these clean-up actions.

Consider another function, moveLayer (Listing 5.29). You already called it, but you haven't seen its code. Insert it into the program.

Listing 5.29. The moveLayer function

```
// Move a line in the kth pit from position No. inz to position No. iz.
function moveLayer(k, inz, iz)
{ var pit = pits[k], i, j, name, depth;


  for (j = 0; j < xx; j++)
  { pit[iz][j].removeMovieClip();
    pit[iz][j] = null;
    if (pit[inz][j])
    { name = pit[inz][j]._name.substr(0, 2);
      depth = dp[k] + iz*xx + j;
      attachMovie(name, name + depth, depth);
      name = eval(name + depth);
      name._x = j*kv + pitx[k];
      name._y = iz*kv + pity[k];
      pit[iz][j] = name;
    }
  }
}
```

Looks sophisticated, huh. Well, if programming were a simple job, there would be programmers everywhere.

You have to move the inzth line to the place of the izth line in the kth pit. This means you should write a loop for j from zero to xx - 1 to iterate through the squares in the line. For the jth square, you first remove its clip from the izth line (as you did in the previous function), check for a clip in the jth position in the inzth line, and, if there is one, create a clip of this square on the jth position in the izth line. If you are attentive enough, you will have noticed that clips aren't removed from the inzth line. This isn't necessary. You'll either move another line to the inzth position or clean this line entirely with the removeLayers function.

So, if pit[inz][j] refers to a clip, you can find out the name of the symbol corresponding to this clip and put it on the required place. The name is one of the following: k0, k1, ..., or k8. It is stored in the _name property of the clip, and consists of two characters. Extract the first two characters of the property and assign them to the name variable:

```
name = pit[inz][j]._name.substr(0,2);
```

Now you should compute the depth of the clip on the new place. To do this, add the depth of the initial square clip in the kth pit, which is dp[k], to the consecutive number of this square, which is the product of the line number and the number of the squares in the line added to the square's position in the line (j):

```
depth = dp[k] + iz*xx + j;
```

You can thus obtain the depth of the clip and its name, consisting of the symbol name and the depth of this symbol's instance. This allows you to call the attachMovie function:

```
attachMovie(name, name + depth, depth);
```

Assign the name variable a reference to this clip:

```
name = eval(name + depth);
```

The X coordinate of the newly-created clip is the sum of the coordinate of the left side of the pit and the product of the position of the clip in the line by the width of a square:

```
name._x = j*kv + pitx[k];
```

A similar formula is true for the Y coordinate:

```
name._y = iz*kv + pity[k];
```

Assign the element of the pit array a reference to this clip to create it logically:

```
pit[iz][j] = name;
```

This, as you can see, is quite tedious. You might think it would be easier to hire a professional.

5.2.7. Coding Motion and Rotation of the Pieces

In the previous section, I described the game engine that allows the pieces to fall down by themselves and processes the gamer's actions. This section describes how to move the pieces to the left or right, and to rotate them. You only need to take the last step. You might be eager to do this, but you have to be patient in order to avoid creating bugs in your program. By the way, do you know the origin of the term *computer bug*? The term came into being on Sept. 9th, 1945, when Grace Hopper repaired a U.S. Navy Mark II electromechanical computing machine by simply removing a moth from a relay. She eventually rose to the rank of Rear Admiral.

But I digress. Take a look at the moveLeft function (Listing 5.30), and copy its code into the program.

Listing 5.30. The moveLeft function

```
// Move both pieces to the left if `possible.
function moveLeft()
{ var i, j, k, fx, fy,
    f = new Array(),
    p = new Array();

  // Check for the possibility.
  for (k = 0; k < 2; k++)
  { fx = figsx[k];
    fy = figsy[k];
    f = figs[k];
    p = pits[k];
    for (i = 0; i < 3; i++)
      for (j = 0; j < 3; j++)
        if (f[i][j] && (j + fx < 1 || (!j || !f[i][j - 1])
          && p[fy + i][fx + j - 1])) return;
  }
  // Carry out the operation
  wipeFigs();
  --figsx[0];
  --figsx[1];
  paintFigs();
  downOrWaitAction(1);
}
```

The only thing that might require explanation is the condition of impossibility to move a piece to the left:

```
f[i][j] && (j + fx < 1 || (!j || !f[i][j - 1]) && p[fy + i][fx + j - 1])
```

Here `f[i][j]` means that there is a square on this place in the array that codes the piece.

The `j + fx < 1` condition means that this piece is at the left side of the pit (its X coordinate is zero). Indeed, to know the X coordinate of a square in the pit, you need to add `fx`, which is the X coordinate of the 3×3 square, to `j`, which is the X coordinate of the square in question inside that 3×3 square. You could also write the condition as `j + fx == 0`.

`!j` means that `j` is equal to zero, that is, the square's X coordinate inside the 3×3 square that codes the piece is zero.

`!f[i][j - 1]` means there is an unused space to the left of this square in the piece.

Now you can group these conditions together:

`!j || !f[i][j - 1]` means the `(i, j)`th square in the piece doesn't have a neighbor to its left.

`p[fy + i][fx + j - 1]` means there is a square in the pit immediately to the left of this square.

Combining the last two conditions, you obtain the following:

```
(!j || !f[i][j-1]) && p[fy + i][fx + j - 1])
```

This means the square doesn't have a neighbor to its left in the piece, but does have a neighbor to its left in the pit.

The entire condition can be rewritten in plain English as follows: "Exit the `moveLeft` function if there is a square on the `(i, j)`th position in the piece and this square is near the left side of the pit, or has a left neighbor not belonging to the piece in the pit". Note that you checked for the left neighbor on the `(j - 1)`th position in the piece only after you have made sure that `j > 0`. The situation is similar with the pit. The element with the `fx + j - 1` coordinates exists because you made sure that `fx + j > 0`.

If the function didn't return control with the `return` statement, the pieces can move to the left. The function removes the pieces using the `wipeFigs` function, reduces their horizontal coordinates by one, and draws the pieces in the new positions. The final action is a call to the `downOrWaitAction` function. A one is passed to it as an argument so that the `downFigs` function that lets the pieces to move one step down starts after the `timestep` interval required for one move down.

. The moveRight function (Listing 5.31) that moves the pieces to the right when possible is similar to moveLeft. Insert its code into the program.

Listing 5.31. The moveRight function

```
// Move both pieces to the right if possible.
function moveRight()
{ var i, j, k, fx, fy,
   f = new Array(),
   p = new Array();

   // Check for the possibility.
   for (k = 0; k < 2; k++)
   { fx = figsx[k];
     fy = figsy[k];
     f = figs[k];
     p = pits[k];
     for (i = 0; i < 3; i++)
       for (j = 0; j < 3; j++)
         if (f[i][j] && (j + fx > xx - 2 || (j == 2 || !f[i][j + 1]) &&
         p[fy + i][fx + j + 1])) return;
   }
   // Carry out the operation.
   wipeFigs();
   ++figsx[0];
   ++figsx[1];
   paintFigs();
   downOrWaitAction(1);
}
```

The sense of the main condition is the following: "Exit the moveRight function if there is a square on the (i, j)th position in the piece, and this square is near the right side of the pit or has a neighbor to its right not belonging to the piece in the pit".

Consider the last function, rotateFigs (Listing 5.32), which rotates the pieces. Insert its code into the program.

Listing 5.32. The `rotateFigs` function

```
// Rotate both pieces if possible.
function rotateFigs()
{ var i, j, k, fx, fy,
    f = new Array(),
    f1 = new Array(),
    p = new Array(),
    pf = new Array();

  // Check both pieces.
  for (k = 0; k < 2; k++)
   { fx = figsx[k];
     fy = figsy[k];
     f = figs[k];
     p = pits[k];
     // Find the pf check array for the figs[k] piece.
     for (j = 0; j < 9; j++)
      if (f == mf[j])
       { pf = ppf[j];
         break;
       }
     // Check for the possibility of rotation.
     for (i = 0; i < 3; i++)
      for (j = 0; j < 3; j++)
       if (pf[i][j] && (fy + i >= yy || fx + j < 0 || fx + j >= xx ||
        p[fy + i][fx + j])) return;
   }
  wipeFigs();
  // Rotate the pieces.
  for (k = 0; k < 2; k++)
   { ffn[k] = (ffn[k] + 1)%4;
     figs[k] = mff[mffn[k]][ffn[k]];
   }
  // Do the operation.
  paintFigs();
  downOrWaitAction(1);
}
```

First, find a reference to the check array to make sure that the piece doesn't encounter a square during rotation or at the end position. For the piece coded with the f0 array, the check array is pf0; for the piece coded with f1, the check array is pf1, and so on. In this case, the f variable refers to the array that codes the piece. How can you find a check array? You should find the number of the array that codes the piece in the mf array that contains such arrays. This can be done in a loop for j:

```
for (j = 0; j < 9; j++)
```

When the condition

```
f == mf[j]
```

is true, the ppf variable is assigned the check array for the piece coded with the f array, and the loop terminates prematurely.

NOTE

The f == mf[j] statement doesn't compare the elements of the arrays, to which the f and mf[j] variables refer. Rather, it compares the contents of these variables. If you create two similar arrays, a = [1,2,3] and b = [1,2,3], a won't be equal to b because these variables refer to different arrays, even though the contents of the arrays are equal. In the rotateFigs function, the comparison operation works because there is the mf array that contains the references to the arrays that code the pieces.

After the reference to the check array is found, the function checks for the possibility of rotation. This is done as follows: It checks what would happen if the pf check array was put into the pit in place of the 3×3 square that contains the piece. If the pf[i][j] element is not equal to zero, and there is a square in the pit on its place, or this element is outside the pit, rotation is impossible:

```
pf[i][j] && (fy + i >= yy || fx + j < 0 || fx + j >= xx || p[fy + i][fx + j])
```

Here you check whether the element is beyond the left or right boundary or the bottom of the pit. You don't check whether it is beyond the top because a piece will never rise above the zero line.

If rotation is possible, the function removes the piece from the pit and looks for the array that codes the new position of the piece being rotated. Now remember the ff0, ff1, ..., and ff8 arrays. For example, if the left current piece is coded in the f3 array (three squares horizontally), a three will be stored in the mff[0] element when the piece appears. This is a kind of index for the piece that can be used to search in the mff array for the ff3 value, which is a reference to the array that codes the positions of rotation for this piece. This array consists of three elements: f3, f4, f3, and f4 that code the positions the piece takes during rotation. If you rotate the piece coded with f3, you'll obtain the piece coded with f4 that is the next element in the ff3 array. When you rotate the piece further, you'll obtain the piece coded with f3. This is the second (counting from zero) element of the ff3 array. Indices in this array are updated cyclically. How can you know the index in the ff3 array for the coding of the current piece? It is stored in the ffn[0] element.

During rotation of the piece in the kth pit, the index of its coding in the ffn array is updated cyclically to obtain its index after the rotation:

```
ffn[k] = (ffn[k] + 1)%4;
```

Then the reference to the array of its new coding is found:

```
figs[k] = mff[mffn[k]][ffn[k]];
```

This doesn't seem too sophisticated.

Start the project. (It is best to start it in the Flash player rather than in the development environment, so that the <Enter> and <Esc> keys are active). Check whether the splash screen disappears after you click a mouse button or press a key. Notice, however, that if you click on the **Sound** button or press the <S> key, you'll exit the splash screen simultaneously with toggling the sound. You can select the speed buttons using the arrow keys, the mouse, or the keys on the numeric pad. You can start the game using the mouse or the <Enter> or <P> key. During the game, when you pause (you can also do this using the <P> key), the **New** button will become inactive to prevent you from starting a new game. If you exit the pause mode, the **New** button will become active, allowing you to start a new came (which can also be done using the <N> key). The checks on the buttons are displayed correctly, the pieces respond to your actions quickly, points are added to the score, the lightning bolts strike the squares, the squares explode, the filled lines disappear, and you can move or rotate the pieces three times after they encounter an obstacle. After the game is over, you can select a speed using the usual methods and start a new game using the <Enter> or <Y> keys. Notice that all of these features take up just 45 K!

You can find the project in the chapter5.2.7.fla and tet5.2.7.as files.

You will also notice a blue panel with the copyright and a button with a link to **www.gameintellect.com**. They are necessary if an owner of the book tries to use this game, for example, on his or her site. It is prohibited to sell, rent, or exchange the game, to distribute its source code, or to derive profit from the game in any other way! The source code is intended only for training purposes.

I should mention that a debugger is incorporated into the Flash development environment, so you can start the movie in the debugging mode using the **Control | Debug Movie** menu item. I don't, however, think you'll like the debugger much. I don't use it when I create games: the `trace` function is enough for me.

5.3. Continuation of the Theme

Besides the two-pit Tetris version, many other versions can be invented (and actually have been). In my opinion, the most interesting variant includes the little figure of a man resembling Alexey Pajitnov, the creator of Tetris. The "man" walks in the game pit and simply gets in the way. If a piece falls on him, the game is over. You can see this and other variants of the game in my Six-Trix program, available at the site **http://www.gameintellect.com/six-trix/**. You can download it using the **http://www.gameintellect.com/six-trix/six-trix_install.exe** link. The size of the distributive file is 1.5 MB.

I believe that you can develop another Flash project based on this one. That project could include one pit, 35 hexamino pieces, rotation about three axes, and the figure of a walking man. I'd be glad to hear about it.

Chapter 6: Interaction between the Game and the Web Server

Up to this point, you have only started the game in the Flash environment or in Flash player. In real life, however, gamers will load it into their browsers from the Internet or start it as an EXE file (see following chapters). You might think that debugging a game loaded from the Internet requires a Web server that supports scripts. However, you can get along with your local computer because of the availability of Windows versions of the Apache Web server, the PHP and Perl interpreters, and even the MySQL database server. What's more, you can get them for free! You can install a full-featured chain of Apache, Perl, PHP, and MySQL on your home computer, even under Windows 98.

6.1. Installing and Setting PHP

The abbreviation PHP stands for *Preprocessor of Home Pages*. It is a scripting language with a syntax resembling those of C, Perl, and Java. Programs written in PHP are embedded into HTML documents (pages), a fact that is very pleasing. Even the creator of such a page can sometimes, however, fail to understand it. The purpose of PHP is to speed up development of dynamic pages. Its official site is **http://www.php.net**.

When a PHP page is requested from the Web server (the server understands this through a special file extension), the server starts the PHP interpreter and passes it this file. PHP looks for the `<?PHP` and `?>` tags (or for a shorter variant, `<?` and `?>`) in this file and executes the code enclosed between them. It then substitutes the tags and the code for the result of execution, that is, for the data output by the code. The rest of the page remains unchanged. PHP passes the processed page back to the Web server, which forwards it to the browser. You can call the PHP interpreter directly from the command line and pass it a file. For example: `php.exe index.php`. The result will be sent to the output stream, the same as is the case with a DOS program.

PHP is supplied as a ZIP archive. No special installation procedures are required — just unpack the archive to a folder. We'll assume here that PHP is installed in the folder C:\php4. The install.txt file describes how to set up the program. Copy the php.ini-dist file to the Windows folder, and rename it php.ini. In this file, comments begin with a semicolon. To enable sessions in PHP, find the following line:

```
session.save_path = /tmp
```

and replace `tmp` with a folder for temporary files, or create a C:\tmp folder. There is no need to change anything else, and the interpreter should now work.

6.2. Installing and Setting the Apache Web Server

The Apache Web server is supplied as an EXE file. Its official site is **http://www.apache.org**. However, you can use another Web server, such as the server that came with your version of Windows, for example.

We'll assume that Apache is installed in the C:\Apache folder. The conf folder includes the configuration file httpd.conf.default. Copy it to the httpd.conf file, and make the changes as follows (remember, comments begin with the # character).

Find the line containing `ServerRoot`, and specify the server root folder:

```
ServerRoot "C:/Apache"
```

Find the line containing `DocumentRoot`. This specifies the document (page) root folder. The line should read:

```
DocumentRoot "C:/Apache/htdocs"
```

The line containing `DirectoryIndex` specifies the default index file names, i.e., the data that should be sent to the browser if no file is specified in an URL request. For example:

```
DirectoryIndex index.html index.shtml index.php
```

Then find `ScriptAlias`, and add a line with the path to PHP:

```
ScriptAlias /cgi-bin/ "C:/Apache/cgi-bin/"
ScriptAlias /php/ "C:/PHP4/"
```

Note that some paths include backslashes, while others include slashes. In addition, some paths end with a slash, while others don't.

Now find `AddType`. If you encounter the following lines:

```
AddType application/x-httpd-php3 .phtml
AddType application/x-httpd-php3-source .phps
```

comment them out, and insert the following lines (or simply edit the available lines):

```
AddType application/x-httpd-php4 .phtml .php
AddType application/x-httpd-php4-source .phps
```

If you're planning to use Perl, insert the following line:

```
AddHandler cgi-script .cgi .pl
```

To use SSI (Server Side Includes), insert the following lines:

```
AddType text/html .shtml
AddHandler server-parsed .shtml
```

Finally, specify an alias for the handler of the application/x-httpd-php4 MIME type. Find the line containing `Action`, and insert:

```
Action application/x-httpd-php4 /php/php.exe
```

PHP (and Perl) should now work with Apache.

To start Apache, type in the command line:

```
C:\Apache\Apache.exe -d "C:\Apache" -s
```

To exit it, type

```
C:\Apache\Apache.exe -d "C:\Apache" -k shutdown
```

Create shortcuts for these commands. The work folder is C:\Apache. In Windows NT, 2000, and higher, you can start Apache as a process. Apache saves all requests in the C:\Apache\logs\access.log file. Erroneous requests are stored in the error.log file. If the Web server is running, it is available to your browser at

```
http://localhost
```

or

```
http://127.0.0.1
```

These are requests to the default file from the C:\Apache\htdocs folder. For example, you can request the C:\Apache\htdocs\mysite\about.html file using the following command:

```
http://localhost/mysite/about.html
```

NOTE

The httpd.conf file doesn't contain the path to the Perl interpreter. The path should be specified in the first line of Perl script. For example, `#!c:/perl/bin/perl.exe`.

6.3. Receiving Game Parameters from the Web Server

You'll receive the following parameters from your Web server:

- ❒ snd — A flag indicating whether the sound is enabled. It can be stored in a cookie on the user's computer.
- ❒ passw — The password for the game that is sent to registered users. The game uses this to determine whether it should run as a full-featured version. The password can also be used to access certain levels in the game. Non-registered users receive an empty string.
- ❒ userpassw — The encrypted password for registered users (others receive an empty string). It can be stored in a cookie in an encrypted form. It is used when sending data to the server for operations that are only permitted for registered users.
- ❒ servres — A flag that indicates whether the results should be sent to the server. It is equal either to zero or one, and the user selects this option when providing the necessary information to be registered.
- ❒ champres — The world record. This is simply information for the gamer. If the table of records is empty, an empty string is sent.
- ❒ time10 — The smallest result in the table of records. (It is assumed that the table contains the top ten records). This value is used to decide whether the result of the game should be sent to the server. If the result is greater than time10, and if servres == 1, then it is sent. At first (when the table of records is empty), time10 contains the zero character ('0').
- ❒ champ — The champion's name. It is displayed during the game.
- ❒ country — The champion's country of residence. This is also displayed.

Let's base our discussion on the project from the previous chapter: the chapter5.2.7.fla and tet5.2.7.as files. Load the project into Flash, and attach the code from Listing 6.1 to the first frame.

Listing 6.1. The code for the first frame

```
var
  vars = new LoadVars();

loadvarsurl = 'http://localhost/lv.php';
addresulturl = 'http://localhost/addres.php';
vars.load(loadvarsurl + '?rand = ' + Math.random().toString().substr(2));
```

This declares that the LoadVars object should load variables into the movie. The object has the load method. In addition, URLs are declared for receiving variables and sending results. These scripts are still to be written. Now, the load method is called to load variables. The URL string contains the rand variable, for which the value is pseudo-random. This is the case because you want to load the result from the server, and not from a cache. To do this, you should specify a unique URL. The first two characters (zero and a period) of the number are deleted using the substr(2) function, so 15 digits remain. From now on, if the Web server isn't running when you start the game in the Flash development environment, the **Output** window will display a message like the following:

```
Error opening URL "http://localhost/lv.php?rand = 373178189620376"
```

Variables are loaded from the Web server asynchronously. Nobody knows if they are loaded completely. The loaded property of the LoadVars object is used as an indicator. When all the variables are loaded, this indicator is equal to true.

Now, enter the third frame, delete the temporary code attached to it, and insert the code from Listing 6.2.

Listing 6.2. The code for the third frame

```
if (_totalframes && _framesloaded == _totalframes && vars.loaded)
{ snd = vars.snd;
  passw = vars.passw;
  userpassw = vars.userpassw;
  servres = vars.servres;
  champres = vars.champres;
```

```
    time10 = vars.time10;
    champ = vars.champ;
    country = vars.country;
    delete(vars);
} else gotoAndPlay(2);
```

The code works as follows: If the _totalframes variable that stores the number of the timeline frames is undefined (or equal to zero), or if the _framesloaded variable that stores the number of loaded frames isn't equal to the number of movie frames, or if the variables aren't loaded yet, the player goes to the second frame. You could write this in another form:

```
gotoAndPlay(_currentframe - 1)
```

This would mean: "Go to the previous frame and play it". If everything is loaded, the code extracts the desired variables from the vars object, assigns their values to the game variables, and destroys the vars object. The data section of the main program ends with the following line:

```
bleep3snd = new Sound();
```

Insert the comment from Listing 6.3 after this line.

Listing 6.3. Data received from the server

```
/*
Parameters received from the server:
snd        - 1/0: sound enabled/disabled
passw      - password to protected levels
userpassw  - encrypted password of the registered user
servres    - 1/0: send/don't send the records to the server
champ      - the champion's name or empty
champres   - the champion's score or empty
time10     - the 10th row in the table of records or '0'
country    - the champion's country of residence or empty
*/
```

You should now write a PHP script that will send data from the server to the game. The data will be stored in the script as literals. A real-life script will retrieve the data from a file with a registered user's profile, from a session, or from the

MySQL database. These details are beyond the scope of this book, and all you have to do is somehow implement the data exchange.

First, consider the script in Listing 6.4 to understand what it sends to the game.

Listing 6.4. A draft of a PHP script that sends data

```php
<?
$snd = 1;
$passw = 12345;
$userpassw = 'AbCdE';
$servres = 1;
$champ = 'Serge Melnikov';
$champres = 25331;
$time10 = '';
$country = 'Greenland';

// Encrypt $userpassw.
for ($i = 0; $i < 5; $i++)
 $userpassw[$i] = chr(ord($userpassw[$i]) ^ 1);

// Set the MIME type (URL coding) for the Web server.
header("Content-Type: application/x-www-urlform-encoded\n\n");

//. Send variables to the Flash movie.
echo 'snd='.$snd.'&passw='.$passw.'&userpassw='.
 urlencode($userpassw).'&servres='.$servres.'&champ='.
 urlencode($champ).'&champres='.$champres.
 '&time10='.$time10.'&country='.urlencode($country);
?>
```

The script begins with the variables that should be sent. A five-character password is then encrypted (although not very securely) using the XOR operation (addition modulo 2). The variables you send should be preceded by a header that tells the Web server the content type, so that the server will know what data it should send in response to the request. In this case, the content type should be application/x-www-urlform-encoded. This is the content type used by the browser to send a filled-in form to the Web server using the GET method. The header should end with an empty line: \n\n. These requirements are set by the HTTP protocol. After you send the header using the header PHP function, send the variables using the `echo` function. The format used by this function is as follows: The variable name is followed by an equal sign and the variable's value. You should then include an ampersand, the name of the next variable, an equal sign, the value, and so on. If the value for a variable can contain characters other than Latin characters, numerical digits, a hyphen, a period, or the underline character, you should process it using the `urlencode` function before sending. This function will replace prohibited characters with sequences consisting of a percentage character followed by two hexadecimal digits. These encode the replaced character. The space character is an exception: It is replaced with a plus sign.

The script file should use Windows encoding. Name it lv.php, save it in the Apache\htdocs folder, and start Apache. In the main program, locate the following line:

```
// *** The beginning of the program ***
```

Insert the following command after the line:

```
trace(champres);
```

This should output the value of the `champres` variable. After the game starts, you'll see 25331 in the **Output** window. This shows that it works!

Now it's time to display the champion's name and country of residence. Create a clip with the name `champname`. It should be a filled rectangle 155 pixels wide and 40 pixels high. Place its upper left corner on the point with the (0, 0) coordinates. Set its color to #C201C2 and the **Alpha** parameter to 33%. Place three text fields — one below the other — on the rectangle. They should be adjacent to each other, or even overlap a little. Their names in the **Var:** fields should be the following (from top to bottom): `text1`, `text2`, and `text3`. Select the **Dynamic text** text type, the **_sans** font, a font size of 11 pts, and the #FFFFCC color. The width of each field should be 155 pixels, while the height should be 17 pixels. The coordinates for the top text field are (0, 0), and each subsequent field is 12 pixels lower than that of the preceding field. The result is shown in Fig. 6.1.

Drag this clip to the main timeline, to the fourth frame of **Layer 2**, and set its coordinates as follows: X = 610, Y = 448. Make sure that you give the clip instance the name `champname` in the properties panel (<Ctrl>+<F3>). Select the instance, copy it to the clipboard using the <Ctrl>+<V> shortcut, and insert it into the fifth frame of the same layer, in the same position, using the <Ctrl>+<Shift>+<V> shortcut. If you don't do this, you won't see the instance in the movie. Why didn't I tell you to drag the clip to the fifth frame from the first? The main program is attached to the fourth frame, and the clip should appear in the movie before values are written into its text fields. You could, however, attach the code to the fifth frame of the movie.

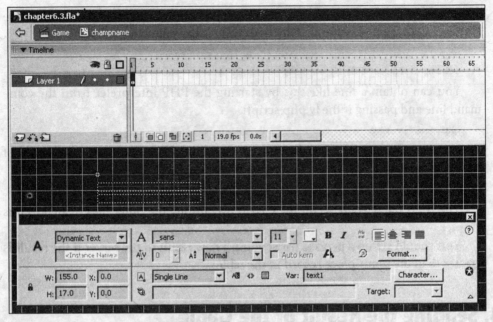

Fig. 6.1. The champname clip

To display these values, insert the code from Listing 6.5 to the beginning of the main program.

Listing 6.5. The code for displaying the champion's name and country of residence

```
if (time10 == '') time10 = 0;
if (champ != '')
 { champname.text1 = 'Champion ('+champres+')';
   champname.text2 = champ+',';
   champname.text3 = country;
 } else champname.text1 = 'Champion: none';
```

After the game starts, you'll see the champion's name, country of residence, and score. Wonderful!

I'd like to point out that a Flash movie can receive data from the server or from a common text file (or from an HTML page that defines the SWF file, for example,

...tetatet.swf?snd = 1&passw = 12345&...). It is important that the variables are URL-encoded. In this example, URL-encoding is the following:

```
snd=1&passw=12345&userpassw=%40cBe%01&servres=1
&champ=Serge%20Melnikov&champres=25331&time10=&country=Greenland
```

You can obtain a line like this by starting the PHP interpreter from the command line and passing it the lv.php script:

```
php.exe lv.php
```

You can test this by replacing the name of the PHP script with the name of a text file (such as lv.txt) in the first frame of the movie:

```
loadvarsurl = 'http://localhost/lv.txt';
```

The lv.txt file is available on the CD-ROM, among the other files related to this chapter.

You should set up a process for sending a new result to the server if the result is greater than the tenth-place record in the table.

6.4. Sending the Result of the Game to the Web Server

The chance to set a world record and carve out their own little chunk of fame will motivate users to visit our site and continue to play until they achieve the final victory. I'll explain how to make this possible. In ActionScript, this can be done using the loadVariables function. It sends results just as the browser sends a form using the GET or POST method. You can use the POST method when the amount of data is large, as Web servers limit the lengths of URL strings to a value between 255 and 1024 characters. In practice, these strings are limited by browsers to a length of approximately 1.5 K. The POST method, however, is unavailable in Flash Player. I recommend that you use the GET method:

```
loadVariables(addresulturl+'?userpassw='+userpassw+'&score='+score+
  '&rand='+getTimer(),'_root');
```

The addresulturl variable is declared in the first frame of the movie. For the sake of security, a Flash movie is only allowed to exchange data with hosts of the domain, from which the movie was loaded. Flash Player can exchange information with any domain. The URL string will also include a unique value, '&rand='+getTimer(), to prevent caching by the browser or a proxy server. If the results of the game were cached, the target server will receive outdated data from a cache, instead of the "hot" information.

To allow the users to send their results, you need two buttons (btSend and btCancel), a clip that contains the buttons and appears every time the results should be sent, and a small function, sendRec1, in the main program. In addition, you should find an appropriate point in the program to call this function. So there is a little more work to do.

Create a new symbol (<Ctrl>+<F8>), name it btSend, and select the **Button** behavior for it. It's not necessary to export it for ActionScript. Draw a 61 × 20-pixel rectangle without an outline. Open the **Color Mixer** window, and select the **Radial** fill. On the color strip, set the markers so that the color is white at the center and yellow at the sides. Click on the center of the button using the **Paint Bucket** tool. For the Send text, select the **_sans** bold font, with a font size of 13 pts and the #FF00FF color. Select the **Static Text** item from the drop-down list. I hope you remember that these operations are carried out in the window containing the properties for the selected object (to open this, use the <Ctrl>+<F3> shortcut). Click on the **Center Justify** button, and check the **Auto Kern** and **Use Device Fonts** checkboxes, if necessary. A screenshot of this stage is provided in Fig. 6.2.

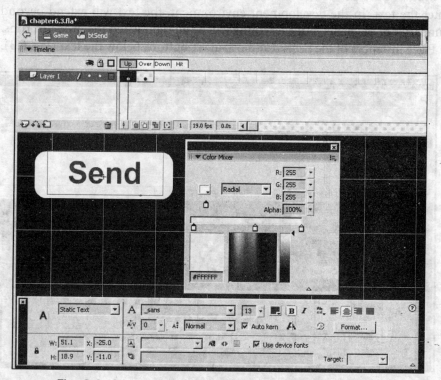

Fig. 6.2. Creating the btSend button (magnification 4x)

These actions were performed in the **Up** frame. Enter the **Over** frame, and press the <F6> key to copy the contents of the **Up** frame to it. In the **Over** frame, change the text color to blue (#0066FF). The button will respond by showing this color when the mouse pointer is moved over it.

Based on the btSend button, create the btCancel button, with the word **Cancel**. To do this, you can use the **Copy Frames** and **Paste Frames** items on the **Edit** menu, or the <Ctrl>+<Alt>+<C> and the <Ctrl>+<Alt>+<V> shortcuts, respectively.

Creating the sendRec1 clip is easy. This is a green, semi-transparent panel, with the two buttons you just created and some text. This can be based on the infoPanel clip.

The sendRec1 name should be exported for ActionScript. In my version of the game, the panel size is 200 × 116 pixels. Place the following text at the top of the panel:

```
            Congratulations!
      Click "Send" to send your
      result to our game server.
```

For the text, select the **_sans** font, a font size of 16 pts, the #FF00CC color, and the **Static Text** type. Check the **Auto Kern** and **Use Device Fonts** checkboxes, and center the text. In the development environment, the text will extend beyond the boundaries of the panel, but everything will be all right when the program runs.

Place instances of the btSend and btCancel buttons below the text (Fig. 6.3).

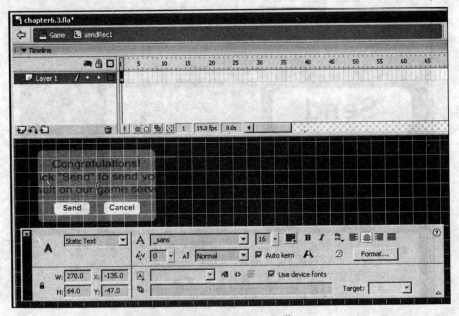

Fig. 6.3. The sendRec1 clip

Now, you have to attach actions to the button instances. To do this, select the btSend instance and press the <F9> key to open the code editor window. Type in the following code:

```
on (release)
{ _root.sendRec(1);
}
```

In a similar manner, attach the following code to the btCancel button instance:

```
on (release)
{ _root.sendRec(0);
}
```

The argument (zero or one) tells the sendRec function whether the gamer has clicked the **Send** or **Cancel** button, i.e., whether or not it should send the data to the server.

Now, write the code for the sendRec function (Listing 6.6).

Listing 6.6. The sendRec1 function

```
// Send the result to the server or cancel.
// The btSend or btCancel button was clicked.
function sendRec(arg)
{ if (arg) loadVariables(addresulturl+'?userpassw='+
    userpassw+'&score='+score+'&rand='+getTimer(),'_root');
  // Remove the sendRec1 clip and display the Game Over panel.
  sendRec1.removeMovieClip();
  menuorOver(0);
}
```

This function also sends the userpassw variable to the server. The movie received this variable from the server so that the server script could determine the registered user in question for the table of records. (The user entered his or her name and country of residence during registration). Place this function in the main program.

You are no doubt eager to learn what data the server script will receive from your game. To see this, write a small PHP script, for which the name, addres.php, is already declared in the code attached to the first frame of the main timeline. On your computer, this script will save the result in a file. What it does on an actual Web server is the concern of a Web developer. Listing 6.7 shows the code for this script. It appends the received variables userpassw and score to the end of the tetatet.txt file.

Listing 6.7. The addres.php script

```
<?
// Add the result to the table of records.
// This script is called from the Flash game.
// The call:
// addres.php?userpassw = <encrypted password>&score = <score>

// Get the password
$userpassw = $HTTP_GET_VARS['userpassw'];
// Decrypt the password
for ($i = 0; $i < 5; $i++) $userpassw[$i] = chr(ord($userpassw[$i]) ^ 1);

// Get the score.
$score = $HTTP_GET_VARS['score'];

// Open the tetatet.txt file and write the data to it.
$fname = 'tetatet.txt';
if (($fp = fopen($fname, 'a+')) == false) exit;
fwrite($fp,"userpassw = $userpassw, score = $score\n");
fclose($fp);
?>
```

The variables sent using the GET method are available to the script in the $HTTP_GET_VARS array. The names of the variables are used as indices for this array. The password is decrypted in the same way as it was encrypted before sending it to the game. The fopen function then opens the tetatet.txt in the append mode. If the file doesn't exist, it will be created. If everything is correct, the function returns the true value. The fwrite function appends the data to the file, after which it is closed by the next function.

To test how the data are sent and received, place the addres.php script in the same folder as lv.php, and make the following changes to the main program:

Locate the line

```
spl();
```

at the end of the program, and insert the following lines before it:

```
score = 12345;
sendRec(1);
```

In the `sendRec` function, you can comment out the last two lines:

```
//sendRec1.removeMovieClip();
//menuorOver(0);
```

If you don't comment these out, however, they are unlikely to affect the test. Then start the game and examine the folder that contains the server scripts. You should find the tetatet.txt file there, and its contents should be the following:

```
userpassw = AbCdE, score = 12345
```

Make sure to undo the changes you made to the main program.

You now need to insert code that actually calls the `sendRec` function. This code should be inserted into the `newFigs` function after the check of whether the pieces overlap. In addition, you have to insert code that will interact with a non-registered gamer. This will limit him or her to playing for only five minutes. To implement this, insert the following lines at the end of the `startGame` function, before the call to the `newFigs` function:

```
endtime = 2000000000;
if (passw != '12345') endtime = getTimer() + 1000*60*5;
```

Insert a declaration of the `endtime` variable into the data section of the main program after the declaration of the `nexttime` variable:

```
endtime,
```

If the `passw` password received from the server is equal to 12345, the `endtime` variable will have a value of 2,000,000,000 ms, which should be large enough for one game. If the `passw` variable does not equal 12345, the `endtime` variable will have the `getTimer() + 1000*60*5` value, that is, five minutes per a game. The updated `startGame` function should look like the one shown in Listing 6.8.

Listing 6.8. The `startGame` function, with game-time limitation

```
// Start a new game. If arg = 1, the function is called with the New button
// before the current game is completed.
function startGame(arg)
{ var i, j, k, p,
  pit = new Array();

  // Remove all clips that could be in the menu.
  gover.removeMovieClip();
  menu.removeMovieClip();
```

```
infoPanel.removeMovieClip();
// Set the initial game speed.
if (arg == 1) speed = speed0;
 else speed0 = speed;
// Reset the score and the numbers of pieces and filled lines to zero.
score = pieces = lines = 0;
// Set the interval (in ms) for one move down that a piece makes on its own.
timestep = 2000 - speed*200;
// Display the speed, the score, pieces, and filled rows.
showNum(speed, 0);
showNum(score, 1);
showNum(pieces, 2);
showNum(lines, 3);
// Clear the game pits.
for (k = 0; k < 2; k++)
 { pit = pits[k];
   for (i = 0; i < yy; i++)
    for (j = 0; j < xx; j++)
     if (p = pit[i][j])
      { p.removeMovieClip();
        pit[i][j] = null;
      }
 }
// Set the event handler.
attachMovie('keydownact', 'keydownact', depth4 + 1);
// Set the game state.
gamestate = gamest;
// Activate the Pause and New buttons.
btPause.useHandCursor = 1;
btNew.useHandCursor = 1;
// Set the nexttime variable to the current time
// to start newFigs() instantly.
nexttime = getTimer();
endtime = 2000000000;
if (passw != '12345') endtime = getTimer() + 1000*60*5;
newFigs();
}
```

Listing 6.9 shows the code for the updated `newFigs` function.

Listing 6.9. The `newFigs` function with game-time limitation

```
// Create and output a pair of pieces.
function newFigs()
{ var i, j, k, t, flag, corr,
  f = new Array(),
  fx,
  fy,
  p = new Array();

  if ((t = getTimer()) < nexttime || ispaused) return;
// Decrease the probability of an inconvenient pair of pieces, No.3 and No.4.
  do
    for (k = 0; k < 2; k++)
      { mffn[k] = Math.floor(Math.random()*9);
        ffn[k] = 0;
        colors[k] = mffn[k];
        figs[k] = mff[mffn[k]][0];
        figsx[k] = 5;
        figsy[k] = 0;
      }
  while (mffn[0] + mffn[1] == 7 && mffn[0]*mffn[1] == 12 && ++corr == 1);
  // Check whether the pieces overlap.
  for (k = 0; k < 2; k++)
  { fx = figsx[k];
    fy = figsy[k];
    f = figs[k];
    p = pits[k];
    for (i = 0; i < 3; i++)
      for (j = 0; j < 3; j++)
        if (f[i][j] && p[fy + i][fx + j]) flag = 1;
  }
  paintFigs();
  showNum(pieces += 2,2);
  if (flag || t > endtime)
    { playSound(goversnd);
      keydownact.removeMovieClip();
      btPause.gotoAndStop(1); btPause.useHandCursor = 0;
```

```
    btNew.gotoAndStop(1); btNew.useHandCursor = 0;
    menuorOver.name = 'gover';
    if (score > time10 && passw == '12345')
   ·{ delete gameact.onEnterFrame;
      attachMovie('sendRec1', 'sendRec1', depth3);
      sendRec1._x = 303;
      sendRec1._y = 207;
    } else menuorOver(t > endtime);
    return;
  }
// Enable control from the keyboard.
controlenabled = 1;
// The gamer can move a piece three times until it moves down.
numact = 3;
// Should the speed be increased?
if (!(pieces%40) && speed < 9)
  { ++speed;
    timestep -= 200;
    showNum(speed, 0);
    playSound(bleep3snd);
  }
showNum(currscore = (speed + 1)*20,4);
downOrWaitAction();
}
```

The changes were introduced into the conditional statement:

```
if (flag || t > endtime)
   { playSound(goversnd);
     keydownact.removeMovieClip();
     btPause.gotoAndStop(1); btPause.useHandCursor = 0;
     btNew.gotoAndStop(1); btNew.useHandCursor = 0;
     menuorOver.name = 'gover';
     if (score > time10 && passw == '12345')
      { delete gameact.onEnterFrame;
        attachMovie('sendRec1', 'sendRec1', depth3);
        sendRec1._x = 303;
        sendRec1._y = 207;
      } else menuorOver(t > endtime);
      return;
   }
```

The condition now contains the following sub-condition:

```
|| t > endtime.
```

As a result, the game will not only stop after a new piece overlaps an existing piece, but also when the current time `t` computed at the beginning of the `newFigs` function exceeds the value contained in the `endtime` variable. The

```
if (score > time10 && passw == '12345')
```

conditional statement checks whether the `score` for the game that just has finished is greater than `time10` (which is in 10th place in the table of records) and whether the `passw` password is correct (i.e., the player is registered). If the condition is met, the `sendRec1` clip is called from the library, and the gamer is given the option send-off sending his or her result to the server. If at least one of the sub-conditions is false, the `menuorOver` function is called, and the `t > endtime` flag is passed to it as an argument to indicate whether the `infoPanel` clip for a non-registered user should be displayed.

You then have to exit the `newFigs` function, as the game is over. This is done using the `return` statement.

To test how the game interacts with a non-registered gamer, insert the following line:

```
spl();
```

near the end of the main program, for example, before the line:

```
passw = '';
```

This will override the password. In the `startGame` function, decrease the value assigned to the `endtime` variable to one minute, so you won't have to wait too long. Start the game. After a minute has passed, you'll see the panel of the `gover` clip and the `infoPanel` clip below it. This will continue to be annoying for a non-registered user, hopefully convincing him or her to pay for registration.

All of the files mentioned in this chapter are available in the Example\Chapter 6 folder on the accompanying CD-ROM.

Chapter 7: Integrating the Flash Project into a Program Shell

This chapter describes how to update your game project to interact with a program shell. All you will need to do is add a few clips and some ActionScript code.

7.1. Adding New Clips

For your game to work in the program shell, you have to update the project files (the FLA file and the AS file). You should provide some new features, including inputting and checking the registration key, displaying the rules for the game and the table of records, and calls to functions from the shell, using the fscommand function.

Create a btExit button, which will allow the gamer to exit the table of records and the program. To create a new clip, press the <Ctrl>+<F8> shortcut, and select the **Button** behavior. Name it btExit. This should be a 45 × 25-pixel rectangle with rounded corners (the radius of the corner should be three). The rectangle's outline should be of the #996699 color and be one-pixel thick. Its fill should be **Linear**, with three color markers: left and right markers of the #577693 color, and a central one with the #978282 color (Fig. 7.1). Remember that you can open the **Color Mixer** panel with the <Shift>+<F9> shortcut.

For the **Exit** text, select the **_sans** bold font with a font size of 16 pts. Select the **Static Text** for the text type and #CC3366 for the text color. Check the **Use Device Fonts** checkbox, and click the **Align Center** button. After you write and justify the text, select the **Over** frame on the timeline, and press the <F6> key to copy the **Up** frame into it. In the **Over** frame, change the text color to #FF9797 and the outline color to #CC00FF. Remember that you should double-click on the outline with the **Arrow** tool before you change the outline color. Now the btExit button is ready, but there are still a few more buttons we need.

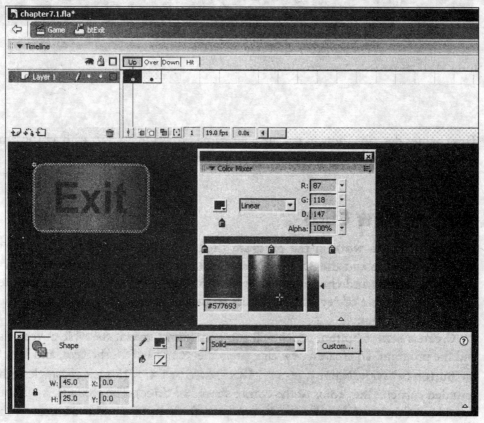

Fig. 7.1. The btExit button (magnified four times)

It is easy to create a btExitHelp button to allow the gamer exit the help display. Create a new button with this name. It should be in the form of a circle with a 30-pixel diameter, with no outline, and with a red cross inside. When the mouse pointer is over it (i.e., when Flash player is in the **Over** frame), it will become pink. Use red tints, as with the previous button. Select the **Radial** fill, moving from the #ABEAFE color in the center to the #7094FE color. The lines that form the cross should have a thickness of three pixels. You should be able to create this button on your own.

To call the Help clip (the clip containing the rules of the game), you need a btHelp clip button. This should be similar to the btNew, btPause, and btSound buttons. Create it based on the btNew button by copying all of its frames (or duplicating the clip in the library) and replacing the label **New** with one reading **Help**. The letter "H" should be underlined. In addition to naming the clip in the **Symbol Properties** panel, make sure to check the **Export for ActionScript** checkbox with the same name, btHelp.

Based on the btExit button created above, create a btOK button. This will be used when entering the gamer's name. The only difference from the btExit button is that, understandably enough, it reads **OK**, rather than **Exit**.

Create another button, btNo. A button of this type was pointless in the browser, but you do need it in a stand-alone program on the **Play again?** panel. The gamer should have the option of rejecting a new game using the **No** button. The btNo button is similar to btYes. It is smaller though (25 × 15 pixels). Its outline should be one pixel thick and its label text should have a font size of 8 pts. The letter "N" should be underlined. Create this button based on the btYes button, open the gover symbol for editing, and place the btNo button to the right of btYes (you might need to move the btYes button to the left a little). Select the btNo button, press the <F9> key, and attach the following code to it in the code editor window:

```
on (release)
{ if (_root.maxscore > _root.topscores[9]) _root.showEnterName ();
    else _root.showTopTen ();
}
```

In this code, the maxscore variable that will be declared later contains the gamer's maximum score for all of the games he or she has played from the beginning to the end of the program. If the score is greater than topscores[9], which is the 10th line of the table of records (remember, the elements of an array are numbered from zero), the showEnterName function is called. Otherwise, the table of records is displayed, using the showTopTen function. This is easy to understand, and all you have to do is implement these functions.

Finally, create a btRegOK button for a panel that will be used to enter a name and registration key. Press the <Ctrl>+<F8> shortcut, give the clip the name btRegOK, and select the **Button** behavior. Draw a 34 × 18.1-pixel rectangle with a **hairline** outline. Select the #FF9900 color for the outline and the #FFFFFF color for fill. In the **Up** frame, write OK using the **_sans** bold font with a font size of 12 pts. The text should be of the **Static Text** type, black, and centered. The **Over** frame differs in its text color, which is red (#FF0000).

Now, create an empty clip symbol, eNameKeyUp. To do this, press the <Ctrl>+<F8> shortcut, and specify this name. Check the **Export for ActionScript** checkbox. Drag the emptyclip symbol from the library into this newly-created symbol, select it, and attach the following code:

```
onClipEvent (keyUp)
  { _root.enterNameKeyUp(1);
  }
```

As a result, the enterNameKeyUp function, which hasn't been written yet, will be called when the gamer releases a keyboard key while typing his or her name and a registration key.

Let's proceed with clips. Create a topten clip to display the table of records. This should be a panel with the header **Top Ten**, ten text fields with the name of the gamer for each of the best scores, and ten text fields for the scores themselves. Each text field will be named to allow you to fill the fields programmatically. There should be a btExit button at the bottom of the panel to allow the gamer to exit the program.

To make the panel more attractive, let's use a picture from a BMP file. In the \Examples\Chapter 7 folder, you will find the topbkgr.bmp file. Select the **File | Import | Import to Library** menu command, and locate this file. It will appear in the library. Move the file to the Images folder. Right-click on the icon for this picture in the library, and open the **Properties** window. If the **Document default quality** parameter is greater than 50%, you can re-import this image with a JPEG 50% quality, which should be more than enough.

Open the **Color Mixer** window, and select the **Bitmap** fill type, the fill from the topbkgr.bmp file, rounded corners, and no outline. In case you cannot see the fill you want in the **Color Mixer** window, select the **Bitmap** fill type window, and the **Import** button will appear to help you. Draw a rectangle 366-pixel wide and 450-pixel high. The coordinates of its upper left corner should be (–183, –189). If your fill looks like tiles (not similar to my sample), highlight it, and click another item in the **Color Mixer** window with the **Fill Color** tool; then click our item again. The fill should be resized to fit into the rectangle. Create a **Layer 2** layer above

Layer 1. At the top of the panel, place a text field with the following properties: **Jikharev, 40 pts, bold, Align Center, Static Text.** The color should be #D7CDBD. Uncheck the **Use Device Fonts** checkbox. Type the text Top Ten. For your reference: The upper left corner of this text field should have the coordinates (−73, −173). Below this text field, place another with the following properties: **Tahoma, 16 pts, bold, Align Left, Dynamic Text, Single Line.** Its color should be #FFFFFF. The field should be 223-pixel wide and 24-pixel high (the height is chosen by the editor, depending on the font size, so don't change the height because this will make the font scale itself). The coordinates for the upper left corner should be (−155, −113). This is a field for the gamer's name. To the right of this, place a similar text field for his or her score. It should differ from the previous field in having **Align Right** property, a width of 66 pixels, and upper-left corner coordinates of (90, −113). Now, duplicate these fields to obtain ten fields in all. To do this, select both fields by clicking them while keeping the <Shift> key pressed. Then, press the <Ctrl> key, and drag one of the fields down while keeping this key pressed. You now have four fields. The vertical spacing is 33 pixels. Create the other fields in a similar way. When you have finished duplicating the fields, name them. This is done in the **Var:** input box on the property panel of the selected object. The top field, with a gamer's name, should have the name n0, the field below it should have n1, and so on to n9. The fields with scores should be named from s0 to s9, respectively. Place the btExit button at the center of the bottom of the panel. To do this, drag it from the library. Select this button, press the <F9> key, and attach the following code to the button:

```
on (release)
  { _root.exitApp();
}
```

The exitApp function will ask the program shell to exit.

Fig. 7.2 shows what this clip looks like on my computer.

The next clip is enterName, which will allow the gamer to enter his or her name in the table of records. Create a clip with this name, and specify the same name for ActionScript to export. Create a **Layer 2** above **Layer 1**. In **Layer 1**, draw a rectangle of 320 × 130 pixels with rounded corners. The coordinates for its upper left corner should be (−160, −45). The outline should be two-pixel thick, with the color #837561. For a fill, use the picture from the topbkgr.bmp file.

Before you draw the rectangle, open the **Color Mixer** window, and select the **Bitmap** fill type. The scroll panel will display the patterns of all of the imported images. Select the image that you imported for the previous panel. The fill can be done inappropriately — showing seams — because the image is larger than the rectangle. To cope with this problem, select the fill using the **Paint Bucket** tool, do another fill, and then redo yours in the **Color Mixer** window.

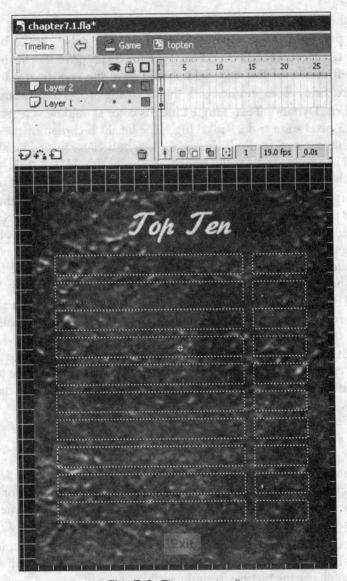

Fig. 7.2. The topten clip

In **Layer 3**, create a header and a text field, and drag the btOK button onto the layer. Using the **Text** tool, draw a box at the top of the panel. Select the **Jikharev bold** font with a font size of 30 pts and the color #cccccc. Select the **Static Text** text type, and center-justify the text. Type in Enter your name:.

Create an input field at the center of the panel. This should be a text field of the **Input Text** type, with the **_sans bold** font, a font size of 16 pts, and be white and left-justified. Its size should be 292 × 79 pixels. Click the **Selectable** button. In the **Var:** field, specify the t name to read this text programmatically. In the **Maximum Characters** field, type 40.

Drag the btOK button from the library, and drop it in the middle of the panel below the input text field. You can place the button in any layer, **Layer 1** or **Layer 2**. Select the button, and attach the following code to it:

```
on (release)
  { _root.enterNameKeyUp(0);
  }
```

Enter the **Layer 1** layer, and create a background rectangle below the text field. The rectangle should have a size of 300 × 30 pixels, the #837561 color, and shouldn't have an outline. Align it with the input text box. The panel for entering a gamer's name should look like the one shown in Fig. 7.3.

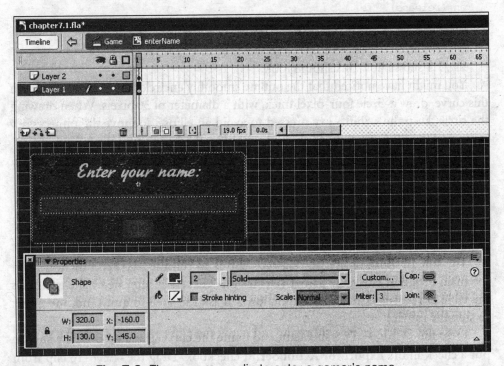

Fig. 7.3. The enterName clip to enter a gamer's name

We now need to create the `help` clip to display the game rules. This name should also be exported for ActionScript. I couldn't think of any other option than a rectangle with rounded corners and the background from the previous clip. This clip should also consist of two layers. The upper layer will contain some text, while the lower layer will contain the rest of the objects. Let's begin with the text. Select the **Arial** bold font, a font size of 16 pts, and the color white. Check the **Use Device Fonts** checkbox, and left-justify the text. Type in the following:

```
Control keys:
Left arrow - move pieces to left
Right arrow - move pieces to right
Up arrow - rotate pieces
Down arrow or space - drop pieces
```

In **Layer 1** (or **Layer 2**), place the `btExitHelp` button in the upper right corner of the **help** panel by dragging the button from the symbol library. Attach the following code to the button:

```
on (release)
 { _root.returnHelp();
 }
```

Fig. 7.4 shows how this should look.

You might have noticed that the outline smoothly encircles the button. To obtain this curve, draw a circle four-pixel thick, with a diameter of 30 pixels. When drawing the circle, keep the <Shift> key pressed to avoid an ellipse. Remove the unnecessary portion of the circle using the **Erase** tool, and place the rest around the button.

Create one more empty clip, `toptenKeyUp`. It should contain another empty clip, `emtyclip`, to which the following code should be attached:

```
onClipEvent (keyUp)
 { if (Key.getCode() == Key.ESCAPE) _root.exitApp();
 }
```

The sole purpose of the `toptenKeyUp` clip is to call the `exitApp` function from the main program when the gamer releases the <Esc> key after he or she examines the table of records. The `exitApp` function will ask the shell to quit (and, therefore, to stop the movie).

Press the <Ctrl>+<F8> shortcut, and name the clip `toptenKeyUp`. Make sure to put a check in the **Export for ActionScript** checkbox. Drag the `emtyclip` clip from the library to this clip and attach the code shown earlier to the `emtyclip` clip.

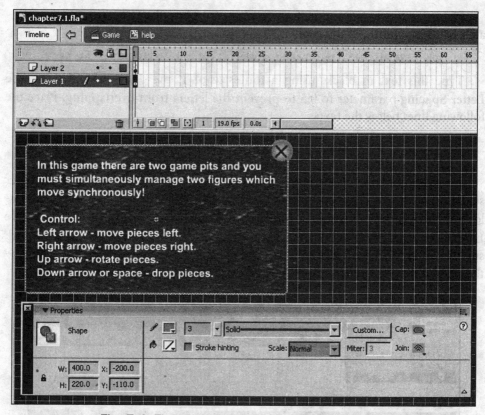

Fig. 7.4. The `help` clip to display the game rules

Finally, create the `sorry` clip. This will appear after a non-registered gamer has played for five minutes. The clip will contain text expressing regret that the gamer couldn't play for long enough, text fields for entering a name and a registration key, and the `btRegOK` button. Create the `sorry` clip using the <Ctrl>+<F8> shortcut, and export its name for ActionScript. Create two more layers: **Layer 2** above **Layer 1**, and **Layer 3** above these. In **Layer 1**, select the **Rectangle** tool, a two-pixel outline, the `#FFCC00` color, rounded corners, and the fill color `#FFFF66`. Draw a 320 × 210-pixel rectangle. Center it using the <Ctrl>+<Alt>+<2> and <Ctrl>+<Alt>+<5> shortcuts or the **Modify | Align** menu command. Select the **Static Text** text type and the **Arial** font. Check the **Use Device Fonts** checkbox. In the **Layer 3** layer, type the following center-justified red text, using a font size of 16 pts:

```
Sorry, you can only play this unregistered version of
Tet-a-Tetris for 5 minutes. Game closed.
```

Place this text in the top half of the clip, and place the following text immediately below the center of the clip:

```
If you have already purchased a registration code, enter it here.
```

Type this text in black, using a font size of 12 pts. For both texts, set the **Letter Spacing** parameter to 0.5 to prevent the letters from overlapping. Place the following lines below the texts:

```
Registration name:
Registration key:
```

For these lines, return the **Letter Spacing** parameter to zero, and leave the other settings unchanged. Place **Input Text** fields to the right of these lines. Select the following settings: the **_sans** font, a font size of 12 pts, black, left-justified, and **Single Line, Selectable**. Each field should have a size of 220 × 12 pixels. In the **Var:** field, specify names for these fields: regname and regkey. Place the btRegOK button below the fields at the center of the panel. You can place the button in **Layer 2** or **Layer 3**.

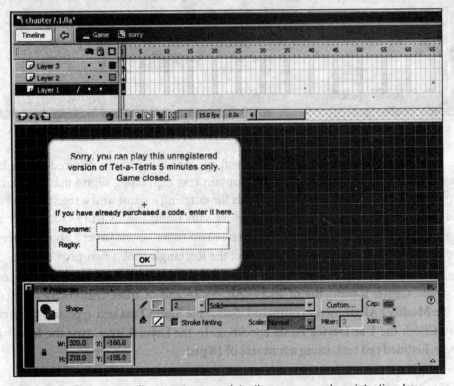

Fig. 7.5. The sorry clip to enter a registration name and registration key

Enter **Layer 2**, and create a background and borders for the input fields. This should be a rectangle of the same size as the input fields, that is, 220×18 pixels. Select the **hairline** outline with the #FF9900 color, and select white as the fill color. Duplicate the rectangle, and place it and the copy right behind the input fields. The result is shown in Fig. 7.5.

You have added a few clips to the project, and now you can remove one clip. This is the infoPanel clip, which became unnecessary after the sorry clip appeared. Select this symbol in the library, and press the <Del> key, or use the pop-up menu that will appear after you right-click on the symbol.

7.2. Updating the ActionScript Code for Work with the Shell

In the stand-alone version, your project will call certain functions of the program shell that will start the game. In addition, you need some code to work with the newly-created clips. You should also update the fragments of the code that interacted with the server.

Locate the following line in the data section of the main program:

```
controlenabled,
```

Insert the snd0 variable after the line:

```
controlenabled,
 // The initial value of the snd flag
 snd0,
```

From now on, the indication whether the sound is enabled will be stored in a configuration file on the hard disk, rather than received from the server. The game will receive the indication from the shell.

Locate another line:

```
nexttime,
```

Insert the following code after this line:

```
// The end time and time limit in milliseconds
// (Time Limit)
 // These are for the non-registered version of the game
 et, tl = 1000*60*5,
 // A flag to display the sorry clip
```

```
imsorry,
 // The lengths of the strings with the gamer name
 // and the registration key
 lname, lkey,
 // Arrays of names and scores for the topten table
 topnames = new Array(10), topscores = new Array(10), namekey = new Array(2),
 // The maximum score for all of the games
 // and the name of the gamer who achieved each of these
 maxscore = 0, maxname,
```

I'd like to comment·on the last two variables. The gamer can play as many games as he or she likes until he or she exits the program shell. While the gamer is playing, the best score is stored in the maxscore variable, and the name for the gamer who achieved it is stored in the maxname variable. Before the program shell closes, if the maxscore value is greater than the score in the tenth row of the table, it will write these variables into the file with the table of records. Therefore, only one result per session, and not the results of all games, will be saved in the file.

You should also update the startGame function a little. Listing 7.1 contains a new version. Replace the old version with this.

Listing 7.1. The updated startGame function

```
// Start a new game. If arg = 1, the function is called
// with the New button before the current game has been completed.
function startGame(arg)
{ var i, j, k, p,
  pit = new Array();

  // Remove all clips that could be in the menu.
  gover.removeMovieClip();
  menu.removeMovieClip();
  btHelp.removeMovieClip();
  // Set the initial game speed.
  if (arg == 1) speed = speed0;
   else speed0 = speed;
  // Reset the score and the numbers of pieces and filled lines to zero.
  score = pieces = lines = imsorry = 0;
  // Set the interval (in ms) for one move down that a piece makes on its own.
  timestep = 2000 - speed*200;
  // Display the speed, the score, pieces, and filled rows.
  showNum(speed, 0);
```

```
showNum(score, 1);
showNum(pieces, 2);
showNum(lines, 3);
// Clear the game pits.
for (k = 0; k < 2; k++)
 { pit = pits[k];
   for (i = 0; i < yy; i++)
    for (j = 0; j < xx; j++)
     if (p = pit[i][j])
       { p.removeMovieClip();
         pit[i][j] = null;
       }
 }
// Set the event handler.
attachMovie('keydownact', 'keydownact', depth4 + 1);
// Set the game state.
gamestate = gamest;
// Activate the Pause and New buttons.
btPause.useHandCursor = 1;
btNew.useHandCursor = 1;
// Set the nexttime variable to the current time
// to start newFigs() instantly.
nexttime = getTimer();
// Set the game termination time (5 minutes for the non-registered
// version and no limit for a registered version).
et = getTimer() + tl;
newFigs();
}
```

The code that accessed the `infoPanel` clip was replaced with the following code:

```
btHelp.removeMovieClip();
```

This code removes the `btHelp` button before the game starts. Code that assigns the value zero to the `imsorry` variable was inserted. Finally, the following code was inserted:

```
et = getTimer() + tl;
```

This assigns the `et` variable the time, at which the game should terminate. (The non-registered version should terminate in five minutes, while the registered version could run for longer than the player would be able to stay awake).

You should also update the keyUp function (Listing 7.2).

Listing 7.2. The updated keyUp function

```
// Handle releasing a key in the menu and during the game
// (during the game, this is only for the Sound, Pause, and New clips).
function keyUp()
{ var key1, name, l1, l2;

  // Indication that the key is pressed
  // This is necessary to exit the splash screen using a key.
  keyisdown = 1;
  // Store the pressed key in the key1 variable.
  key1 = Key.getCode();
  // Is the clip with the rules displayed?
  if (typeof(help) == 'movieclip')
      // Hide the game rules when the gamer presses <Esc>.
    { if (key1 == Key.ESCAPE) returnHelp();
      // Toggle sound when the gamer presses S or s.
      if (key1 == 83) btsound.s._visible = snd ^= 1;
      return;
    }
  switch (key1)
      // The S (s) key was released. This is for the Sound button.
    { case 83: btsound.s._visible = snd ^= 1;
      break;
      // The P (p) key was released. This is for the Pause button
      case 80: if (typeof(menu) == 'movieclip') startGame();
      else togglePause();
      break;
      // The Y (y) key was released. This is for the Yes button.
      case 89: if (typeof(gover) == 'movieclip') startGame();
      break;
      //Hh
      case 72: if (gamestate == menust) showHelp();
      break;
      //F1
      case 112: if (gamestate == menust) showHelp();
      break;
      // The N (n) key was released. This is for the New button.
```

```
    case 78: if (gamestate == gamest && !ispaused) startGame(1); else
      if (typeof(gover) == 'movieclip')
        if (maxscore > topscores[9]) showEnterName(); else showTopTen();
  }
// Exit if this isn't the menu.
if (gamestate != menust) return;
// In the menu, <Enter> can start the game.
if (key1 == Key.ENTER) startGame();
// Assign the name variable the id of the clip ('menu' or 'gover').
name = rel.name;
if (key1 == Key.LEFT && speed > 0)
  { // Skim over the speed selection buttons from right to left.
    eval(name + '.is.d' + speed).gotoAndStop(1);
    eval(name + '.is.d' + --speed).gotoAndStop(2);
  }
if (key1 == Key.RIGHT && speed < 9)
  { // Skim over the speed selection buttons from left to right.
    eval(name + '.is.d' + speed).gotoAndStop(1);
    eval(name + '.is.d' + ++speed).gotoAndStop(2);
  }
if (key1 > 47 && key1 < 58)
  { // Select the game speed using the keys from <0> to <9>.
    eval(name + '.is.d' + speed).gotoAndStop(1);
    eval(name + '.is.d' + (speed = key1 - 48)).gotoAndStop(2);
  }
}
```

The following code was inserted into the keyUp function:

```
if (typeof(help) == 'movieclip')
      // Hide the game rules when the gamer presses <Esc>.
    { if (key1 == Key.ESCAPE) returnHelp();
      // Toggle sound when the gamer presses S or s.
      if (key1 == 83) btsound.s._visible = snd ^= 1;
      return;
    }
```

This code processes key strokes when the game rules are displayed. When the gamer presses <Esc>, the clip with the game rules is removed, and the clip with the menu is displayed. This is carried out in the returnHelp function.

The code that displays the `help` clip after the \<H\>, \<h\>, or \<F1\> key is released was added to the `keyUp` function:

```
// The <H> or <h> key is released.
    case 72: if (gamestate == menust) showHelp();
     break;
    // The <F1> key is released.
    case 112: if (gamestate == menust) showHelp();
     break;
```

The code that processes strokes of the \<N\> and \<n\> keys should be aware of the `btNo` button that appeared in the menu:

```
// The N (n) key was released. This is for the New button.
    case 78: if (gamestate == gamest && !ispaused) startGame(1);
     else if (typeof(gover) == 'movieclip')
      if (maxscore > topscores[9]) showEnterName();
       else showTopTen();
```

The `btNo` button is processed after the first `else` keyword. When the `gover` clip is displayed, the \<N\> key relates to the `btNo` button. Pressing this key indicates that the gamer wants to exit the program. You should check whether the gamer achieved a score greater than the value in the tenth row of the table of records. If he or she did, the `showEnterName` function is called. This displays the `enterName` clip, which allows the user to enter his or her name, and then displays the table of records. If the gamer didn't break into the Top Ten, the `showTopTen` function is called directly.

Some code was added to the `menuorOver` function and the code related to the `infoPanel` clip (which was discarded) was removed, as was the `arg` parameter (Listing 7.3).

Listing 7.3. The updated `menuorOver` function

```
// Display the menu or the GameOver panel.
function menuorOver()
{ var i, name,
  name1 = menuorOver.name;

  delete gameact.onEnterFrame;
  attachMovie(name1, name1, depth3);
  name = eval(name1);
  name._x = 303;
```

```
name._y = 230;
// Is this a non-registerd version?
if (imsorry)
   // Display the sorry clip by attaching it
   // to the menu or gameover clip.
 { name._y = 130;
   name.attachMovie('sorry', 'sorry', 1);
   name.sorry._x = 0;
   name.sorry._y = 292;
   // Fill in the name and key fields with the values entered earlier.
   name.sorry.regname = namekey[0];
   name.sorry.regkey = namekey[1];
 }
speed = 0;
gamestate = menust;
// Display the btHelp button.
attachMovie('btHelp', 'btHelp', 0);
btHelp._x = 692;
btHelp._y = 412;
btHelp.onRollOver = function()
 { this.gotoAndStop(2);
 }
btHelp.onDragOver = function()
 { this.gotoAndStop(2);
 }
btHelp.onRollOut = function()
 { this.gotoAndStop(1);
 }
btHelp.onDragOut = function()
 { this.gotoAndStop(1);
 }
btHelp.onRelease = function()
 { showHelp();
 }
// Write the game speed values on the d0, d1, ..., and d9 clips.
for (i = 0; i < 10; i++)
 { name = eval(name1 + '.is.d' + i);
   name.t = i;
   // Highlight the clip with the current game speed.
   if (i == speed) name.gotoAndStop(2);
```

```
// Create mouse event handlers for
// ten game speed-selection clips.
name.onRollOver = name.onDragOver = go2;
name.onRollOut = name.onDragOut = go1;
rel.name = name1;
name.onRelease = rel;
}
}
```

If the gamer plays a non-registered version (which is detected at the beginning of the program by checking the name and the key in a key file), you should display the sorry clip:

```
if (imsorry)
     // Display the sorry clip by attaching it
     // to the menu or gameover clip.
  { name._y = 130;
    name.attachMovie('sorry', 'sorry', 1);
    name.sorry._x = 0;
    name.sorry._y = 292;
    // Fill in the name and key fields with the values entered earlier.
    name.sorry.regname = namekey[0];
    name.sorry.regkey = namekey[1];
  }
```

The fields for the registration name and registration key are filled in using the values from the key file. (Just in case the gamer makes a mistake when typing.)

Code displaying the btHelp button was also added. The button behaves in a similar way to the btNew button: When the mouse pointer is over it, it becomes highlighted. When the mouse pointer moves away, the highlight disappears. When the left mouse button is released on this button, the showHelp function is called:

```
attachMovie('btHelp', 'btHelp', 0);
  btHelp._x = 692;
  btHelp._y = 412;
  btHelp.onRollOver = function()
  { this.gotoAndStop(2);
  }
  btHelp.onDragOver = function()
  { this.gotoAndStop(2);
  }
```

```
btHelp.onRollOut = function()
  { this.gotoAndStop(1);
  }
btHelp.onDragOut = function()
  { this.gotoAndStop(1);
  }
btHelp.onRelease = function()
  { showHelp();
  }
```

Finally, the newFigs function was updated (Listing 7.4).

Listing 7.4. The updated newFigs function

```
// Create and output a pair of pieces.
function newFigs()
{ var i, j, k, t, flag, corr,
    f = new Array(),
    fx,
    fy,
    p = new Array();

  if ((t = getTimer()) < nexttime || ispaused) return;
  // Decrease the probability of an inconvenient pair of pieces No.3 and No.4.
  do
    for (k = 0; k < 2; k++)
      { mffn[k] = Math.floor(Math.random()*9);
        ffn[k] = 0;
        colors[k] = mffn[k];
        figs[k] = mff[mffn[k]][0];
        figsx[k] = 5;
        figsy[k] = 0;
      }
  while (mffn[0] + mffn[1] == 7 && mffn[0]*mffn[1] == 12 && ++corr == 1);
  // Check whether the pieces overlap.
  for (k = 0; k < 2; k++)
    { fx = figsx[k];
      fy = figsy[k];
      f = figs[k];
      p = pits[k];
```

```
     for (i = 0; i < 3; i++)
      for (j = 0; j < 3; j++)
       if (f[i][j] && p[fy + i][fx + j]) flag = 1;
  }
  paintFigs();
  showNum(pieces += 2, 2);
  if (flag || (imsorry = t > et))
   { playSound(goversnd);
     if (flag) maxscore = (score > maxscore) ? score : maxscore;
     keydownact.removeMovieClip();
     btPause.gotoAndStop(1);
     btPause.useHandCursor = 0;
     btNew.gotoAndStop(1);
     btNew.useHandCursor = 0;
     menuorOver.name = 'gover';
     menuorOver();
     return;
   }
  // Enable control from the keyboard.
  controlenabled = 1;
  // The gamer can move a piece three times until it moves down.
  numact = 3;
  // Should the speed be increased?
  if (pieces && !(pieces%40) && speed < 9)
   { ++speed;
     timestep -= 200;
     showNum(speed, 0);
     playSound(bleep3snd);
   }
  showNum(currscore = (speed + 1)*20, 4);
  downOrWaitAction();
}
```

The following code was added to the conditional statement:

```
if (flag || (imsorry = t > et))
   { playSound(goversnd);
     if (!imsorry) maxscore = (score > maxscore) ? score : maxscore;
     keydownact.removeMovieClip();
     btPause.gotoAndStop(1);
```

```
btPause.useHandCursor = 0;
btNew.gotoAndStop(1);
btNew.useHandCursor = 0;
menuorOver.name = 'gover';
menuorOver();
return;
}
```

The condition that pieces overlap (which is stored in the `flag` variable) is now accompanied by the `t > et` condition, stored in the `imsorry` global variable. This is the requirement to terminate the game after five minutes have elapsed. If the game terminates normally, you should correct the `maxscore` variable, which stores the maximum score for all the games of the current session. This is carried out in the following statement:

```
if (flag) maxscore = (score > maxscore) ? score : maxscore;
```

If the game terminated because pieces overlapped, and if the current score (`score`) isn't greater than the session's maximum score (`maxscore`), the first value is assigned to the second.

7.3. Adding New Functions and Code to the Main Program

You should now add functions that work with clips, as well as a few auxiliary functions. The `enterNameKeyUp` function (Listing 7.5) is called when the gamer releases a key while entering his or her name, or when he or she clicks on the **OK** button. This happens in the `enterName` clip. Add the code for this function to the main program after the `rotateFigs` function, which should be the last function before the beginning of the program. The next functions described in this section should follow each other.

Listing 7.5. The `enterNameKeyUp` function

```
// If press == 1, a key was pressed;
// otherwise, the mouse button was clicked.
function enterNameKeyUp(press)
{ if (!press || press && Key.getCode() == Key.ENTER)
```

```
{ maxname = enterName.t;
  showTopTen();
}
}
```

If the gamer clicked the **OK** button or released the <Enter> key, the function assigns the entered name (which is currently stored in the `enterName.t` clip variable) to the `maxname` global variable, and calls the `showTopTen` function to display the table of records.

The `chNK` function, the name of which is an abbreviation of *check name key*, checks the validity of the key (Listing 7.6). The gamer receives the key from the author of the game, who generates the key from the gamer's name using a secret algorithm. The key generation can be carried out using a script on the author's server or on the server of the author's registration provider. To increase the security level of the program, I suggest an approach involving a check performed on one part of the key in the program shell that is yet to be written and checking the other part of the key in the code of the game, that is, in this function.

Listing 7.6. The chNK function

```
// Check whether the key corresponds to the gamer's name.
function chNK()
{ // Check the 1st condition.
  if (namekey[1].charCodeAt(5) != namekey[1].charCodeAt(4) - 4) return;
// Check the 2nd condition
//  if (namekey[1].charCodeAt(7) != namekey[1].charCodeAt(6) - 2) return;
  // Set the game time limit to a very large number.
  tl = 1000000000;
}
```

This function checks the requirement that the subtraction of four from the code of the fourth character of the key should result in the code of the fifth character of the key. If this is not the case, the key is a fake, and the function returns control. The `tl` variable will store a value equal to the game start time plus five minutes. In this case, the game will last for five minutes. If somebody discloses the key-generating algorithm, and if a key generator appears on the Internet, you'll have to check the second condition, which is currently commented out. You can choose another key generator and change the conditions.

If the key appears to be valid, the `tl` variable will be assigned a very large value. If fact, the gamer will be able to play 1,000,000,000 ms or, approximately, about three weeks.

The `enterNameKey` function (Listing 7.7) gains control when the gamer clicks the **OK** button after he or she enters his or her name in the `sorry` clip. First, the name is stored in the zero element of the `namekey` global array, and the key is stored in the first element of this array. The string containing the name and the key is then passed to the program shell using the `fscommand` global function. Remember that this function passes two strings to the program that hosts the Flash movie. The first string, `'savename'`, is used by the shell to determine what kind of information is passed to it. The second is the information being passed.

Listing 7.7. The `enterNameKey` function

```
// This is called with a click on the btRegOK button in the sorry clip.
function enterNameKey()
{ // Read the name the key entered by the user.
  namekey[0] = gover.sorry.regname;
  namekey[1] = gover.sorry.regkey;
  // Call the shell and pass it the string that contains the name
  // and the key separated with the '|' character.
  fscommand('savename', gover.sorry.regname + '|' + gover.sorry.regkey);
  // Remove the sorry clip while the gover clip remains on the screen.
  gover.sorry.removeMovieClip();
  // Check the validity of the key.
  chNK();
}
```

The `showHelp` function displays the clip with the game rules (Listing 7.8). It is called when the gamer clicks on the `btHelp` button or releases the <H> or <F1> key.

Listing 7.8. The `showHelp` function

```
// Display the game rules.
function showHelp()
{ // Hide the menu or gover clip. The name is stored
  // in the function's property menuorOver.name.
  eval(menuorOver.name)._visible = 0;
```

```
// Display the help clip.
attachMovie('help', 'help', depth4 + 1);
help._x = 310;
help._y = 250;
}
```

The `returnHelp` function (Listing 7.9.) does the reverse: It hides the `help` clip and unhides the `menu` or `gover` clip. This function is called when the gamer clicks on the `btExitHelp` button (the one with a cross on it) on the `help` clip or releases the <Esc> key when the `help` clip is displayed.

Listing 7.9. The `returnHelp` function

```
// Hide the game rules.
function returnHelp()
{ // Remove the help clip.
  help.removeMovieClip();
  // Display the menu or gover clip.
  eval(menuorOver.name)._visible = 1;
}
```

The `showEnterName` function shows the panel for entering the gamer's name for the table of records (Listing 7.10). How it works is clear from the comments. I should also point out that the focus and the blinking cursor are set to the input field using the `setFocus` property of the `Selection` global object. If this wasn't the case, the user would have to click on the input field to set the cursor inside it.

Listing 7.10. The `showEnterName` function

```
// Show the enterName for entering the gamer's name
// for the table of records.
function showEnterName()
{ // Remove the keyupact and keydownact clips that control the game
  // because the previous game was the last in this session.
  keydownact.removeMovieClip();
  keyupact.removeMovieClip();
  // Remove the btHelp button.
  btHelp.removeMovieClip();
  // Display the enterName clip.
```

```
attachMovie('enterName', 'enterName', depth3);
enterName._x = 302;
enterName._y = 230;
// Clear the input field in the clip.
enterName.t = '';
// Set the focus and the blinking cursor on the input field.
Selection.setFocus('enterName.t');
// Call the eNameKeyUp empty clip to call
// the enterNameKeyUp function when the keys are released.
attachMovie('eNameKeyUp', 'eNameKeyUp', depth5);
}
```

The showTopTen function (Listing 7.11) displays the table of records and passes it to the program shell, which will save the table in a file. This is the case because a Flash movie cannot write data into files.

Listing 7.11. The showTopTen function

```
// Show the table of records and pass it to the shell,
// along with the indication whether the sound is enabled in the game.
function showTopTen()
{ var i, s;

// Remove clips that are no longer needed.
  enterName.removeMovieClip();
  gover.removeMovieClip();
  eNameKeyUp.removeMovieClip();
  attachMovie('topten', 'topten', depth4);
  topten._x = 304;
  topten._y = 250;
  // Does the last row of the table contain a score that is less
  // than the gamer's score?
  if (topscores[9] < maxscore)
   { // Remove the '|' characters from maxname.
     while ((i = maxname.indexOf('|')) > -1)
      maxname = maxname.substr(0,i) + maxname.substr(i + 1);
     // Insert maxname and maxscore into topnames and topscores.
     for (i = 0; i < 10; i++)
      if (topscores[i] < maxscore)
```

```
       { for (j = 9; j > i; j--)
         { topnames[j] = topnames[j - 1];
           topscores[j] = topscores[j - 1];
         }
         topnames[i] = maxname;
         topscores[i] = maxscore;
         break;
      }
    // Store the table of records and the snd variable
    // in a string to pass it to the shell.
    for (i = 0; i < 10; i++) s += topnames[i] + '|' + topscores[i] + '|';
    s += snd.toString(10);
    // Call the shell and pass the table to it along with
    // the indication whether the sound is enabled in the game.
    fscommand('savetopten', s);
  }
// Rewrite the names and the scores to the topten clip.
topten.n0 = topnames[0];
topten.n1 = topnames[1];
topten.n2 = topnames[2];
topten.n3 = topnames[3];
topten.n4 = topnames[4];
topten.n5 = topnames[5];
topten.n6 = topnames[6];
topten.n7 = topnames[7];
topten.n8 = topnames[8];
topten.n9 = topnames[9];
topten.s0 = topscores[0];
topten.s1 = topscores[1];
topten.s2 = topscores[2];
topten.s3 = topscores[3];
topten.s4 = topscores[4];
topten.s5 = topscores[5];
topten.s6 = topscores[6];
topten.s7 = topscores[7];
topten.s8 = topscores[8];
topten.s9 = topscores[9];
attachMovie('toptenKeyUp', 'toptenKeyUp', depth5);
}
```

Everything is clear up to the point where the `topten` clip is outputted. First, I'll explain how this function inserts the gamer's name `maxname` and his or her maximum score in the session into the table of records. The table consists of two arrays of ten elements each: `topnames` contains gamers' names, and `topscores` contains their scores. A score is inserted in the table only when it is greater than the table's tenth row, `topscores[9]`. This is checked in the following condition:

```
if (topscores[9] < maxscore)
```

When the condition is true, you should include the result in the table after you shift the lesser results down, ousting the tenth result. However, you should first delete all of the '|' characters from the `maxname` variable, because the shell considers them to be delimiters between the names and the scores (the table of records is passed to the shell as one string). ActionScript misses a built-in function that could delete characters from a string. Therefore, the `substr` function, which returns a specified number of the string's characters starting from a specified position, is used. The required position `i` of the '|' character in the `maxname` string is found as follows:

```
while ((i = maxname.indexOf('|')) > -1)
```

If `i` is greater than –1, the `maxname` string contains this character (perhaps, the gamer decided to test whether your program is foolproof). To delete the `i`th character, extract the first `i` characters (from 0th to `(i-1)`th) from `maxname`, and extract all of the characters that follow the `i`th. Then assign these two substrings to the `maxname` string:

```
maxname = maxname.substr(0, i) + maxname.substr(i + 1);
```

Repeat this in the `while` loop until you have deleted all of the '|' characters from `maxname`. You should then find the first value lower than `maxscore` in the `topscores` array. This value exists because the condition you checked earlier was true. This search is carried out using the following loop:

```
for (i = 0; i < 10; i++)
  if (topscores[i] < maxscore)
```

When this condition is true, the `i` variable is equal to the index of the sought value in the `topscores` array. You should shift all the values in the `topnames` and `topscores` arrays, beginning with the `i`th (the tenth name and score will be lost), to the right, and insert the `maxname` and `maxscore` values into the `i`th positions:

```
{ for (j = 9; j > i; j--)
  { topnames[j] = topnames[j - 1];
    topscores[j] = topscores[j - 1];
```

```
      }
   topnames[i] = maxname;
   topscores[i] = maxscore;
   break;
  }
```

When this is done, the `break` statement interrupts the loop because the values should be inserted only once. When the values are inserted into the tenth position (`i` is equal to nine), the loop for `j` will not work, so everything will be in order.

You should then write the entire table into one string, `s`, using the `'|'` characters as delimiters between the array elements. This is done in the following loop:

```
   for (i = 0; i < 10; i++) s += topnames[i] + '|' + topscores[i] + '|';
```

Finally, the indication whether sound is enabled is added to the `s` string:

```
   s += snd.toString(10);
```

This statement converts the `snd` variable to a string using the decimal numeric base. The result is either the `'0'` or `'1'` string.

In order to show the table of records to the user, you should rewrite the `topnames` and `topscores` arrays into the text fields of the `topten` clip. I'm afraid that it is impossible to do this in a loop, so you'll have to write 20 assignment statements:

```
   topten.n0 = topnames[0];
   ...
   topten.s9 = topscores[9];
```

Finally, you should attach the `toptenKeyUp` clip to the movie, to allow the gamer exit the program with the <Esc> key release at the moment of the table of records displaying, and not only with a click on the **Exit** button.

The `exitApp` function (Listing 7.12) accesses the program shell and passes it the exit string, so that the shell exits.

Listing 7.12. The `exitApp` function

```
// Exit the program when the table of records is shown.
function exitApp()
{ fscommand('exit', '');
```

In addition to providing these functions, there is still more code to be written. First, remove the following statement from the third frame of the main timeline:

```
   snd = 1;
```

Then, click on the first frame of the **Actions** layer, and attach the code from Listing 7.13 to the frame.

Listing 7.13. The code for the first frame of the main timeline

---

```
var topnames1, topscores1, snd, namekey1;


fscommand('showmenu', false);
fscommand('gettopten', '');
fscommand('readname', '');
```

This code declares the `topnames1` and `topscores1` variables. These are strings, in which the shell will store the names and scores from the table of records after it receives the following command:

```
fscommand('gettopten', '');
```

If the records are saved on the disk (in the tetatet.top file), `topnames1` contains the record-holders' names, delimited with the `'|'` characters. For empty lines, the shell will use a special value, `<Empty>`. If the tetatet.top file is missing from the folder with the game, the shell will create and initialize it.

The `topscores` variable contains the record scores, also delimited by `'|'` characters. Remember that the shell exchanges data with the Flash movie using Unicode strings. The `snd` variable contains an appropriate value, because the sound indication is stored at the end of the file that contains the table of records. The indication is separated from the last string of the table using the `'|'` delimiter.

The command

```
fscommand('readname', '');
```

makes the shell read the gamer's name and key from the tetatet.k file, and write them into the `namekey1` string, putting the `'|'` delimiter between them. This, however, will only happen if the validation check in the shell confirms that the key corresponds to the name. If the key turns out to be a fake, nothing will be assigned to the `namekey1` string, so it will remain undefined.

You have probably already guessed that, before you send information from the shell to the Flash movie's variables, you should create (declare) these variables first. This is done at the beginning of the program.

There is still one command that should be explained:

```
fscommand('showmenu', false);
```

This hides the menu of Flash player when the user right-clicks on the program window.

To test your game as a stand-alone Windows application, add the small fragment of code in the tet7.1.as file to the main program. Locate the following line:

```
// *** The beginning of the program ***
```

and insert the code from Listing 7.14 after it.

Listing 7.14. The code to insert at the beginning of the main program

```
// Convert the sound indication from a string to a binary value.
snd0 = snd = parseInt(snd);
// Move the names and the scores to the table of records.
topnames = topnames1.split('|');
topscores = topscores1.split('|');
// Store the name in namekey[0] and the key in namekey[1].
// If you use the split() function for empty strings,
// the target array will be lost!
i = length(namekey1);
j = namekey1.indexOf('|');
if (i > 13 && j == i - 11)
  { namekey = namekey1.split('|');
    chNK();
  }
```

The shell assigned the snd variable a string that is either '0' or '1'. The statement

```
snd0 = snd = parseInt(snd);
```

converts the string to numeric form and stores the result both in the snd and snd0 variables. This will be used at the end of the game to determine whether the gamer toggled the sound. If the snd and snd0 variables are equal at the end of the program, and the gamer couldn't make it into the table of records, the shell doesn't need to update the tetatet.top file. However, if these variables aren't equal, the file should be updated with the new sound indication.

The lines of code

```
topnames = topnames1.split('|');
topscores = topscores1.split('|')
```

split the strings containing the names and scores from the table of records by the '|' delimiters. The resulting substrings are stored in the topnames and topscores arrays.

Before you split the `namekey1` variable, you should check whether it contains the '|' character, and that it consists of at least three characters. Only in this case can you apply the `split` method to the `namekey1` variable to split it into the name and the key to store them in the `namekey[0]` and `namekey[1]` array elements, respectively. Experience shows that, if you fail to perform this check, the target array will be lost, i.e., it will become undefined. You should be aware of this incomprehensible feature of ActionScript (or of some Flash player versions). I hope that the bug will be eliminated in future versions. After the name and the key are separated, the `chNK` function is called to check the second requirement for the characters of the key. If the key doesn't comply with this requirement, the gamer will only be able to play for five minutes. If the key is valid, the gamer will be able to play each game for three weeks. This should be more than sufficient.

So, you have now completed updating the project files to work with the program shell. The result is in the files in the \Chapter 7 folder. The shell itself, however, is still missing. You'll create this in *Chapter 9*.

Chapter 8: Creating a Key Generator

You already know how a key is checked in the ActionScript program. Now let's write a key generator as a CGI (Common Gateway Interface) script in Perl. You'll also create key generators in Delphi and in Microsoft Visual C++ as small Windows applications. If you have chosen RegNow (**www.regnow.com**) as your registration provider, my Perl script can be used unchanged for automatic key generation at the moment of purchase. RegNow allows you to maintain a remote key generator on your server that will be called from RegNow's server. However, this requires the introduction of minor changes in my program so that it conforms to CGI specifications. The program in Delphi can be used to generate keys and send them to the purchaser from your computer. In addition, it can be used as a prototype key generator for another famous registration provider: ShareIt! (**www.shareit.com**). On ShareIt!'s server, key generators are executed as DLL or EXE programs for Windows, according to their specifications. You can see examples in the registration provider's control panel.

8.1. The Key-Generating Algorithm

You can change this algorithm and complicate the function that generates a key from the user's name example as you like. The suggested procedure is simple.

1. Receive the `username` character string and delete leading and tail characters, for which the codes are less than 33 (i.e., spaces and control characters).
2. If the user name is shorter than three characters, return an error message.
3. If the user name is longer than 10 characters, leave only the first ten characters.
4. If the user name is shorter than 10 characters, increase it to 10 characters by repeating its characters cyclically, starting from the first. For example, if the user name is `John`, the supplemented name will be `JohnJohnJo`.
5. For the 10-character key obtained, use the following alphabet: `ALPH = 'abcdefghjkmnopqrstuvwxyz23456789'`. It consists of lowercase letters and digits excluding `i`, `1`, `0`, and `1` to avoid confusion between characters that look alike. For the XOR operation, use 10 numbers between 0 and 256: `XORKEY - (145, 133, 94, 160, 196, 165, 123, 54, 167, 146)`. Create a loop for `i` from zero to nine, iterating all of the characters from the user name. In the loop, replace each character of the user name with a character from the `ALPH` alphabet, according to the following rule: The ith character of `username` is added modulo 2 to the ith element of the `XORKEY` (using the XOR operation). The result is divided by the length of the `ALPH` string (which is 32), and the remainder from this division operation is used as the code of the ith character of the key. In this example, all the indices start from zero.
6. For the code of the fifth character of the key, use the code of the fourth character, decreased by four. If this code is missing from `ALPH`, use `'o'` (whose ASCII code is 111) as the fifth character, and replace the fourth character with `'s'` (code 115).
7. For the code of the seventh character of the key, use the code of the sixth character, decreased by two. If this code is missing from `ALPH`, use `'6'` (code 54) as the seventh character, and replace the sixth character with `'8'` (code 115).
8. The key file should have the name tetatet.k and be 40 bytes long. The user name is contained in the first 30 characters. If it is shorter, it is supplemented with spaces at the right; if it is longer, it is truncated. The key follows immediately after the name.

The shell will check whether the first four characters of the name and the key agree with each other. For this purpose, the shell will contain a fragment of the key-generating algorithm. The ActionScript program will check whether the sixth item of the algorithm was fulfilled (i.e., whether the fourth character's code, minus four, is equal to the fifth character's code). The other check (for the seventh item) is reserved in case a key generator for this game appears on the Internet. I mentioned this in the previous chapter, when describing the chNK function.

8.2. A Perl Key Generator

Consider the Perl script in Listing 8.1.

Listing 8.1. A key generator in Perl

```perl
#!/usr/local/bin/perl -w

use strict;
use integer;

my $userName = $ARGV[0];
my $ALPH = 'abcdefghjkmnopqrstuvwxyz23456789';

# Compute a key from a user name.
sub generatekey($)
{ my @XORKEY = (145, 133, 94, 160, 196, 165, 123, 54, 167, 146);
  my ($ls, $i, $j);
  my $c = 0;
  my $s = shift @_;
  my $la = length $ALPH;

  # Delete leading and tail non-printing characters.
  $s = ~s/^[\000-\040]+//;
  $s = ~s/[\000-\040]+$//;
  $ls = length $s;

  # The name should be at least 3 characters long.
  return "ERROR: Regname too short\n" if $ls < 3;

  # If the name length is greater than ten, discard the extra characters.
  if ($ls > 10)
    { $s = substr $s, 0, 10;
```

```
    $ls = 10;
  }


# Supplement the $s variable to ten characters.
for ($i = $ls, $j = 0; $i < 10; $i++)
 { vec($s, $i, 8) = vec($s, $j, 8);
   $j = ($j+1) % $ls;
 }


# Substitute ten characters of the $s variable with new ones.
for ($i = 0; $i < 10; $i++)
   { vec($s, $i, 8) = vec($ALPH, (vec($s, $i, 8) ^ $XORKEY[$i]) % $la, 8);
   }


# Rewrite the 4th and 6th characters of the key.
vec($s, 5, 8) = vec($s, 4, 8) - 4;
# If the 5th character is missing from ALPH,
# assign the 4th and 5th characters
# predefined values.
if (index($ALPH, chr vec($s, 5, 8)) < 0)
 { vec($s, 4, 8) = 115;  # s
   vec($s, 5, 8) = 111;  # o
 }
vec($s, 7, 8) = vec($s, 6, 8) - 2;
# If the 7th character is missing from ALPH,
# assign the 6th and 7th characters
# predefined values.
if (index($ALPH, chr vec($s, 7, 8)) < 0)
 { vec($s, 6, 8) = 56;  # 8
   vec($s, 7, 8) = 54;  # 6
 }
 return $s;
}


# The main program
#$userName = 'Serge Melnikov'; # For debugging
my $regCode = &generatekey($userName);
print "$regCode\n";


# Create the key file.
```

```
#$userName = ~s/^[\000-\040]+//;
#$userName = ~s/[\000-\040]+$//;
#my $ls = length $userName;
#exit if $ls < 3;
#$userName = substr($userName, 0, 30) if $ls > 30;
#$userName. = ' ' x (30-$ls) if $ls < 30;

#open F, ">perl-tetatet.k";
#print F "$userName$regCode";
#close F;
```

The first line

```
#!/usr/local/bin/perl -w
```

tells the operating system where the Perl interpreter is. The -w switch enables warning messages. In some hosting providers, the path to the interpreter can be different:

```
#!/usr/bin/perl -w
```

To clear this up, refer to the control panel of your hosting providers.
On RegNow's server, the user name is passed to a script as $ARGV[0]:

```
my $userName = $ARGV[0];
```

The generatekey function implements the algorithm described in the previous section. It takes the user name as an argument, and returns a key or an error message. The main program calls this function and outputs the key to the caller script on RegNow's server:

```
print "$regCode\n";
```

The following line is commented out:

```
# $userName = 'Serge Melnikov'; # For debugging
```

It is only used for debugging when generating keys manually on your home computer.
The following lines are also commented out:

```
# Create the key file
# $userName = ~s/^[\000-\040]+//;
# $userName = ~s/[\000-\040]+$//;
# my $ls = length $userName;
# exit if $ls < 3;
```

```
# $userName = substr($userName, 0, 30) if $ls > 30;
# $userName. = ' ' x (30-$ls) if $ls < 30;

# open F, ">perl-tetatet.k";
# print F "$userName$regCode";
# close F;
```

Remove the comment characters ('#') if you want to operate the key file on your computer and send it to the buyer.

When using this key generator, be aware of the following: Non-ASCII characters have different codes in DOS and Windows, and console applications, including this Perl script, use DOS encoding during a DOS session.

8.3. A Delphi Key Generator

Listing 8.2 contains a Delphi application that achieves the same results as the Perl script from the previous section.

Listing 8.2. A key generator in Delphi

```
{$I+}
unit Unit1;

interface

uses
  SysUtils, Forms, Classes, Controls, StdCtrls;

type
  TForm1 = class(TForm)
    Edit1: TEdit;
    Label1: TLabel;
    Label2: TLabel;
    Edit2: TEdit;
    Button1: TButton;
    procedure Button1Click(Sender: TObject);
  private
    { Private declarations }
  public
```

```
    { Public declarations }
  end;

var
  Form1: TForm1;

implementation

{$R *.DFM}

// Compute a key from a user name
function GenKey(username: string): string;
const
 ALPH: string = 'abcdefghjkmnopqrstuvwxyz23456789';
 XORKEY: array[1..10] of byte = (145, 133, 94, 160, 196, 165, 123, 54, 167, 146);
var
 ls, la, i, j : integer;
 s, c: string;

begin
// Delete leading and tail non-printing characters.
s := Trim(username);
ls := Length(s);
// The name should be at least 3 characters long.
if ls < 3 then
 begin
 Result := 'ERROR: Regname too short';
 Exit;
 end;
// If the name length is greater than 10, discard the extra characters.
if ls > 10 then
 begin
 SetLength(s, 10);
 ls := 10;
 end;
// Supplement the s variable to 10 characters.
j := 1;
for i := ls + 1 to 10 do
 begin
 s := s + s[j];
```

```
 j := j mod ls + 1;
 end;
// Substitute 10 characters of the s variable with new ones.
la := Length(ALPH);
for i := 1 to 10 do
 s[i] := chr(byte(ALPH[(byte(s[i]) xor XORKEY[i]) mod la + 1]));
// Rewrite the 4th and 6th characters of the key (numbered from zero)
s[6] := chr(byte(s[5]) - 4);
c := s[6];
// If the 5th character is missing from ALPH,
// assign the 4th and 5th characters
// predefined values.
if Pos(c, ALPH) < 1 then
 begin
 s[5] := chr(115);  // s
 s[6] := chr(111);  // o
 end;
s[8] := chr(byte(s[7]) - 2);
c := s[8];
// If the 7th character is missing from ALPH,
// assign the 6th and 7th characters
// predefined values.
if Pos(c, ALPH) < 1 then
 begin
 s[7] := chr(56);  // 8
 s[8] := chr(54);  // 6
 end;
Result := s;
end; {GenKey}

procedure TForm1.Button1Click(Sender: TObject);
var
 l: integer;
 name: string;
 f: TextFile;
begin
Edit2.Text := GenKey(Edit1.Text);

name := Trim(Edit1.Text);
l := Length(name);
```

```
if l < 3 then Exit;
// Create the key file.
AssignFile(f, ExtractFilePath(Application.ExeName) + 'delphi - tetatet.k');
Rewrite(f);
if l > 30 then SetLength(name, 30);
if l < 30 then name := name + StringOfChar(#32, 30 - l);
Write(f, name + Edit2.Text);
CloseFile(f);
end;

end.
```

8.4. A C++ Key Generator

A key generator written in Microsoft Visual C++ and all of the auxiliary files are located in the Examples\Chapter 8\MSVC folder on the accompanying CD-ROM.

Chapter 9: Integrating a Flash Movie into a Delphi Program

This chapter teaches you how to install the Shockwave Flash component in Delphi and write a shell for your Flash game.

9.1. Installing the Shockwave Flash Component in Delphi

To display Flash movies using a Delphi program, you should install the Shockwave Flash component that should be present in your system if Flash player is installed.

Start Delphi and select the **Component | Import ActiveX Control...** menu command. The **Import ActiveX Control** dialog box will open. In the **Registered Controls** section, select **Shockwave Flash**. In the **Palette Page** section, select the page, on which the component should be placed after installation. By default, this is the **ActiveX** page. In the **Unit Dir Name** section, select the path to the folder that should contain the component. It is best to accept all of the default settings in this window.

Click on the **Install** button. A window asking you to choose a package for the component will appear. You can choose a new or an existing package. A window for editing the selected package will open, and you'll be asked: "**...Package will be rebuilt. Continue?**" Answer **Yes**. After this, you will be able to use Flash in your applications.

The new ShockwaveFlashObjects_TLB.dcu module and its source file, ShockwaveFlashObjects_TLB.pas, will appear in the Imports folder. You'll need this module when creating applications, so the ShockwaveFlashObjects_TLB.dcu file should be placed in one of Delphi library folders so that it will be available during compiling. The simplest way to do this is to place the ShockwaveFlashObjects_TLB.pas file in your current project folder.

Base your new project on the chapter7.1.fla and tet7.1.as files from *Chapter 7*. I saved with new names tetatet.fla and tetatet.as in the Examples\Chapter 9 folder. When renaming the AS file, make sure to correct its name in the ActionScript code attached to the fourth frame of the main timeline.

Create a folder for your new Delphi project and place the ShockwaveFlashObjects_TLB.pas file in it. In addition, translate the tetatet.fla file and place the result, that is, the tetatet.swf file, in the same folder. To do this, press the <Shift>+<F12> shortcut in the Flash development environment. Then, start Delphi and select the **File | New | Application** menu command. Delphi will create a new form, Form1, for the new project. In the **Object Inspector** window, write the Tet-a-Tetris name as the form's **Caption** property. This form will only contain the ShockwaveFlash control. To drag its icon onto the form, scroll through the component palette until the **ActiveX** tab appears. In this tab, click on the **ShockwaveFlash** button so that it remains pressed. Then click anywhere on the **Form1** form (Fig. 9.1).

In the **Object Inspector** window (which can be opened using the <F11> key), the **Properties** tab will open. It contains the properties of the **ShockwaveFlash1** object. Resize the form by dragging its lower right corner so that the window of your game, for which the size is 769 × 564 pixels, fits in the form. Now enter the following settings for the ShockwaveFlash1 object's properties: set Top and Left to zero, Width to 769, and Height to 564. If scrollbars appear on the form, stretch the form further until they disappear. Save the project. To do this, select the **File | Save All** menu command, and locate the folder already containing two files for your project. When saving the project file, rename it from Project1.dpr to Tetatet.dpr. Continue setting the game window properties. Set the Movie property to the full path to the tetatet.swf file, otherwise Delphi will fail to find the project. Now you can run the project. To do this, press the <F9> key. Everything should work, except there will be no sound. To hear the sounds, click the **Sound** button or press the <S> key.

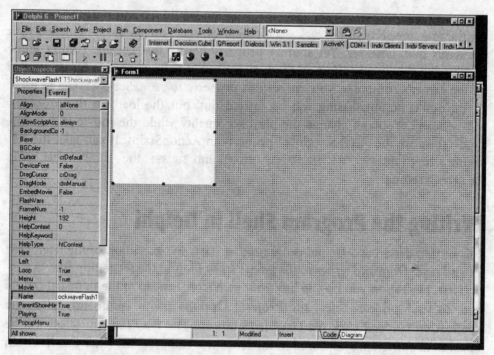

Fig. 9.1. Linking the **Shockwave Flash** component to the program

After you have examined the empty table of records, you won't be able to exit the program using the **Exit** button. This is to be expected, because the sound indicator is passed to the game by the shell, the shell is responsible for exiting, and you have yet to write the required procedures. In addition, you should adjust the program form to the game window and select an appropriate window style to prevent the user from resizing it. To exit the program, click the close button (the button with a cross) or press the <Alt>+<F4> shortcut. Move to the **Form1** tab in the **Object Inspector** window by clicking on an unused area in the form or by selecting **Form1** from the drop-down list. Set the BorderStyle property to bsSingle, and set ClientHeight and ClientWidth to 564 pixels and 769 pixels, respectively (these values are the dimensions of the movie window). If you then start the application, it will look as it should.

Notice that the Flash player menu appears if you right-click on the game while it is running. Let's hide the menu. Move to the tab with the properties for the ShockwaveFlash1 object, and set Menu to False. Set Loop to False as well. By the way, your game will start immediately after loading, because the Playing property is set to True. If this wasn't the case, the program would have to start the game using the Play property of the ShockwaveFlash1 object. You should be satisfied with the status quo, however. Yet another property here is DeviceFont. I don't know whether it can have any affect on Flash player but, if your game uses fonts installed on the gamer's computer, you can set this property to True. Set Quality2 to High. If you don't, no antialiasing will be carried out, but the load on the processor will be lower. You can change the playback quality while the movie is running. To do this, use the _quality global property in ActionScript. It can take the following string values: 'LOW', 'MEDIUM', 'HIGH', and 'BEST', the 'HIGH' value being the default setting.

9.2. Writing the Program Shell in Delphi

This section describes a Delphi program that starts the execution of the tetatet.swf file and reads from and writes to the tetatet.k key file and the tetatet.top file.

First, I will show you how to link your own icon, instead of the standard Delphi icon, to your project. Select the **Project | Options** menu command, select the **Application** tab, and click the **Load Icon** button. The ICO file you select will be linked to the program and stored in the tetatet.res resource file. After this has been done, the icon will appear in the program window caption. If you're wondering how can you create an icon, this can be done using a special editor; you can find such editor on the CD accompanying this book.

In the **Object Inspector** window, move to the properties for the Form1 form, and open the **Events** tab. Locate the line with the OnClose event, and double-click on its input field, located to the right of OnClose. A dummy for a handler of this event will appear in the code window:

```
procedure TForm1.FormClose...
```

This procedure will be called when the gamer uses any method to try to close the application (pressing the <Alt>+<F4> shortcut, clicking on the close button in the system menu, or on the **Exit** button below the table of records). Before closing the program, you should check whether the gamer has changed the snd variable, which is the sound indicator. If he or she has, the latest value should be written at the end of the table of records. This is an instance when the snd0 variable comes to your aid.

Create a dummy for an OnShow event handler in the same way. This event takes place when the form appears on the screen. On this event, you'll create a file with the table of records (if there isn't any) and pass its contents to the game.

In the **Object Inspector** window, move to the properties of the tetatet object, and create a dummy for an OnFSCommand event handler. It will handle the following calls from the game to the fscommand procedure:

❏ readname — Used to pass the gamer's name and registration key and to check the validity of the registration key.

❏ savename — Used to write the gamer's name and registration key to the tetatet.k file. It is unwise to give this file a KEY extension, because files with these extensions are used to write to the Registry. In addition, some mail services, such as AOL, delete files with these extensions, making it difficult to send them via e-mail.

❏ gettopten — Used to read the tetatet.top file and pass the table of records to the game.

❏ savetopten — Used to save the table of records received from the game in the file.

❏ exit — Used to exit the program when the **Exit** button on the topten clip is clicked.

The Delphi procedure will receive two string parameters: the command and the data being passed. These strings are of the WideString type, i.e., each character is encoded using two bytes. This isn't a problem when you use Delphi, because it takes care of type conversion between the common strings of the String type and WideString strings. Procedures that process common strings can also be used for wide strings.

9.2.1. The Type and Global Data Section of the Program

In Delphi, move to the code window for the **fmMain** form. Its code is stored in the fmMain.pas file. To switch between the form's appearance and its code window, use the <F12> key.

Locate the following string:

```
{$R *.dfm}
```

and insert the code from Listing 9.1 after it.

___

Listing 9.1. The type and global data section of the program

___

```
type
 mb = array[1..999999] of byte;
const
```

```
  // The name of the top ten file
  TOPNAME = 'tetatet.top';
  // The name of the SWF file
  SWFNAME = 'tetatet.swf';
  // The name of the file with the user name and key
  KEYNAME = 'tetatet.k';
var
  pathtop, pathswf, pathkey: string;
  topten, topnames, topscores: WideString;
  globname: string;
```

The mb type will be used when reading the SWF file which, generally speaking, can be encrypted to hamper its use outside this shell. This is done in the EncodeSWF procedure that encrypts the first 2,048 bytes of the tetatet.swf file. However, I put the exit command at the beginning of this procedure to bypass encryption for the sake of debugging convenience. You can enable encryption if you wish, but be aware that the normal state of the tetatet.swf file will be encrypted, and it will only be able to work with the shell. To encrypt or decrypt the tetatet.swf file outside the shell, use a small console program EncodeSWF.dpr, which is a copy of the procedure with the same name used in the main program. In addition, you can rename the tetatet.swf file as, for instance, tetatet.dat to conceal its purpose. To do this, you should also change the value of the SWFNAME variable in the EncodeSWF.dpr console program. However, I advise you not to encrypt the SWF file, as it could cause other problems.

The pathtop, pathswf, and pathkey variables will store the full names (including the disk name and the paths) of the top ten file, the SWF file, and the key file, respectively. The topten, topnames, and topscores wide strings will store the table of records, ten names, and ten scores, respectively. These variables are necessary for exchanging data with the Flash game, so their type is WideString. The globname variable will store the name and the key read from the tetatet.k file.

Insert the code for the EncodeSWF procedure (Listing 9.2) after the type and global data section of the program.

Listing 9.2. The EncodeSWF procedure

```
// Encrypt and decrypt the SWF file
procedure EncodeSWF;
const
  NUMB = 2048;
var
```

```
  f: file;
  p: ^mb;
  i: integer;

begin
// Exit the procedure.
exit;
// Open the SWF file.
AssignFile(f, pathswf);
Reset(f, 1);
// Allocate NUMB bytes of memory.
GetMem(p, NUMB);
// Read the first NUMB bytes and store them in p^.
BlockRead(f, p^, NUMB);
// Encrypt (or decrypt) the first 2, 048 bytes.
for i := 1 to NUMB do p^[i] := p^[i] xor byte(6000 - i);
// Set the read/write pointer to the beginning of the file.
Seek(f, 0);
// Write the first NUMB bytes into the file.
BlockWrite(f, p^, NUMB);
CloseFile(f);
FreeMem(p);
end; {EncodeSWF}
```

This procedure is straightforward. For encryption, the XOR operation is used. It is addition modulo 2 of bytes read from the file and bytes computed from the i loop counter. The decryption is carried out using the same procedure.

Now, insert the EncodeTopTen procedure to encrypt and decrypt the table of records (Listing 9.3). It is encrypted to prevent anybody from putting him or herself in first place. Because the table of records is stored in a WideString string, it has an even number of bytes and, therefore, can be encrypted using words.

Listing 9.3. The EncodeTopTen procedure

```
// Encrypt and decrypt the table of records.
procedure EncodeTopTen;
var
  i, l: integer;
```

```
begin
l := Length(topten);
for i := 1 to l do word(topten[i]) := word(topten[i]) xor (i + 2000);
end; {EncodeTopTen}
```

This procedure needs no explanation.

The CheckNK function checks whether the first four characters of the key correspond to the first four characters of the name (Listing 9.4). It actually contains a fragment of key generator code. If the key is invalid, the function returns FALSE. Otherwise, it returns TRUE.

Listing 9.4. The CheckNK function

```
// Check whether the first four characters of the key
// correspond to the first four characters of the name.
function CheckNK(name, key: string): boolean;
const
 ALPH: string = 'abcdefghjkmnopqrstuvwxyz23456789';
 XORKEY: array[1..4] of byte = (145, 133, 94, 160);
var
 la, i : integer;
 s: string;
begin
Result := FALSE;
if (Length(name) < 3) or (Length(key) <> 10) then Exit;
s := name;
if Length(s) = 3 then s := s + s[1];
la := Length(ALPH);
for i := 1 to 4 do
 if chr(byte(ALPH[(byte(s[i]) xor XORKEY[i]) mod la+1)])) <> key[i] then
Exit;
Result := TRUE;
end; {CheckNK}
```

The next three procedures already have dummies that you created earlier. So you need only to insert the appropriate code into them (Listing 9.5).

Listing 9.5. The FormShow procedure

```
// Handle the form show event.
procedure TForm1.FormShow(Sender: TObject);
label 10, 20;
const
 MINSIZE = 44;
 MAXSIZE = 844;
var
 f: file;
 size, size2, i, ind: integer;

begin
// Find the path to the program.
pathswf := ExtractFilePath(Application.ExeName);
// Find the path to the table of records.
pathtop := pathswf + TOPNAME;
// Find the path to the key file.
pathkey := pathswf + KEYNAME;
// Find the path to the SWF file.
pathswf := pathswf + SWFNAME;
AssignFile(f, pathtop);
// If the tetatet.top file doesn't exist...
if not FileExists(pathtop) then
 begin
 // ...create a file for the table of records.
10:
 // The first row contains the author's record.
 topten := 'Author|26121|';
 // The other nine rows are empty.
 for i := 0 to 8 do topten :=  topten + '<empty>|0|';
 // Append the sound indicator.
 topten := topten + '1';
 // Encrypt the table.
 EncodeTopTen;
 // Create the tetatet.top file.
 Rewrite(f, 1);
 // Write the table into the file.
 // Don't forget that a character consists of two bytes!
 BlockWrite(f, topten[1], Length(topten)*2);
```

```
CloseFile(f);
// Go to reading the table of records.
goto 20;
end else
 // The topten.top file exists. Read it and store it in the topten string.
 begin
 // Open the file.
 Reset(f, 1);
 // Store the file size in bytes in the size variable
 // and store the file size in characters in the size2 variable.
 size :=  FileSize(f);
 size2 :=  size div 2;
 // Check whether the file size is appropriate and even.
 if (size < MINSIZE) or (size > MAXSIZE) or Odd(size) then goto 10;
 // Set the length of the topten wide string
 // equal to the file size.
 SetLength(topten, size2);
 // Read the file and store it in the topten variable.
 BlockRead(f, topten[1], size);
 CloseFile(f);
 // Rewrite the names to the topnames string and the scores
 // to the topscores string.
20:
 // Decrypt topten.
 EncodeTopTen;
 topnames := '';
 topscores := '';
 for i := 0 to 9 do
  begin
  // Find the next '|' character.
  ind := Pos('|', topten);
  // If there isn't any, this is an error.
  if (ind = 0) then goto 10;
  // Read the next name
  topnames := topnames + Copy(topten, 1, ind);
  // Delete it from the topten string.
  Delete(topten, 1, ind);
  // Find the next '|' character
  ind := Pos('|', topten);
```

```
    // If there isn't any, this is an error.
    if (ind = 0) then goto 10;
    // Read the next score.
    topscores := topscores + Copy(topten, 1, ind);
    // Delete it from the topten string.
    Delete(topten, 1, ind);
    end;
  // Remove the last '|' character.
  SetLength(topnames, Length(topnames) - 1);
  SetLength(topscores, Length(topscores) - 1);
  // One '|' character should remain in topten.
  // If there isn't any, this is an error.
  if (Length(topten) <> 1) then goto 10;
  end;
// Decrypt the SWF file.
EncodeSWF;
// Load the Flash movie.
tetatet.LoadMovie(0, pathswf);
// Encrypt the SWF file.
EncodeSWF;
// The game will start on its own because the Playing property
// is equal to True.
// This is why you don't need to start the game.
// tetatet.Play;
end; {TForm1.FormShow}
```

First, the procedure creates the full paths for the SWF file, the key file, and the file with the table of records. The ExtractFilePath function is used.

NOTE

In the Delphi environment, you can get online help about its every procedure or function, or about a method or a property of any object. Just move the cursor onto the name, and press the <Ctrl>+<F1> shortcut.

The procedure then checks whether the top ten file exists. If it doesn't, it is created and initialized. The internal representation of the table of records is the following string:

```
'Author|26121|<empty>|0|<empty>|0|<empty>|0|<empty>|0|<empty>|0|
<empty>|0|<empty>|0|<empty>|0|<empty>|0|1'
```

Gamers' names, followed by scores, are repeated ten times. The table ends with a one, indicating that sound is enabled. The first row is filled with the game author's name and score. After the table of records is created, it is encrypted and saved in a file. Control is then passed to processing the read table.

If the tetatet.top file exists, its contents are stored in the topten string. Note that, before you do this, you should allocate the required memory for the string variable, using the SetLength function.

NOTE

For a WideString string, memory is allocated in words, so the size2 variable equal to the half of the file size is used. When you use the BlockRead low-level function, you pass it the number of bytes to read, i.e., the size variable. When using the BlockRead and BlockWrite functions, pass them the first element of the string, i.e., topten[1]. If you pass the topten string itself, the data won't be stored in it. Rather, they will be stored in a memory area containing a four-byte pointer to the contents of the topten string. As a result, the memory area will be ruined, and the program will not function properly.

The procedure then decrypts the topten string and writes the names and the scores into different strings, topnames and topscores, to make it easier to store the names and scores in the arrays in ActionScript. In the topnames and topscores strings, the data are also separated with '|' characters. During the process, the procedure also checks whether the tetatet.top file is correct. If it finds an error, it jumps to creating a new file.

The procedure then loads the SWF file:

```
tetatet.LoadMovie(0, pathswf);
```

To do this, it uses the LoadMovie method of the tetatet object. To see all the methods and properties of this object, type

```
tetatet.
```

and wait for a while. A tip window will appear at the position of the text cursor. You can see the same tip in the ShockwaveFlashObjects_TLB.pas file in the project folder.

NOTE

Don't expect all of these methods to work correctly. Some of them can "freeze" the program. However, the methods used in this program don't cause any problems.

Before the SWF file is loaded, it is decrypted. It is encrypted again after loading.

Consider the work of the `tetatetFSCommand` method. It will be called when the game calls the `fscommand` function. Two arguments of this function (which are `WideString` strings) will be passed to the `tetatetFSCommand` method.

Listing 9.6. The `tetatetFSCommand` procedure

```
// Process calls to the fscommand function from the Flash movie.
procedure TForm1.tetatetFSCommand(Sender: TObject; const command,
  args: WideString);
var
 f: file;
 namekey, name, key: string;
 wname: WideString;
 ipos, lname, lkey: integer;

begin
// A test output of the strings received from the Flash movie
if (command = 'test') then ShowMessage(args);

// Process the 'readname' command.
if (command = 'readname') then
 begin
 // If there is no key file, exit.
 if not FileExists(pathkey) then Exit;
 AssignFile(f, pathkey);
 // Open the tetatet.k file.
 Reset(f, 1);
 // The size of the key file should be exactly 40 bytes.
 if (FileSize(f) <> 40) then
  begin
  CloseFile(f);
  Exit;
  end;
 // Set the length of the name string to 40 bytes.
 SetLength(namekey, 40);
 // Read the tetate.k file, and store it in the name string.
 BlockRead(f, namekey[1], 40);
 CloseFile(f);
 name := Trim(Copy(namekey, 1, 30));
 if Length(name) < 3 then Exit;
```

```
key := Copy(namekey, 31, 10);
// Check whether the first four characters of the key are valid.
if not CheckNK(name, key) then Exit;
// Copy the name and the key to a wide string to send them
// to the Flash movie.
wname := name + '|' + key;
// Store the name and the key in a global variable.
globname := name + '|' + key;
// Store the wname string in the namekey variable of the Flash movie.
tetatet.SetVariable('namekey1', wname);
end;


// Process the 'savename' command.
if (command = 'savename') then
begin
// Get the position of the delimiter.
ipos := Pos('|', args);
// The name should be at least 3 characters long.
if (ipos < 4) then Exit;
// Copy the name to a variable.
name := Trim(Copy(args, 1, ipos - 1));
// Copy the key to another variable.
key := Trim(Copy(args, ipos + 1, Length(args) - ipos));
// The gamer's input shouldn't contain any '|' characters.
if (Pos('|', key) > 0) then Exit;
lname := Length(name);
lkey := Length(key);
// Check whether the length of the name and the key are correct.
if ((lname < 3) or (lkey <> 10)) then Exit;
// Truncate the name to 30 characters.
if (lname > 30) then
 begin
 lname := 30;
 SetLength(name, 30);
 end;
// If the name is shorter than 30 characters, supplement it with spaces.
if (lname < 30) then name := name + StringOfChar(#32, 30 - lname);
AssignFile(f, pathkey);
Rewrite(f, 1);
// Save the name and the key in the tetatet.k file.
```

```
    BlockWrite(f, name[1], 30);
    BlockWrite(f, key[1], 10);
    CloseFile(f);
    end;

// Process the 'gettopten' command.
if (command = 'gettopten') then
  { Store the names, the scores, and the sound indicator in the clip's
variables.}
  with tetatet do
    begin
    SetVariable('topnames1', topnames);
    SetVariable('topscores1', topscores);
    SetVariable('snd', topten);
    end;

// Process the 'savetopten' command.
if (command = 'savetopten') then
  begin
  AssignFile(f, pathtop);
  Rewrite(f, 1);
  topten := args;
  // Encrypt the table of records.
  EncodeTopTen;
  // Save it in the file.
  BlockWrite(f, topten[1], Length(topten)*2);
  CloseFile(f);
  end;

// Process the 'exit' command.
if (command = 'exit') then close;
end; {TForm1.tetatetFSCommand}
```

The `tetatetFSCommand` procedure is a series of conditional statements in the following form:

```
if (command = '...') then ...;
```

Each of these checks whether the received command is a particular string, and executes the command if this is the case.

The `'test'` command makes the procedure display the received data.

The `'readname'` command is executed as follows: The procedure reads the key file and checks for the validity of the first four characters of the key, using the CheckNK function. If the key is invalid, the name and the key aren't sent to the game. You can use another key generator and carry out other checks. It is also useful to put a few additional requirements on the key, just in case somebody creates a key generator for your program. If an illegal key generator like this appears on the Internet, you'll be able to void it by checking another condition.

The format of the tetatet.k file is the following: The first 30 bytes contain the registration name in Windows encoding. If the name entered by the gamer into the sorry clip is shorter than 30 characters, it is supplemented with spaces. The name is followed by a key that is 30 bytes long. It can contain lowercase letters and digits, but not 0, 1, i, and l, because they can be confused.

When processing the key file, the procedure deletes the spaces, stores the name and the key separated by a 'l' character in the wname wide string, and sends it to the game using the following method.

```
tetatet.SetVariable('namekey1', wname);
```

Note that the name of the namekey1 variable declared in the first frame of the Flash game is sent as a string. As a result, the wname string is assigned to the namekey1 variable. The getVariable method is complementary to setVariable. It takes one parameter, the name of an ActionScript variable, and returns the value of the variable as a WideString string. Numbers are also sent as strings. This is how the shell exchanges data with the Flash movie.

The `'savename'` command is executed as follows: The procedure receives the name and key entered by the gamer into the sorry clip. This is sent by the Flash game as one string. In the string, the name and the key are separated by a 'l' character. The procedure checks whether the input format is correct and supplements the name with spaces, if necessary. It then saves the name and the key in the tetatet.k file.

The `'gettopten'` command makes the procedure assign the topnames1, topscores1, and snd variables the values read by the shell from the tetatet.top file, or values that are newly-created if the file didn't exist.

The `'savetopten'` command tells the procedure that the args variable contains the table of records and the sound indicator received from the Flash game. The procedure should encrypt it and save it in the tetatet.top file.

The `'exit'` command is the simplest. It is sent by the game when the gamer clicks the **Exit** button below the table of records (or releases the <Esc> key). The procedure simply calls the close method of the program's only form.

Before the program exits, the FormClose event occurs. It is handled by the FormClose method of the Form1 form (Listing 9.7).

Listing 9.7. The FormClose procedure

```
// Handle the FormClose event.
procedure TForm1.FormClose(Sender: TObject; var Action: TCloseAction);
var
 f: file;
 l, size: integer;
 c: WideString;
begin
 with tetatet do
  // If the gamer toggled the sound indicator,
  // write it to the tetatet.top file.
  if (GetVariable('snd') <> GetVariable('snd0')) then
   begin
   // Assign the c variable the snd value received from the Flash movie.
   c := GetVariable('snd');
   AssignFile(f, pathtop);
   Reset(f, 1);
   size := FileSize(f);
   // Set the topten wide string
   // to the file size.
   SetLength(topten, size div 2);
   // Read tetatet.top and store its contents in the topten string.
   BlockRead(f, topten[1], size);
   l := Length(topten);
   // Decrypt the table of records.
   EncodeTopTen;
   if (l > 0) then
    begin
    // Update the sound indicator.
    SetLength(topten, l - 1);
    topten := topten + c;
    // Encrypt the table of records.
    EncodeTopTen;
    Rewrite(f, 1);
    // Save it in the file.
```

```
    BlockWrite(f, topten[1], size);
    end;
    CloseFile(f);
    end;
end; {TForm1.FormClose}
```

This procedure is only needed to compare the snd and snd0 variables and, if they differ (i.e., if the gamer toggled the sound indicator), rewrite the tetatet.top file to toggle between the '0' and '1' characters at the end of the file.

This completes the programming of the Delphi shell for your game. You now can compile it to obtain the Tetatet.exe executable file. The source code is in the Examples\Chapter 9 folder.

To continue with the theme, you can create a **Clear records** button for the table of records so that a gamer can initialize the tetatet.top file by clicking this button. Gamers sometimes wish to clear the table of records, but not all gamers know how to delete the file.

This completes the description of Tet-a-Tetris both as an online game and as a Windows application. You can now create Flash games that are able to interact with the Web server or with a Windows application that starts a game from a SWF file.

Chapter 11 describes how to create a logical Flash game that can "think" and even beat a person if he or she isn't concentrating hard enough. Creating games like this have long been a dream of advanced programmers. Delphi is a very promising tool in this area. A Delphi program can "think over" moves and send them to a Flash game that only displays the computer's moves. The performance of a program like this would be ten, or even one hundred, times greater than that of an ActionScript program. *Chapter 11* demonstrates how to compute moves and win a game called Nim using an ActionScript program. This will allow you to use this game on the Web.

If you were patient and went through all the stages of creating Tet-a-Tetris, you should have no problem with this chapter.

Chapter 10: Integrating Flash Movie into a C++ Program

This chapter describes how you can integrate a Flash animation into a common Windows program and set up interaction between them. Here, you'll create a shell for Tet-a-Tetris. Not only will your program load and play the Flash movie, but it will also input and save a registration key, as well as save top ten results.

Because this program is intended for training purposes, I tried to make it as simple as possible so that you can concentrate on the most important issues without getting distracted with minor details and additional features. I will, however, point out from time to time the ways to improve the program and make it more professional.

I have tried to present the material in a form comprehensible even to a novice programmer. However, it would be best if you can program for Win32 and have a general notion of COM and ActiveX. For my part, I'm going to give you basic information on these topics. You should also know C++, at least at a beginner's level. Unfortunately, I couldn't completely avoid the use of some advanced features of C++, such as template classes, but I tried to use them sparingly and provide all the necessary comments to talk you through. For reasons of space, I cannot go into the details of C++ programming for Win32. My goal is to sketch outlines, and you will need to refer to special sources for more in-depth information.

What are these sources? A great many books on programming under Windows have been written. However, the main source of information is the MSDN Library from Microsoft. It is freely available at **http://msdn.microsoft.com**. A "lightweight" version of it comes with MS Visual Studio. MSDN Library contains comprehensive reference information and many articles and examples. Unfortunately, it is sometimes difficult to find necessary information quickly, but this is not hard to understand, considering the amount of information to be stored there.

To create the program shell, you'll need Microsoft Visual C++. I created the project for this book in Visual C++ version 6.0, but you can compile it in the latest version Visual Studio .NET. Most of information presented in this chapter is basic for Win32 and C++ and doesn't depend on a particular development environment.

10.1. Getting Started with the Project

When creating an application, regardless of its complexity, it is a good practice to increase its functionality step by step. At each stage, you should either include a new feature, upgrade an existing one, or simply remove bugs. It is important that you continually maintain the integrity of your project so that it is possible to compile and run the project at each stage. Let's stick to these principles.

You don't have to repeat every step described in this chapter. You can simply open the example project located on the accompanying CD-ROM. However, it is more convenient to describe the project in the order, in which it was developed. In addition, even this small project allows me to demonstrate the step-by-step method for creating an application. This method is very convenient and effective in practice.

So let's start with creating a simple application for opening an empty window. I can't assume that every reader is skilled at programming in Win32, so I'll touch on some of the basics here.

10.1.1. Precompiled Headers

I'm not going to teach you how to use Visual Studio, create a new project, and so on. I hope that you are at least experienced at using Windows, and you'll find appropriate menu items and buttons on your own. I cannot, however, ignore an interesting feature that is unknown even to some of the most experienced users. The feature is *precompiled headers*.

Note the stdafx.h and stdafx.cpp files in the example project. Visual Studio usually creates them when you create a new project. (In this case, you should select the **Win32 application** project type.) However, you can create them on your own when necessary. To do this, you should make the appropriate project settings (**C++ | Precompiled Headers**) first.

How does this feature work? The stdafx.cpp file usually contains the only line, `#include "stdafx.h"`. Information obtained when compiling this is saved in a special file. The other CPP files begin by including the same stdafx.h file, and the compiler loads the data saved on the disk rather than compile the stdafx.h file anew. As a rule, stdafx.h contains system headers and the headers of third-party libraries. As files describing system and library functions and classes are usually large, this method allows you to speed up the compilation. Although the difference is almost unnoticeable when working on a small project like the one in this chapter, this trick will speed up your work on large projects, because you have to compile your programs repeatedly when debugging them.

For now, include only the windows.h file in stdafx.h. In windows.h, most of Win32 API functions are declared:

```
#define STRICT
#include <windows.h>
```

The STRICT preprocessor symbol affects the compilation of the windows.h file. When it is defined, the control of data types used in Windows functions is strict. I recommend that you always use this option.

In the next section, *ATL (Active Template Library)* headers will be added to this file.

10.1.2. Registering the Main Window Style

Let's get started with the program. The execution of any Windows program begins with the WinMain function. In this function, you should create the main window of your application and arrange a main message loop.

In Windows, a window is created in two stages. First, you have register its class (don't confuse window classes with C++ classes) using the RegisterClassEx function:

```
const TCHAR c_szClassName[] = TEXT("1334FE45-5CC8-444f-97E1-FEA2518BA742");

WNDCLASSEX wndclassex;
wndclassex.cbSize = sizeof(WNDCLASSEX);
wndclassex.style = 0;
wndclassex.lpfnWndProc = WindowProc;
wndclassex.cbClsExtra = 0;
```

```
wndclassex.cbWndExtra = 0;
wndclassex.hInstance = _hInstance;
wndclassex.hIcon = ::LoadIcon( _hInstance, MAKEINTRESOURCE(IDI_MAIN) );
wndclassex.hCursor = ::LoadCursor( NULL, IDC_ARROW );
wndclassex.hbrBackground = (HBRUSH)( 1 + COLOR_APPWORKSPACE );
wndclassex.lpszMenuName = NULL;
wndclassex.lpszClassName = c_szClassName;
wndclassex.hIconSm = NULL;
ATOM atomWndClass = ::RegisterClassEx( &wndclassex );
if( !atomWndClass ) {
 ErrorMessage();
 return 1;
}
```

The RegisterClassEx function takes only one parameter, which is a pointer to the WNDCLASSEX structure. The structure contains parameters for the window being created, such as the icon in the window caption, the default cursor, the background color, the menu, and so on. I won't describe all of them here, but there are two that are the most important. The first is lpfnWndProc, a pointer to the window function. This function controls the window during the window's entire life span. I'll describe it later. The second important parameter is lpszClassName, which is a pointer to the class name. Deep down, the main purpose of the RegisterClassEx function is to link the window function to the name, so that you can create windows by specifying the class name. Once you have registered a class, you can create as many windows of this class as you like.

Why is such a two-step approach used? In most cases, the addresses of window functions aren't known until the application is loaded into the memory. However, class names are known in advance. This fact is used, for example, to create dialog boxes. A dialog template contains the class names of its controls. When a dialog box is loaded, the system reads these names, creates necessary windows, and places them on the dialog box according to the template. So this two-step approach makes creation of windows flexible.

You can choose any character string for the class name. For example, you could specify it to be OurSuperMegaRulesTetATetrisGame. The only requirement is that the name should be unique, in order to avoid it to coincidentally match with another window class name used in your program, including system names and window class names used in libraries linked to your program. To be sure that this does not happen, I use a GUID (Global Unique Identifier) as a class name. It can be generated using the GuidGen utility.

Note that the type of the class name and of the other strings in the program is TCHAR, rather than char, and the class-name string is declared using the TEXT macro. This will allow you to compile your program as Unicode, if necessary.

If the RegisterClassEx function fails, it will return zero. This can be the result of a mistake on your part, like incorrectly defining one of the parameters in the WNDCLASSEX structure, for example, or of the fact that a class with this name might have already been registered. A system error is also likely, for example, if the program runs out of memory. The same is true for each system function. This is why you should always try to foresee such an event and check whether a system call was successful.

Handling all conceivable errors would be a topic for an entire separate chapter, or even a book. Not only should a good application inform the user about an error, but it should also describe the error comprehensively. Win32 offers you special tools for this purpose. The GetLastError function returns an error code, and the FormatMessage function allows you to retrieve a text message describing the error. In C++ programs, it is convenient to use exceptions for error handling. An important and difficult problem related to error handling is that a function in an erroneous situation should free up the resources it uses (deallocate the memory, close files, etc.), in addition to terminating correctly. Some C++ features, such as exceptions and destructors, allow you to cope with the problem easily. Unfortunately, describing them would require an enormous digression here. To avoid unnecessarily complication of the program, you'll simply call the ErrorMessage function displaying an error message for the user, and exit the program if an error occurs.

10.1.3. Creating the Main Window of the Program

After you've successfully registered the class, you can proceed with creating the main window. However, there is one problem you need to deal with first. The Tet-a-Tetris work area that you'll put into the window should have a fixed size of 769×564 pixels. You could set the size of the window when creating it using the CreateWindowsEx function, or you could resize the window later, using the MoveWindow function. However, you should pass any of the functions the external size of the window, including the border, the caption, and the menu, whereas you need to fix size of the client area within the window. Fortunately, Win32 offers you a special function, AdjustWindowRectEx, which computes the entire size of the window from a given size of the client area.

```
const unsigned int c_nClientWidth = 769;
const unsigned int c_nClientHeight = 564;
```

```
const DWORD c_dwWndStyle = WS_BORDER |
              WS_CAPTION |
              WS_CLIPCHILDREN |
              WS_MINIMIZEBOX |
              WS_OVERLAPPED |
              WS_SYSMENU;
const DWORD c_dwWndStyleEx = WS_EX_APPWINDOW |
              WS_EX_CLIENTEDGE |
              WS_EX_CONTROLPARENT;
RECT rect;
rect.left = 0;
rect.right = c_nClientWidth;
rect.top = 0;
rect.bottom = c_nClientHeight;
BOOL isOk = ::AdjustWindowRectEx( &rect, c_dwWndStyle, FALSE,
c_dwWndStyleEx );
if( !isOk ) {
    ErrorMessage();
    return 1;
}
unsigned int nWindowWidth = rect.right - rect.left;
unsigned int nWindowHeight = rect.bottom - rect.top;
```

You should pass this function the parameters of the window style that are also passed to the CreateWindowEx function:

```
g_hMainWindow = ::CreateWindowEx(  c_dwWndStyleEx,
              c_szClassName,
              TEXT("Tet-a-Tetris"),
              c_dwWndStyle,
              CW_USEDEFAULT,
              CW_USEDEFAULT,
              nWindowWidth,
              nWindowHeight,
              NULL,
              NULL,
              _hInstance,
              NULL );
if(!g_hMainWindow ) {
  ErrorMessage();
  return 1;
  }
```

A *window style* is a set of bit flags specifying how the window should look, whether it should have a border, a caption, and so on. There are so many flags that one 32-bit variable cannot hold all of them. This is why the `CreateWindowEx` function has two flag parameters: `dwStyle` and `dwExStyle`. Perhaps the most important of the window styles is `WS_OVERLAPPED`. It specifies an *overlapped* window, i.e., a common application window. If you use the `WS_CHILD` style, you'll create a *child* window linked to its parent window. As a rule, controls (buttons, lists, input boxes, etc.) have this style of window.

You might have noticed that many system-function names have an `Ex` suffix. This is for historical reasons. When upgrading from the 16-bit Windows version to Win32, Microsoft tried to simplify porting applications to the new platform as much as possible. Most of the Win32 functions are actually Windows 3.1 functions with the types of their arguments upgraded. Their extended versions appeared at the same time. For example, `CreateWindowEx` differs from `CreateWindow` in an additional parameter, `dwExStyle`, which is a set of additional style flags. Because the only purpose of the earlier functions is to provide compatibility, it is preferable to have the latest versions. However, be aware that some Win32 functions only appeared in new Windows versions. For example, Windows XP has many new functions. To avoid compatibility problems, always refer to MSDN Library, which describes each Win32 function and indicates, which Windows versions support it.

So now you created the main window of your application. Its handle, which will come in handy for controlling the window, is stored in the `g_hMainWindow` global variable. Before you proceed, you should call two more functions:

```
::ShowWindow( g_hMainWindow, _idCmdShow );
::UpdateWindow( g_hMainWindow );
```

The first displays the window, because the `CreateWindowEx` function creates an invisible window if the `WS_VISIBLE` style isn't specified. The second parameter of this function is very important. It determines how the window should be displayed (maximized, minimized, or in another way). The system passes this parameter to your program as the fourth argument of the `WinMain` function, and you should pass it to `ShowWindow`. The `UpdateWindow` function redraws the window so that, at last, it appears on the screen.

10.1.4. A Message Loop

The final part of the `WinMain` function is its message loop.

```
MSG msg;
for(;;) {
```

```
int idResult = ::GetMessage( &msg, NULL, 0, 0 );
switch( idResult ) {
case 0:        // WM_QUIT received
    return 0;

case -1:
    ErrorMessage();
    return 1;
}

::TranslateMessage( &msg );
::DispatchMessage( &msg );
}
```

Most of the messages received by your program are sent by the operating system. They contain information about system events such as movements of the mouse pointer, pressing of keys by the user, and so on. You can send your own messages using the SendMessage and PostMessage functions. I'll discuss messages later in this chapter.

The message loop calls two functions repeatedly. The GetMessage function retrieves a message from the system message queue and stores some information about the message in the MSG structure. The DispatchMessage function sends the message further to the function of the window, to which the message is addressed. If the GetMessage function returns zero, this means it has received a special message WM_QUIT, and the message loop (and the application) should terminate.

Why is the message loop required, since the system could arrange such a loop on its own? What's more, some functions, for example, DialogBox, have their own message loops. The point is that you can handle the received messages between the GetMessage and DispatchMessage functions. For example, you call the TranslateMessage function that translates keyboard messages. However, the main handling is carried out by the window function described in the next section.

10.1.5. The Window Function

Almost all interaction between the system and your application is based on exchanging window messages. The system sends messages to your window when the user moves the mouse pointer over it, presses the keys, moves or resizes your window, and so on. Most of the message handling is carried out by the window function specified when registering the window class.

The system passes the window function four parameters. The first parameter is the window handle (this approach allows the function to control several windows). The second is the message code, and the third and fourth contain additional data depending on a particular event. Sometimes, they aren't used at all. The most important parameter is the message code. It determines the contents of the message. For example, when the WM_MOUSEMOVE message (which is sent to a window when the mouse pointer moves in it) is mentioned in an article or a book, the author means a message whose code is WM_MOUSEMOVE. If you open the winuser.h system header file, you'll see that WM_MOUSEMOVE is a preprocessor symbol defined as 0x200.

Jumping ahead a little, I will tell you that you'll handle three messages: WM_CREATE, WM_SIZE, and WM_DESTROY. The first message is sent to a window immediately after it has been created, and the last is sent when the window is about to be destroyed. The WM_SIZE message indicates the resizing of the window. To prevent the window function from becoming too large and incomprehensible, create an individual handler function for each message. Name them OnCreate, OnSize, and OnDestroy:

```
LRESULT __stdcall WindowProc(  HWND _hWnd,
                UINT _idMsg,
                WPARAM _wParam,
                LPARAM _lParam )
{
switch( _idMsg ) {
case WM_CREATE:
    return OnCreate( _hWnd );

case WM_SIZE:
    return OnSize( _hWnd );

case WM_DESTROY:
    return OnDestroy( _hWnd );
}

return ::DefWindowProc( _hWnd, _idMsg, _wParam, _lParam );
}
```

Note that when you don't handle a message on your own, you call the DefWindowProc function. It is a default window message handler that is very useful. For example, when you click the close button in the window caption, the window isn't, as you might expect, destroyed immediately. Instead, the WM_CLOSE message is sent to the window. To destroy the window, you need to call the DestroyWindow function. This is what the DefWindowProc function does when it receives the WM_CLOSE message, because this response is natural for most windows. However, you can change things by handling the WM_CLOSE message on your own. Sometimes, it makes sense to ask the user whether he or she indeed wants to close the application, whether all the data have been saved, and so on. In this program, you'll agree with the standard response of the DefWindowProc function.

I will postpone a description of the OnCreate and OnSize functions till the next section. As for the PostQuitMessage function, you should call it for the WM_DESTROY message. Otherwise, the application won't quit when the window is closed.

```
LRESULT OnDestroy( HWND _hWnd )
{
    ::PostQuitMessage( 0 );
    return 0;
}
```

The PostQuitMessage sends a special message: WM_QUIT. Note that you cannot send it using common functions like PostMessage and SendMessage. When the GetMessage function encounters this message in the queue, it will return zero to terminate the message loop. When the loop terminates, so will the WinMain function, and, therefore, the application will quit.

At this stage, you can compile and run your application. You'll see an empty window. Though it does nothing interesting, your subsequent work will be based on it.

10.2. Working with ActiveX Using ATL

This section describes how to place the Shockwave Flash ActiveX control on the window you created in the previous section, and how to load animation into the control. To do this, use ATL that comes with Microsoft Visual C++ and is intended to make it easier for you to work with COM and OLE and ActiveX components and create your own components.

10.2.1. Linking ATL

Begin with including ATL headers into stdafx.h:

```
//  #define _ATL_DLL_IMPL
#include <atldef.h>
#include <atliface.h>
```

```
#include <atlbase.h>
extern CComModule _Module;
#include <atlcom.h>
```

Authors of articles about ATL usually recommend defining the `_ATL_DLL_IMPL` preprocessor symbol. In this case, some of ATL functions will be called dynamically from the atl.dll library, rather than be directly included in your program. However, the authors often fail to mention that atl.dll will be used by your application in any case. Many ATL functions are called from atl.dll regardless of whether the `_ATL_DLL_IMPL` symbol is defined. Therefore, if you're planning to distribute your program, you should take care that atl.dll is installed with it, if necessary. Fortunately, it only takes up about 70 Kb, and usually doesn't present any problems. Make sure to add atl.lib to the library list for the linker.

The `extern CComModule _Module` line is only necessary for compiling the atlcom.h file. In fact, you won't use the `_Module` variable in your project. It is only necessary when you create your own COM components, which you won't do here.

In your program, you first need to initialize ATL or, more precisely, the part of it responsible for work with ActiveX controls. To do this, call the `AtlAxWinInit` function. Place a call to it at the beginning of the `WinMain` function. Everything is ready now for the creation of an ActiveX control.

10.2.2. Loading the Shockwave Flash ActiveX Control

Now, after you have initialized ATL, it's time to load Shockwave Flash. You have created the main window, so you can create its child controls. The best place for this operation is the handler of the `WM_CREATE` message.

Creating an ActiveX control using ATL is almost the same as creating a common window. Use the same `CreateWindowEx` function you used to create the main window. The only difference is that you should create a child window rather than one that overlaps. This is why you specify the `WS_CHILD` style and make sure to specify the parent window's handle.

```
LRESULT OnCreate( HWND _hWnd )
{
 g_hFlashContainerWindow = ::CreateWindowEx( 0,
                 TEXT("AtlAxWin"),
                 TEXT("ShockwaveFlash.ShockwaveFlash"),
                 WS_CHILD | WS_TABSTOP | WS_VISIBLE,
                 CW_USEDEFAULT,
                 CW_USEDEFAULT,
```

```
                    CW_USEDEFAULT,
                    CW_USEDEFAULT,
                    _hWnd,
                    NULL,
                    g_hInstance,
                    NULL );
    if( !g_hFlashContainerWindow ) {
        ErrorMessage( TEXT("Error! Cannot create Flash control.") );
        return -1;
    }
```

Specify AtlAxWin as a window class. This window class is controlled with ATL, and it was registered when you called the AtlAxWinInit function. (In the latest ATL version that comes with Visual Studio .NET, this class is named AtlAxWin7, but older programs often use the previous name.) Specify the name of the ActiveX control for the window caption. In this case, it is ShockwaveFlash.ShockwaveFlash. Alternatively, you could specify its GUID, but this isn't the best option. The GUID can change after a new Flash version appears. If you want to use the latest Flash Player version installed in the system, specify the name, and the system will determine its GUID on its own.

That did the trick! You can now use this window like any other. For example, to resize or move it, you can use the MoveWindow Win32 API function. Every time the window is resized, it receives the WM_SIZE message. Even when the window size is fixed, as is the case in your project, the window receives this message at least once, immediately after the WM_CREATE message. For the Flash movie to take up the entire window, specify the size of the client area in the handler of the WM_SIZE message, and stretch Flash window so that its takes up the entire client area:

```
LRESULT OnSize( HWND _hWnd )
{
RECT rect;
BOOL isOk = ::GetClientRect( _hWnd, &rect );
if( !isOk ) {
    ErrorMessage();
    return 0;
}

isOk = ::MoveWindow( g_hFlashContainerWindow,
        rect.left,
        rect.top,
        rect.right - rect.left,
```

```
            rect.bottom - rect.top,
            TRUE );
    if( !isOk ) {
        ErrorMessage();
        return 0;
    }


    return 0;
}
```

Of course, since the window should have a fixed size, you could simply specify the size of the Flash control when creating it. I set the size in the WM_SIZE event handler deliberately, to illustrate that you can use common Win32 functions to work with an ActiveX component created using ATL. In addition, this approach allows you to make the window of your application resizable if you wish: Simply add the WS_THICKFRAME parameter to the window style, and a thick frame allowing the user to resize the window will appear.

The window you created is just a container for the ActiveX control. A low-level API for work with ActiveX controls is quite complicated. It contains a dozen *COM (Component Object Model) interfaces*, and some of them should be implemented with the control while others are implemented with its container. This solution is universal, and can be used in any situation. However, it is cumbersome and complicated. This is the case where ATL comes to your aid. It creates a container window that implements all necessary interfaces. From experience, 99 percent of the functionality of low-level ActiveX interfaces isn't claimed, and container windows are convenient to use.

10.2.3. ActiveX and COM Interfaces

So, you have already created the window containing the Flash ActiveX control and know that you can use common functions such as MoveWindow to work with it. However, you also need to control Flash animation. For example, you need to load the SWF file with Tet-a-Tetris first. In addition, you need to prohibit the Flash movie from displaying a pop-up menu in response to a right mouse click. Let's see how you can do this.

While standard controls such as buttons and drop-down lists are managed using window messages, this is not the case with ActiveX controls, for which COM interfaces are used. You shouldn't confuse these with COM ports used to connect modems and older models of computer mice to computers. (Perhaps Microsoft, which brought this technology to the market, decided to name it ActiveX to avoid confusion.) Unfortunately, there is not enough room here to describe COM comprehensively. I'll simply mention that a COM interface is a set of pointers to various functions. It is designed so that a C++ programmer can use virtual functions. Thanks to this, it is easy to use COM interfaces in C++ programs. Each COM interface is defined as a special class that contains nothing but a set of virtual functions. All these functions are always abstract, that is, they aren't implemented in the interface class. The only purpose of the interface is to declare a set of methods, and implementation of the methods is the responsibility of subclasses of COM components. The same interface can be implemented in different component classes. The user of a particular component usually only knows a pointer to the interface. He or she doesn't need to know, which component implements the interface, but can easily use its methods. This allows the programmer to achieve a goal that is only partly achieved by C++: to separate an interface and its implementation completely.

The most important advantage of COM interfaces in comparison to traditional API or window messages is that they are *object-oriented*. Just as you can create multiple instances of one class in C++, you can create as many instances of a COM component as you like. In fact, when you program in C++, you build a COM component as a separate class. As a result, a COM interface is both a pointer to a particular instance of a COM component and a set of methods (functions) for working with it. Not only COM itself is object-oriented, but it is convenient to use it in object-oriented programming.

If you are a novice programmer, you might get frightened by terms such as "virtual function". Don't worry. It is very easy to use COM interfaces. A call to a COM interface method looks exactly like a call to a class method when you know a pointer to this class. Unfortunately, this isn't the case with building COM components that implement interfaces. Though COM is based on simple principles, their combination involves quite a complicated system. When implementing it, a programmer should take into account many of nuances, not all of which even ATL can hide. If you wish to learn this technology in detail, refer to the excellent book *Inside COM*, by Dale Rogerson (Microsoft Press; Bk&CD-Rom edition, Feb. 1, 1997). Fortunately, you won't create your own COM components in this project, but will use ready-made ones instead.

Let's proceed from theory to practice. Shockwave Flash ActiveX implements a special COM interface, called `IshockwaveFlash`, which allows you to control the component. However, you should access it first. This is done in two steps. For the sake of convenience, I implemented them in a separate function:

```
void GetFlash( IShockwaveFlash** _ppFlash )
{
CComPtr<IUnknown> pFlashUnknown;
HRESULT hResult = AtlAxGetControl( g_hFlashContainerWindow,
          &pFlashUnknown );
if( FAILED(hResult) ) {
    ErrorMessage();
    return;
}

hResult = pFlashUnknown.QueryInterface( _ppFlash );
if( FAILED(hResult) ) {
    ErrorMessage();
    return;
}
}
```

The `AtlAxGetControl` ATL function gives you direct access to interfaces of an ActiveX control loaded into a container window. In this code, you pass this function the handle of the window you created earlier.

The `AtlAxGetControl` function returns a result of the HRESULT type. This is typical of almost all COM interface methods, as well as of functions that are not related to COM but are members of an interface. The HRESULT result indicates whether this function terminated successfully. In addition, it can contain some information on errors. To determine the actual result, use special macros SUCCEEDED and FAILED, as shown in this example.

Using the second parameter, the `AtlAxGetControl`, returns you a pointer to the IUnknown interface. This is a special interface that is the basis for any other COM interface. It consists of three methods:

```
struct IUnknown {
public:
  virtual HRESULT STDMETHODCALLTYPE QueryInterface( REFIID riid, void**
ppvObject ) = 0;
  virtual ULONG STDMETHODCALLTYPE AddRef( void ) = 0;
  virtual ULONG STDMETHODCALLTYPE Release( void ) = 0;
};
```

The `AddRef` and `Release` methods are designed for work with a *reference counter*, which every COM component should have. The principle behind the reference counter is simple. When you want to store a pointer to the interface for later use, call the `AddRef` method, which increments the counter by one. When you no longer need the interface, call the `Release` method, which decreases the counter by one. When the counter becomes equal to zero, this means no function needs the object. The object will destroy itself in this case. Such an approach allows you to use the same interface in different parts of your program without the risk that it will be destroyed in an untimely manner.

Compare the reference counter to a common approach used when working with files. Two functions are used: One opens a file, and the other closes it. Suppose that two independent procedures in a program access the same file. You open the file and pass its handle to both procedures. When one of them completes, it shouldn't close the file if it isn't sure that the other procedure doesn't yet need the file. However, when the reference counter is used, the problem is manageable. If two procedures use the same COM interface, each of them calls the `Release` function when it completes and doesn't pay attention to whether the other procedure has completed. (Of course, both procedures should have called `AddRef` when they started.) The object will only be destroyed after both procedures release it.

The reference counter is a convenient and elegant solution for determining the lifetime of an object. However, the flip side of the coin is that this approach requires you to be very careful when using the `AddRef` and `Release` methods directly. If you are not experienced enough, you can unnecessarily call one of these methods or, conversely, fail to do this. At best, such a mistake can result in resource leakage when an unused object remains in the memory. At worst, the program can fail if an object is destroyed in an untimely manner. To avoid mistakes, use the `CComPtr` class, like in this example. It is a special ATL template class of a smart pointer to a COM interface. The most important feature of this class is that it calls the `AddRef` and `Release` methods automatically and prevents mistakes of this kind.

The `CComPtr` class was designed using many C++ tricks such as overloaded operators. This allowed its developers to build the class so that it looks like a common pointer. For example, if you work with a variable of the `CComPtr<IShockwaveFlash>` type, you can imagine it as a variable of the `IShockwaveFlash*` type. You won't notice a difference, at least outwardly. In combination with automatically watching the reference counter, this feature makes it easy and convenient to use the `CComPtr` class.

The third method of the `IUnknown` interface is called `QueryInterface`. It allows you to access any interface supported by the COM component. This is what you want in this case, because `AtlAxGetControl` returned you a pointer to the

`IUnknown` interface, while you need `IShockwaveFlash`. The `QueryInterface` method requires an IID, the ID of the requested interface, as a parameter:

```
hResult = pFlashUnknown->QueryInterface( __uuidof(IShockwaveFlash),
_ppFlash );
```

Note this feature: Because `IUnknown` is a base for any other COM interface, you can access any other interface it supports if you have a pointer to any interface of a COM component.

However, it is convenient to call the `QueryInterface` method through the mediation of the `QueryInterface` method of the `CComPtr` smart pointer, rather than to call it directly. A trick is that it can determine the necessary IID automatically, using C++ type control, so the notation is simpler and shorter:

```
hResult = pFlashUnknown.QueryInterface( _ppFlash );
```

I should note at this point that the `__uuidof` keyword isn't standard for C++, and it isn't a Microsoft extension. It is most likely, therefore, to fail in another compiler. Orthodox C++ programmers that struggle for pure C++ will gnash their teeth when they see this notation. As for me, I always view any extension with suspicion. However, in this case the `uuid` and `__uuidof` keywords are apt and make it easier to work with COM components. At worst, if you need to port your program to another compiler some day, you'll have to edit it slightly. So, if you're planning to work only with Visual C++ in the near future, you can safely use this extension.

Summarizing, to access the `Ishockwaveflash` interface, you should first call the `AtlAxGetControl` function to get the `IUnknown` interface of the ActiveX control, and then call its `QueryInterface` method to get the `IShockwaveFlash` interface itself.

10.2.4. Finding Information about an Interface

In the previous section, I demonstrated how to access the `IShockwaveFlash` interface. Before I proceed with its use, I will tell you how I came to find the interface and its description.

To do this, I used the Visual Studio's OLE/COM Object Viewer tool. It shows you information about all COM components registered in your system. You should find **Shockwave Flash Object** among them easilly. OLE/COM Object Viewer will also show you a list of interfaces supported by the object, including `IShockwaveFlash`. In addition, you'll see a set of standard ActiveX control interfaces, such as `IOleObject`, `IViewObject`, and others. The most interesting fact is that this object is declared in the Flash.ocx type library. Type libraries are intended for use primarily in RAD authoring environments such as Visual Basic. They contain comprehensive information about COM components and their interfaces including descriptions of all methods and their arguments. You can view the library using the same Object Viewer. To open the OCX file, either select the **View TypeLib** menu item or find the library in the list in the **Type Libraries** section and double-click on its name. You'll see classes and interfaces declared in the library.

OLE/COM Object Viewer allows you to save the type library contents in an IDL file. *IDL (Interface Definition Language)* is a specialized programming language for defining COM interfaces. I obtained a Flash.idl file, and placed it together with the other files of this project. Using a specialized compiler, MIDL, which also comes with Visual C++, you can compile this file. Type the following command:

```
MIDL Flash.idl /h Flash.h
```

You'll get a Flash.h header file that C++ compiler can read. This is used in this project.

10.2.5. Loading the Flash Movie

The Flash.idl and Flash.h files contain descriptions of all methods of IShockwaveFlash. Their names are self-explanatory and they are easy to use. Let's start with disabling the pop-up menu:

```
HRESULT hResult = pFlash->put_Menu( VARIANT_FALSE );
if( FAILED(hResult) ) {
  ErrorMessage();
}
```

In a programming language such as Visual Basic, the Flash object would have the Menu property. In fact, an object's property is a pair of methods: one to read the property and the other to write it. In this case, these are get_Menu and put_Menu.

The argument of the put_Menu is a variable of the VARIANT_BOOL type. Note that the "true" and "false" values of this variable are VARIANT_TRUE and VARIANT_FALSE. These constants are defined as –1 and 0, while common TRUE and FALSE are defined as 1 and 0. The latter are used in Win32 functions that have parameters of the BOOL type. Don't confuse these pairs of values!

At last, you can now load the Flash game to your project. You just need to set the Movie property using the put_Movie method:

```
TCHAR szFilePath[MAX_PATH + 1];
if( !MakeFilePath( szFilePath, TEXT("tetatet.swf") ) ) return -1;

CComBSTR bstrFile = szFilePath;
```

```
hResult = pFlash->put_Movie( bstrFile );
if( FAILED(hResult) ) {
  ErrorMessage( TEXT("Error! Cannot open Flash movie.") );
  return -1;
}
```

The tetatet.swf file is in the same folder as the program. I wrote a special function, `MakeFilePath`, which builds a full path to a file from the path to your program and the name of the file. You'll use this function later.

The `Movie` property is of the `BSTR` type. It is a standard string type used in ActiveX interfaces. In system header files, the `BSTR` type is declared as a pointer to a Unicode string. However, you should be aware of one nuance: For system functions to work with `BSTR` correctly, the memory for this string should be allocated using the `SysAllocString` system function. It is convenient to use ATL for this purpose. It offers you the `CComBSTR` class, which is a wrapper for the `BSTR` type. The constructor of this class allocates memory and converts a specified string to Unicode, while the destructor frees the memory up. As a result, your code is simple and compact.

You now know how to include the Shockwave Flash ActiveX control and how to use it. If you compile and run your program, Tet-a-Tetris will start. However, the project isn't complete yet. Although you know how to use this ActiveX control, you need closer interaction between it and your program.

10.3. Handling the ActiveX Component's Events

You now need to learn how to receive and handle events that the ActiveX component sends to your program. More precisely, you'll have to handle the `FSCommand` event sent by Flash.

You cannot get around creating your own C++ class in this part of your program. Because I know that inexperienced programmers often feel uncomfortable working with classes, I have avoided using classes so far, using only global functions and variables instead. But I did this only because I'm providing a training program. In a real-life program, this approach would be inappropriate. You should always include all your functions into classes. If you are a novice programmer, you might think this requirement is too strict. Well, when you group functions related to each other into a class, you make the structure of the program clear and easy-to-understand. Another programmer will read your code easily, and you'll avoid confusion. The clarity of the source code is as important as the performance of the program.

Unfortunately, some beginners stick to this rule thoughtlessly. They go to the other extreme and create classes without necessity, which does nothing to make their programs clearer. The art of creating classes is beyond the scope of this book. Perhaps, only your own experience will allow you to master this art well enough.

10.3.1. Sending Events from the Flash Control to Your Program Shell

Before you proceed, you should know what the events of an ActiveX component are. In fact, they are a COM interface. However, unlike the case with an ordinary interface, such as IShockwaveFlash, this one should be implemented in your program, and the component will call methods of this interface to inform your program about events that occur. Therefore, an event interface is, so to speak, a reverse COM interface.

A component capable of sending events should always implement the special interfaces IConnectionPointContainer and IConnectionPoint. Connecting a handler is always done in two steps. The IConnectionPointContainer::FindConnectionPoint method allows you to get the required connection point by specifying the GUID of the event interface, and the IConnectionPoint::Advise method connects the interface of a particular event receiver to the component. This two-step arrangement allows one component to support multiple different connection interfaces, and multiple clients can connect to each of them. However, you won't call these methods directly in this project.

Consider the interface that Flash will use to inform you about events. This is how it is declared in the IDL file containing the extract from the type library:

```
[
    uuid(D27CDB6D-AE6D-11CF-96B8-444553540000),
    helpstring("Event interface for Shockwave Flash"),
    hidden
]
dispinterface _IShockwaveFlashEvents {
    properties:
    methods:
        [id(0xfffffd9f)]
        void OnReadyStateChange(long newState);
        [id(0x000007a6)]
        void OnProgress(long percentDone);
        [id(0x00000096)]
```

```
        void FSCommand( [in] BSTR command,
                        [in] BSTR args);
};
```

It declares three event functions, including FSCommand, in which we have an interest. If you look at what the MIDL compiler made of this declaration, you might be surprised:

```
MIDL_INTERFACE("D27CDB6D-AE6D-11CF-96B8-444553540000")
_IShockwaveFlashEvents : public IDispatch
{
};
```

This declaration for C++ contains no methods, and the interface seems to be empty. How could this happen?

This is because _IshockwaveFlashEvents is a dispatch interface. It is based on a special interface called Idispatch, and is intended for use by RAD environments, such as Visual Basic, VBScript, and VBA. As a rule, systems of this type cannot directly call methods of COM interfaces for dynamically-linked components. Rather, they use the IDispatch interface that has the Invoke method, which takes the ID of the function being called (the ID is specified in the IDL file) and a set of parameters. The Invoke method performs the required actions. Many interfaces exist in two forms: as an ordinary COM interface, to be called directly using C++ or a similar language, and as an interface based on Idispatch, to be called using a language of the Visual Basic family. Such interfaces are called *dual*. By the way, the IShockwaveFlash interface is one of these. Some interfaces, however, are available only through IDispatch. Most often, these are event interfaces, and _IShockwaveFlashEvents is among them. As you can see, Shockwave Flash ActiveX is designed so that it can be used in RAD authoring environments.

In this project, you'll use an ATL wrapper class that will conceal these details from you. Nevertheless, I am convinced that, even when you use a wrapper, you should understand what is inside. This knowledge will allow you to use ATL classes effectively.

10.3.2. Creating a Handler Class

Now, when you know the structure of the event interface of the Flash control, you can use it in practice. You should implement the _IShockwaveFlashEvents interface and connect it to the control.

While I was writing this training program, I considered two variants. As an alternative to the use of ATL, I could also suggest that you implement the

`_IShockwaveFlashEvents` interface. In any case, you don't need a full-featured COM component, so most methods of the `IDispatch` and `IUnknown` interfaces can be left empty. This variant wouldn't be more complicated than the use of ATL. In addition, it would be a good illustration of the theory presented in the previous section. However, since ATL is a standard for building and using ActiveX and COM components, I have chosen the variant with the wrapper class included in ATL.

Consider what ATL offers for building event handlers based on the `IDispatch` interface. There are two similar template classes: `IDispEventImpl` and `IDispEventSimpleImpl`. They differ in that the first accesses the type library. I suggest that you use the second. It is a little simpler and doesn't require the type library, but you'll have to provide it with some information that the first class retrieves from the type library on its own.

Name the event handler class `ClTetatetFSCommand`. It should look like follows:

```
class ClTetatetFSCommand : public IDispEventSimpleImpl< 0,

ClTetatetFSCommand,

&__uuidof(_IShockwaveFlashEvents)>{
public:    // methods
        void Advise( IShockwaveFlash* _pFlash );
        void Unadvise( void );

public:    // sink map
    BEGIN_SINK_MAP(ClTetatetFSCommand)
        SINK_ENTRY_INFO( 0,
                    __uuidof(IShockwaveFlashEvents),
                    0x00000096,
                    OnFSCommand,
                    &s_atlOnFSCommandInfo )
    END_SINK_MAP()

    void __stdcall OnFSCommand( BSTR _bstrCommand, BSTR _bstrArgs );

private:    // data
    static _ATL_FUNC_INFO s_atlOnFSCommandInfo;

    CComPtr<IShockwaveFlash> m_pFlash;
};
```

Its base class is the `IDispEventSimpleImpl` template class. Note that the template's second parameter is its subclass. This might seem strange, but the construction is valid in C++ and is often convenient. The third parameter is a pointer to the GUID of the event interface. As with the first parameter, it is an identifier to your liking. It is used to allow one class to support several event interfaces. From now on, you should specify it as the first parameter of the `SINK_ENTRY_INFO` macro.

The `Advise` method stores a pointer to the `IShockwaveFlash` interface in the `m_pFlash` variable, because you'll need it when handling events later. Then, the `DispEventAdvise` method belonging to the `IDispEventSimpleImpl` template is called:

```
void ClTetatetFSCommand::Advise( IShockwaveFlash* _pFlash )
{
 m_pFlash = _pFlash;

 DispEventAdvise( _pFlash, &__uuidof(_IShockwaveFlashEvents) );
}
```

The `DispEventAdvise` method connects the event interface to the ActiveX component using the `IConnectionPointContainer` and `IConnectionPoint` interfaces. You can verify this if you find the implementation of this method in ATL header files.

The `Unadvise` method carries out the reverse operation:

```
void ClTetatetFSCommand::Unadvise( void )
{
 if( !m_pFlash ) return;

 DispEventUnadvise( m_pFlash, &__uuidof(_IShockwaveFlashEvents) );

 m_pFlash.Release();
}
```

The `IDispEventSimpleImpl` class requires that its event handler subclass declare a sink map. Special macros are used for this purpose: `BEGIN_SINK_MAP`, `SINK_ENTRY_INFO`, and `END_SINK_MAP`. From the IDL file, you know that the `_IShockwaveFlashEvents` interface supports three kinds of events: `OnReadyStateChange`, `OnProgress`, and `FSCommand`. You'll only need the third. You will also notice that two parameters of the `BSTR` type accompany this event. Therefore, the sink for the `FSCommand` event should be declared as follows:

```
void __stdcall OnFSCommand( BSTR _bstrCommand, BSTR _bstrArgs );
```

Using the `SINK_ENTRY_INFO` macro, this sink is added to the sink map as shown earlier. The parameters of this macro are the following: the identifier specified in the `IDispEventSimpleImpl` template, the interface GUID, the event ID that can be found in the IDL file, the name of the sink method, and a pointer to a structure of the `_ATL_FUNC_INFO` type that declares the sink method. The structure that declares the `OnFSCommand` method should be included in the class as a static member. Name it `s_atlOnFSCommandInfo`. It describes a call convention for your method, the return type, and the number and types of the arguments:

```
_ATL_FUNC_INFO ClTetatetFSCommand::s_atlOnFSCommandInfo = {
CC_STDCALL,
VT_EMPTY,
2,
{ VT_BSTR, VT_BSTR }
};
```

Create a simplified version of the `OnFSCommand` method first. Let it just handle the `test` command and display its argument:

```
void __stdcall ClTetatetFSCommand::OnFSCommand( BSTR _bstrCommand,
  BSTR _bstrArgs )
{
USES_CONVERSION;

if( ::wcscmp( _bstrCommand, L"test" ) == 0 ) {
    const TCHAR* pszArgs = OLE2CT( _bstrArgs );
    ::MessageBox( g_hMainWindow, pszArgs, "test", MB_OK );
    return;
  }
}
```

To convert a BSTR string to a common ASCII string, the `OLE2CT` macro is used. ATL offers you a set of macros for the conversion of strings between ASCII and Unicode. For the macros to work correctly, the `USES_CONVERSION` macro is required at the beginning of the function.

The `ClTetatetFSCommand` class has now been created, and you need to insert it into the main program. For the sake of simplicity, create an instance of this class as a global variable:

```
ClTetatetFSCommand tetatetFSCommandHandler;
```

Include the connection of this event into the `WM_CREATE` event handler immediately following the point where the ActiveX control is created:

```
LRESULT OnCreate( HWND _hWnd )
{
...
```

```
// Creating the ActiveX control as described earlier
...
CComPtr<IShockwaveFlash> pFlash;
GetFlash( &pFlash );
if( !pFlash ) return -1;
tetatetFSCommandHandler.Advise( pFlash );
...
}
```

The last thing to implement is the disconnection of the event handler as a response to the WM_DESTROY message. Otherwise, the program won't be able to quit correctly:

```
LRESULT OnDestroy( HWND _hWnd )
{
tetatetFSCommandHandler.Unadvise();

::PostQuitMessage( 0 );
return 0;
}
```

Done! You can compile the program and see how the test command works.

As you see, passing events from ActiveX elements to a shell program isn't simple. Unfortunately, the ATL that conceals low-level details offers an arrangement that is no less complicated. However, if you don't understand this approach completely, you can use this example as a base for your other programs.

10.4. Creating a Shell for Tet-a-Tetris

So you have learned methods for including the Flash ActiveX control in your program. You have built a base program, included the Shockwave Flash control in it, and learned how to use it and receive events from it. The last thing you have to do is upgrade the program and implement functions required by Tet-a-Tetris.

Most of upgrading is related to responses to commands received with the FSCommand event. So let's upgrade the sink method for this event:

```
void __stdcall ClTetatetFSCommand::OnFSCommand( BSTR _bstrCommand,
                      BSTR _bstrArgs )
{
if( ::wcscmp( _bstrCommand, L"exit" ) == 0 ) {
    VERIFY( ::PostMessage( g_hMainWindow, WM_CLOSE, 0, 0 ) );
```

```
        return;
    }

    if( ::wcscmp( _bstrCommand, L"readname" ) == 0 ) {
        OnReadName();
        return;
    }

    if( ::wcscmp( _bstrCommand, L"savename" ) == 0 ) {
        OnSaveName( _bstrArgs );
        return;
    }

    if( ::wcscmp( _bstrCommand, L"savetopten" ) == 0 ) {
        OnSaveTopTen( _bstrArgs );
        return;
    }

    if( ::wcscmp( _bstrCommand, L"gettopten" ) == 0 ) {
        OnGetTopTen();
        return;
    }
}
```

Because the commands are received as Unicode strings, the wcscmp function, which is a Unicode version of the strcmp function, is used. The string constants have an L prefix, so the compiler create them in the Unicode format.

At the exit command, the handler sends the main window the WM_CLOSE message, which is equivalent to clicking the close button in the window caption. You could close the window immediately using the DestroyWindow function. However, sending the WM_CLOSE message allows you to use its handler if necessary. The handler isn't defined in this example, but you could write it, for example, to ask the user whether he or she indeed wants to close the game.

To avoid complicating the OnFSCommand method, the other command handlers are separated into individual functions. Because I described the handling techniques earlier, it makes no sense to present the source code for these functions. I'll describe their functionality briefly.

At the readname command, the handler should read the user's name and registration key from the tetatet.k file, check them for validity, and send them to Flash inside the namekey1 variable. The tetatet.k file has a fixed size of 40 bytes, 30 of which are allocated for the user's name, and 10 for the key. They should be sent to Flash in another format: as one string containing the name and key separated with the '|' character. The savename command performs the reverse operation. It saves the name and key in the file.

The gettopten and savetopten commands are used to read and write the tetatet.top file that contains the top ten results achieved by gamers. To prevent gamers from changing the data in this file, the results are encrypted using a simple algorithm. They are stored in the file as a sequence of alternated strings with names and scores separated with the '|' characters. In this format, they are received along with the savetopten command, and the only thing the handler should do is encrypt this string and write it to the file. This information is sent back to Flash in another format: as two individual strings for the names and scores (and the sound indicator variable appended). Therefore, at the gettopten command, the handler should read and decrypt the file and perform the required format conversion.

The tetatet.top file contains an indicator of whether sound is enabled in the game. When the game terminates, you should check whether the indicator has been changed by the user, and correct its value in the tetatet.top file if it was. This is done with the SaveSoundFlag method called from the main window as a response to the WM_DESTROY message.

You can study details of these functions if you open the example project located in the Examples\Chapter 10 folder on the CD-ROM.

Summarizing, this example program illustrates all the main stages of work with the ISockwaveFlash ActiveX control: creating the control, managing it using the ISockwaveFlash COM interface, and receiving and handling Flash events sent via the _IShockwaveFlashEvents interface. ATL is used at each stage. Using the techniques described in this chapter, you can create your own programs that use Shockwave Flash and other ActiveX controls.

For required information, refer to *Chapter 9.*

Chapter 11: Nim: Programming a Logical Game

This chapter will teach you how to skim through variants of moves when looking for the best move, how to limit the depth of this skimming, and how to implement heuristic algorithms.

11.1. A Description of Nim

A game where the players removed little stones from several groups, taking any number of stones from one group at a time, was known of as long ago as in ancient China. I'll describe a variant of this game, called Nim. There are three groups of three, four, and five pieces each. Two players take turns removing the pieces. A player can remove anywhere from one to all of the pieces from one group. The player who removes the last piece wins.

   This game was popular in Europe and America about 100 years ago. Men played it in bars with coins laid out in three rows, and the loser paid for the next whisky or beer. However, at the beginning of 20th century, an American mathematician found a method to determine whether a particular position is winning, and to find the best move if this is the case. To prevent you from being disappointed,

I won't disclose the winning strategy. Few people know it, and the value of Nim is that it allows me to demonstrate how you can create a function that skims through moves and finds the winning move, if it exists. Since my site is called **GameIntellect.com**, I'm compelled to teach you how to write this game. The program will play fair: It will skim through variants like a human would do. When you learn how to skim through the possible moves in your program, you'll be able to write similar programs playing other intellectual games. If you fail, you can ask me for advice.

Unlike Java, C, Delphi, and other authoring environments, Macromedia Flash doesn't offer you many tools for writing "thinking" game programs. Like JavaScript, Perl, and PHP, ActionScript is an interpreted language, and its code is executed tens, or even hundreds times slower than a common program. Java applets are processed by browsers using JIT (Just In Time) compilers. They translate Java bytecode into processor code, and a Java applet works as quickly as a Windows application. However, ActionScript bytecode is executed by Flash player. If code attached to a frame or an object is executed for longer than 15 seconds, Flash Player will display the window shown in Fig. 11.1.

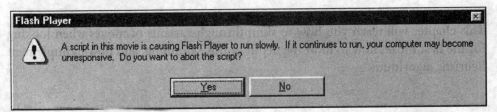

Fig. 11.1. Flash Player's message

The message will appear every 15 seconds while the program computes without moving the playing head to another frame. This window indicates that the script hampers Flash Player, and the player "suspects" that the script has entered an infinite loop. A click on the **No** button will continue the execution of the script, but does the user want to click on the button every 15 seconds? This is why your program should think over its move within 14 seconds. You'll avoid these problems if moves are thought over by a shell while the Flash movie just displays them. You already know how to write a shell. For online games, however, you'll have to optimize the thinking function so that it conforms to actual connection conditions.

11.2. Preparing Game Graphics

Start a new project and name it nim.fla. Open the **Document Properties** panel by double-clicking on the **12.0 fps** panel located below the timeline, and set the movie size to 385 × 375 pixels. Set the frame rate to 19 fps. I advise you to choose the background color after you finish the project. It would be best to have the color match that of your home page. Press the <Shift>+<F2> shortcut, and re-name the scene **Game**.

Select the third frame on the main timeline, and press <F6>. Attach the fol-lowing code to the second frame (which is also a key frame):

```
if (!_totalframes || _framesloaded != _totalframes) gotoAndPlay(1);
```

This code should be familiar to you. Attach the following code to the third frame:

```
#include "nim.as"
```

The main program will be contained in a separate file, named nim.as.

11.2.1. A Game Board Square

Start creating graphics with a square of the game board. Let its side be 70 pixels long. However, create the square's shadow first. Create a new clip, name it square (<Ctrl>+<F8>), and export this name for ActionScript. Select the **Rectangle** tool and disable the outline. (To do this, select **Stroke Color** on the toolbar, and click on the crossed square with the **No Color** hint). Select the #666666 fill color. While keeping the <Shift> key pressed, draw a square with a side of 70 pixels. To know the precise values, use the **Info** panel or this square's property panel. To use the latter, select the square, and press the <Ctrl>+<F3> shortcut. Center the square using the <Ctrl>+<Alt>+<2> and <Ctrl>+<Alt>+<5> short-cuts, and move it 5 pixels down and to the right. This can be done with the right and down arrow keys. Now, draw the board square itself. For its outline, select the #3399FF color and a **Solid** line, two-pixel thick. Select the **Radial** fill. To do this, open the **Color Mixer** panel (using the <Shift>+<F9> shortcut), make the left marker white, and select the #878787 color for the right marker. Draw a square on an unused place, and set its size to 70 × 70 pixels. Center the square in the same way as its shadow. (The square should partially overlap the shadow.) Adjust the fill so that its center is from 8 pixels to 10 pixels above and to the left of the center of the square, as shown in Fig. 11.2.

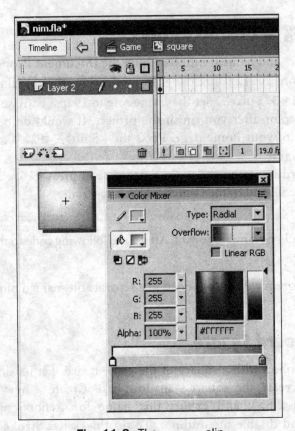

Fig. 11.2. The `square` clip

NOTE

You could create the shadow on a separate layer under the square, and this would allow you to move it from behind the square so that it is seen a little. Then you would select the square and move it to the layer with the shadow using the **Edit | Paste in Place** menu command. However, a piece shouldn't have a shadow below it. This would spoil the impression of the piece's disappearance, because the pieces in this game disappear by gradually increasing their transparency.

11.2.2. A Piece

Create a new clip, name it `piece`, and also export this name for ActionScript. First create a shadow with the same color as the square shadow. It should be a circle with a diameter of 55 pixels. Center it and move it four or five pixels down and to the right. Draw a circle without an outline on an unused place, and center it in the same way you centered the square. Select the **Radial** fill. Set the left and right markers to the colors #66CCFF and #0066FF, respectively. Shift the fill center in the same way as with the square.

To create a **Shape** animation, in which the piece disappears after the gamer removes it from the board, select the fifth frame on the timeline and make it a key frame, by pressing the <F6> key. In the fifth frame, select only the piece, so that its fill is displayed in the **Color Mixer** window, and set the **Alpha** parameter to 30 percent, using the slider. You will need to set the opacity of 30% for both markers at the gradient bar, by clicking on them. Repeat this with the shadow.

The **Shape** animation type is selected in the drop-down list in the property panel of the selected object. Select all the frames and set animation for them. The animated frames on the timeline will acquire a green background, and an arrow from the first to the fifth frame will appear. All that remains now is to write some code. Select the first frame and attach the following code to it:

```
stop();
```

Attach the following code to the fifth frame:

```
this.removeMovieClip();
```

You should remember this code from Tet-a-Tetris.

11.2.3. Buttons

You should now create three buttons that differ only in their labels. Create a new button with the name btNewGame without exporting for ActionScript. Create a shadow for this button. It should be a rectangle, 61-pixel wide and 36-pixel high, with the #666666 color, and with a corner radius equal to four. Draw such a rectangle, center it, and move it 4 pixels down and to the right. As for the fill, it should be of the **Linear** type, and its left and right markers on the **Color Mixer** should have the #0066FF color, the central marker having the #61D7FE color. There should be no outline. Draw a rectangle of the same size as the shadow and center it. The New game text should take up two lines. Select the following settings for the text: the **Static Text** type, the **Tahoma** font, a font size of 12 pts, the bold typeface, the **Align Center** alignment, the **Use Device Fonts** checkbox unchecked, and the #FF6600 color. Click the **Edit format options** button and set all the values on the **Format Options** panel to zero. Type the text on the button, move to the **Over** frame, and press <F6> to create a key frame. Select the text on the button, and change its color to #FFFF00. Create two more buttons, btOK and btYou, in the same manner. The first should bear the **OK** text, and the second should have the text **Comp. begins** over two lines. For the **OK** text, set **Letter Spacing** to three to move the letters apart (this input box is located immediately below the **Font** drop-down list).

My btNewGame button is shown in Fig. 11.3.

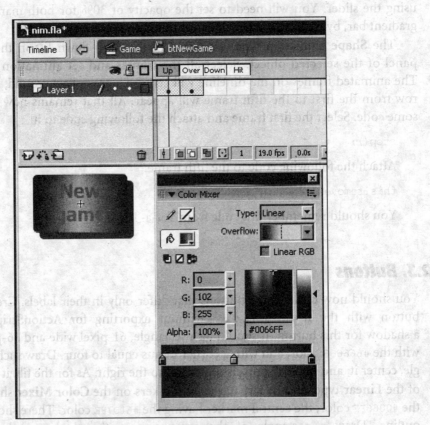

Fig. 11.3. The btNewGame button (magnified two times)

Drag these buttons from the library to the work area or, more precisely, to the third frame. Set their coordinates as follows: X = 12 for the btOK button, X = 99 for the btYou button, X = 183 for the btNewGame button, and Y = 325 for all the buttons.

The purpose of these buttons is following: The btOK button is used for configuration of the gamer's move; the btYou button is used to let the computer make the first move; and the btNewGame button is used to start a new game at any moment. Attach the following code to the buttons:

```
on (release)
    { userMove();
    }
```

to the btOK button,

```
on (release)
  { youBegin();
  }
```

to the btYou button, and

```
on (release)
    { newGame();
    }
```

to the btNewGame button.

These functions (and many others) will be written later.

11.2.4. An Empty Clip for Event Handling

Create another empty clip and name it gameact. You'll attach an event handler to it later. Don't export the clip name for ActionScript. In the third frame of the main timeline, drag this clip to an unused place on the movie work area, or even outside this area. Set the **Instance Name** parameter to gameact. You should remember that this is done on the property panel of the selected object, and the panel is opened using the <Ctrl>+<F3> shortcut.

11.2.5. Clips for Messages

Create four identical clips to display messages.

☐ gameover — With the **Game Over!** text
☐ think — With the **Thinking...** text
☐ youlost — With the **You lose** text
☐ youwon — With the **You win!** text

Rectangles with these labels should have shadows, and you already know how to create them. You can draw shadows in a separate layer. This will allow you to adjust the clip size to a shorter or longer label. The rectangles should have rounded corners, no outlines, yellow (#FFFF99) fill color, and the #6666FF text color. The text font should be **Tahoma, 24 pts, Static Text, bold, Align Center**. The registration points of all the clips should be in the upper left corner. The gameover clip's rectangle should be 170-pixel wide, and the other rectangles should have a width of 150 pixels. All the rectangles are 50-pixel high.

The gameover clip is shown in Fig. 11.4.

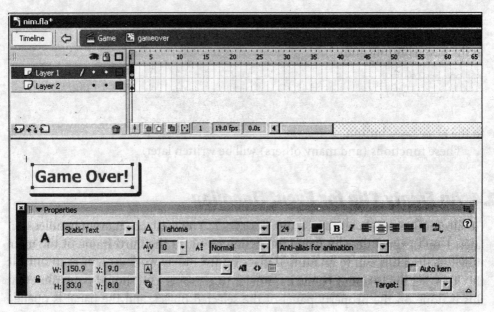

Fig. 11.4. The gameover clip

11.2.6. A Clip for Marking Pieces

What else do you need to allow players to make moves? They should be able to mark pieces they want to be removed from the board after a click on the btOK button. Create a clip for this purpose and name it mark. It should be a semi-transparent circle with a cross (Fig. 11.5).

To create this clip, press the <Ctrl>+<F8> shortcut, set the mark name, and check the **Export for ActionScript** checkbox. Select a line width of 3 pixels, the #FF6600 color, and **Alpha** equal to 50 percent. Using the **Oval** tool, draw a circle with a diameter of 25 pixels (be sure to keep the <Shift> button pressed). Align the circle with the center of the work area. Draw a cross with the same line width. If your cross juts out of the circle, trim it using the <Del> key.

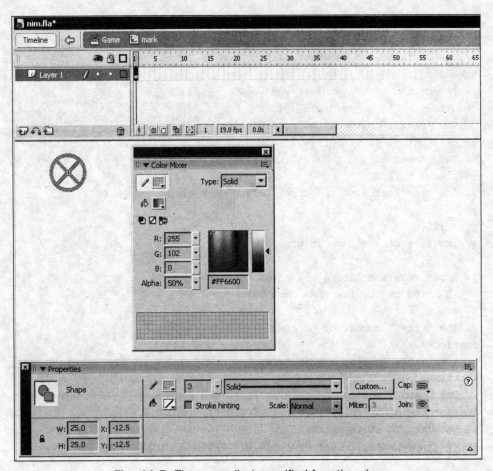

Fig. 11.5. The `mark` clip (magnified four times)

11.3. Writing Auxiliary Functions

Create a nim.as file in the project folder, and open it in a text editor.

11.3.1. The Data Section of the Program

Let's start writing the program with the data section (Listing 11.1).

Listing 11.1. The data section of the program

```
var
  // The depth of the think clip
  thinkdepth = 1,
  // The depth of the gameover clip
  gameoverdepth = 1,
  // The depths of the youlost and youwon clips
  resultdepth = gameoverdepth + 1,
  // The initial depth of the square clips
  squaredepth = resultdepth + 1,
  // The number of the squares (and pieces) on the board
  maxpieces = 12,
  // The coordinates of the upper left square clip
  x0 = 50,
  y0 = 125,
  // The size of a square in pixels
  sqx = 70,
  // A variable indicating who makes the move
  // (0 - the gamer, 1 - the computer)
  mymove,
  // The current number of pieces
  numpieces,
  // A variable setting a time delay
  waittime,
  // The board (3 groups containing 3, 4, and 5 pieces)
  board = new Array([0,0,0,0,0], [0,0,0,0,0], [0,0,0,0,0]),
  // An array to store marks
  marked = new Array([0,0,0,0,0], [0,0,0,0,0], [0,0,0,0,0]);
```

I believe you understand the purpose of the variables from the comments. I'll describe them in more detail later.

11.3.2. The Code of the Main Program (without Functions)

Leave three empty lines after the data section and enter the code of the main program (Listing 11.2).

Listing 11.2. The main program

```
//*** The main program ***
// Draw the board.
var sdepth = squaredepth;
for (var i = 0; i < 3; i++)
 for (var j = 0; j < 5; j++)
  { if (j < i + 3)
     { attachMovie('square', 'square' + j + i, sdepth);
       eval('square' + j + i)._x = x0 + sqx*j;
       eval('square' + j + i)._y = y0 + sqx*i;
     }
    ++sdepth;
  }
newGame();
stop();
```

This code needs some explanation. First, it draws 12 squares that will remain untouched during the game. There can be pieces on the squares, so you'll attach a piece to a square using the `attachMovie` function. In addition, there can be markers put on the pieces by the gamer. So you have three clips, two of which are attached to the master clip. The `board` and `marked` arrays have five elements in each line, but only the first three elements are used in the first line, and four used in the second. (Generally, ActionScript allows you to declare different dimensions for an array.) To make the program simpler, let's assign depths to the squares as if there are five elements in each line. That is, the first square in the upper line has a depth of `sdepth = squaredepth`, the depth of its neighbor to the right is greater by one, the depth of the first square in the second line is `sdepth + 5`, and that of the first square in the third line is `sdepth + 10`. This is why the `++sdepth` statement is located outside the conditional statement. You should name the squares so that it is easy to attach pieces to squares and markers to pieces in a loop. So the square in the `i`th line and `j`th column should be named `'square' + j + i`. For example, the first square will have the name `square00`, and the last will have the name `square42`. This is done in the following statement:

```
attachMovie('square', 'square' + j + i, sdepth);
```

The `if (j < i + 3)` condition "cuts off" unused elements in the first two lines.

The statements

```
eval('square' + j + i)._x = x0 + sqx*j;
eval('square' + j + i)._y = y0 + sqx*i;
```

assign each newly-created square coordinates in pixels, computed from its logical coordinates j and i. The eval('square' + j + i) function returns a reference to the square object, given its name.

After all the squares are arranged, the newGame function is called, and the stop() command is given. The command will stop the movie in the third frame to prevent it from playing cyclically from the first frame to the third. (You might remember that you attached this command to a main timeline frame in Tet-a-Tetris.)

11.3.3. Functions of the Main Program

Put the functions from Listings 11.3—11.7 between the data section and the main program. However, the order of the functions isn't important in ActionScript.

Listing 11.3. The showThinking function

```
// Displays "Thinking..." when arg != 0
// and hides when arg == 0.
function showThinking(arg)
{ if (arg)
   { attachMovie('think', 'think', thinkdepth);
     think._x = 185;
     think._y = 12;
   }
   else think.removeMovieClip();
}
```

Listing 11.4. The showGameOver function

```
// Displays "Game over" when arg != 0
// and hides when arg == 0.
   function showGameOver(arg)
   { if (arg)
      { attachMovie('gameover', 'gameover', gameoverdepth);
        gameover._x = 185;
        gameover._y = 12;
      }
      else gameover.removeMovieClip();
   }
```

Listing 11.5. The showResult function

```
// When arg == 0, hides the "You lost" or "You won" text.
// When arg == 1, displays "You lost".
// When arg == 2, displays "You won".
function showResult(arg)
{ var names = new Array('', 'youlost', 'youwon');

  if (!arg)
    { youlost.removeMovieClip();
      youwon.removeMovieClip();
    } else
    { attachMovie(names[arg], names[arg], resultdepth);
      var name = eval(names[arg]);
      name._x = 12;
      name._y = 12;
    }
}
```

Listing 11.6. The thinking function

```
// Displays "Thinking..." and calls the computerMove function
// after a delay of 1,500 ms.
function thinking()
{ if (getTimer() < waittime) return;
  showThinking(1);
  waittime = getTimer() + 1500;
  gameact.onEnterFrame = computerMove;
}
```

This function is called before the computer starts thinking over its move. Delays before and after the appearance of the **Thinking...** text are necessary to avoid displaying the text and making a move almost simultaneously.

Listing 11.7. The youBegin function

```
// This is called after the gamer releases the mouse button
// on the "Comp begins" button.
function youBegin()
{ if (numpieces == maxpieces)
```

```
// If all pieces are on the board, make a random move.
anyMove();
}
```

If the computer makes the first move, the function checks whether all pieces are on the board. When this is the case, it calls the anyMove function (Listing 11.8) to make a random move. If the program computed all variants before the first move, it would always win (at least in this position, and with these rules), so the gamer would see the **You lose** message instantly. Our program is friendly, and it warns the gamer, who will inevitably lose, that he or she can start a new game.

Listing 11.8. The anyMove function

```
// Making a random move
function anyMove()
{ var i, j, k, rows = new Array(0, 0, 0);

  // Assigning the rows array the number of pieces in three rows
  for (i = 0; i < 3; i++)
   for (j = 0; j < i + 3; j++)
    rows[i] += board[i][j];
  // Finding the row with the maximum number of pieces
  i = 2;
  if (rows[1] > rows[2]) i = 1;
  if (rows[0] > rows[1]) i = 0;
  // Removing k pieces from the ith row
  k = 2;
  if (rows[i] < 3 || Math.random() < 0.67) k = 1;
  for (j = 0; j < i + 3; j++)
   if (board[i][j])
    { showPiece(0, j, i);
      if (!--k) break;
    }
  // The gamer's move
  mymove = 0;
  // Hide "Thinking..."
  showThinking(0);
}
```

You should be careful when making a random move. It is desirable to avoid positions that the gamer can easily analyze. Therefore, the computer should delete few pieces, for example, one or two, and shouldn't leave empty rows after its move. Later, when you learn how to skim through variants, you'll know another method for making a "good" random move. In this function, you declare an array of three elements and assign them the numbers of pieces in each row. Then you assign the i variable the number of the row with the maximum number of pieces. You then call the Math.random method of the Math object to decide whether one or two pieces should be removed. The computer removes one piece when the ith row contains less than three pieces or when the Math.random method returns a number less than 0.67 (the probability of which is 2/3). A loop then iterates through all the pieces in the ith row:

```
for (j = 0; j < i + 3; j++)
if (board[i][j])
    { showPiece(0, j, i);
      if (!--k) break;
    }
```

The loop finds a square with a piece (board[i][j]) and removes the piece by calling the showPiece function (Listing 11.9). It then subtracts one from the k variable and terminates when k becomes equal to zero.

Listing 11.9. The showPiece function

```
// Shows the piece with the (x, y) coordinates when arg != 0
// and hides the pieces when arg == 0.
function showPiece(arg, x, y)
{ var
    // The reference to the square containing the piece
    name = eval('square' + x + y);

  if (arg)
    { // Attaching the piece to the square (the piece depth is 1)
      name.attachMovie('piece', 'piece', 1);
      // Computing a reference to the piece clip from the piece name
      name = eval('name.piece');
      // placing the piece in the center of the square
      name._x = 0;
      name._y = 0;
```

```
    // Store the coordinates of the piece in its properties j and i
    // to compute the coordinates when the gamer clicks on the piece.
    name.j = x;
    name.i = y;
    // Each piece will pass its coordinates from the j and i
    // properties to the rel function.
    name.onRelease = function()
      { rel(this.j, this.i);
      }
    // Creating a piece logically removing a piece from the board
    board[y][x] = 1;
  } else
  { // The piece gradually disappears.
    --numpieces;
    board[y][x] = marked[y][x] = 0;
// The piece disappears gradually.
    eval('name.piece').play();
  }
}
```

The following fragment of the showPiece function needs some explanation:

```
name.j = x;
name.i = y;
// Each piece will pass its coordinates from the j and i
// properties to the rel function.
name.onRelease = function()
{ rel(this.j, this.i);
}
```

When you create an instance of the piece clip, you add the j and i properties to it. Thanks to this, each instance of the piece clip stores its board coordinates (j is the column number, and i is the row number, where numbering begins from zero). In addition, a handler of the mouse-release event is created for each piece instance. As a result, when a gamer releases the mouse button on a piece, it passes the rel function its coordinates, to inform the main program, which piece is clicked. You could implement computation of coordinates in another way, by finding the pixel coordinates of the mouse pointer when the user releases the mouse button, and converting these to the logical coordinates of a square of the board. However, you would also have to check whether there is a piece on the square. The solution where the piece tells its coordinates on its own is more convenient.

After the piece is removed, numpieces is decremented by one, zeroes are assigned to the appropriate elements of the board and marked arrays, and the play method of the appropriate piece is called. The piece gradually disappears from the board and destroys itself along with its onRelease event handler, using the ActionScript code attached to the piece.

Listing 11.10. The newGame function

```
// Preparing for a new game
function newGame()
{ var i, j;

  for (var i = 0; i < 3; i++)
   for (var j = 0; j < 5; j++)
    if (j < i + 3) showPiece(1, j, i);
  // Setting the current number of pieces to the maximum number
  numpieces = maxpieces;
  // The gamer can make a move.
  mymove = 0;
  // Hiding the clip with the result
  showResult(0);
  // Hiding the gameover clip
  showGameOver(0);
}
```

The function in Listing 11.10 puts the pieces by calling the showPiece function, hides any messages, and allows the gamer to make the first move.

Listing 11.11. The rel function

```
// This function is called when the gamer releases the mouse button
// on any piece. It takes the coordinates of the piece: x and y.
function rel(x, y)
{ // If this is the computer's move, return.
  if (mymove) return;
  // Is the piece in the x column and the y row marked?
  if (marked[y][x])
   { // Removing the mark clip from the piece
     eval('square' + x + y + '.piece.mark').removeMovieClip();
```

```
    // Removing the mark logically
    marked[y][x] = 0;
    return;
  }
// The gamer clicked on an unmarked piece. Checking for marked
// pieces in the other rows
for (var i = 0; i < 3; i++)
  { // Skipping the current row
    if (i == y) continue;
    for (var j = 0; j < i + 3; j++)
    // A marked piece is found in another row. The attempt
    // at an illegal move is ignored.
    if (marked[i][j]) return;
  }
// Marking the piece and
// finding a reference to the required clip from its name
var name = eval('square' + x + y + '.piece');
// Attaching the mark clip to the piece (whose depth is 1)
name.attachMovie('mark', 'mark', 1);
// Getting a reference to the mark clip instance
name = eval('name.mark');
// Putting it in the center of the piece
name._x = 0;
name._y = 0;
// Marking the piece logically
marked[y][x] = 1;
}
```

Listing 11.11 contains the `rel` function that is called from the `onRelease` event handlers attached to every piece. If the piece that passed its coordinates to `rel` is marked, the function should remove the mark from the piece. In other words, it should remove the `mark` clip attached to the piece, and set `marked[y][x]` to zero. The `mark` clip can be accessed using its full name `eval('square' + x + y + '.piece.mark').removeMovieClip()`. Here, `'square' + x + y` is the name of the square on the board. Appending the `'.piece'` string to this name gives you the name of the piece on this square. If you append `'.mark'` to the result, you'll get access to the instance of the `mark` clip attached to the piece. When you know the name of an object, you can call the `eval` function to obtain a reference to the object, and use its methods and properties.

If the gamer clicked an unmarked piece, the function should mark it by attaching an instance of the mark clip to the piece. The function should first, however, check for marked pieces in the other rows. If the check is successful, the function gets a reference to the instance of the piece: name = eval('square' + x + y + '.piece'). It then uses the name reference to get a reference to the instance of the mark clip attached to the piece: name = eval('name.mark'). You might be surprised, but this code, where the name reference is inside a string, works correctly.

Generally speaking, when you attach a piece to a square and a mark to a piece, you don't need to set their coordinates to zeroes, because these are default values. However, you can test this code, for example, by setting the _x property of the mark clip to ten: name._x = 10. You'll see that the marks on the pieces move ten pixels to the right.

Listing 11.12. The userMove function

```
// The user's move
// This function is called when the btOK button is clicked.
function userMove()
{ var flag = 0;

  // If this is the computer's move, exit the function.
  if (mymove) return;
  // Removing all the marked pieces
  for (var i = 0; i < 3; i++)
   for (var j = 0; j < i + 3; j++)
    if (marked[i][j])
    { showPiece(0, j, i);
      // Setting an indication that at least one piece was removed
      flag = 1;
    }
  // If there were no move, nothing happens.
  if (flag)
   { if (!numpieces)
     // There are no pieces left. The game is over.
     { // You won!
       showResult(2);
       // Game over
       showGameOver(1);
       return;
```

```
    }
    // It is the computer's move now.
    mymove = 1;
    // The thinking function will start in 0.1 second.
    // It will display "Thinking..."
    gameact.onEnterFrame = thinking;
    waittime = getTimer() + 100;
  }
}
```

After the gamer marks pieces to be removed, he or she clicks the btOK button. However, some people can click this button needlessly, just for fun. The userMove function (Listing 11.12) foresees both situations. While removing the marked pieces in the loop, the function sets the flag variable indicating whether at least one piece was removed. Then it examines the indicator. If no pieces were removed, the function does nothing. Otherwise, it checks whether the game is over by analyzing the numpieces variable. If the variable is equal to zero, the gamer has won. Otherwise, it is the computer's turn to make a move. The function calls the thinking function, which calls the computerMove function. Both calls are made after delays, so that the **Thinking...** text isn't displayed simultaneously with the disappearance of the piece.

11.4. Computing and Making Moves

To be able to play with your program, you only need to implement the last two functions: computerMove, which makes a move, and an auxiliary function, isWin, which determines whether a given move is winning. The latter function will analyze the position after the move. This function is the most important, though very small. Without it, the program would make random pointless moves. Interaction between these two functions is the following: The computerMove function skims through all possible moves in the current position. It passes the resulting positions to the isWin function, asking it whether the position is winning. If isWin answers: "Yes", the computerMove function makes the move and allows the gamer to make his or hers. If no winning move is found, the anyMove function that makes a random move is called.

In which form is the position passed to the isWin function? Only three variables are necessary for describing a position. They should store the numbers of pieces in each row. Indeed, the locations of the pieces in the columns are insignificant.

For the sake of convenience, these variables are combined in an array, although working with indexed variables is slower than with scalar ones.

Before I show you the `isWin` function, I should digress. This function calls itself, and the functions like this have not been presented in the book so far.

11.4.1. Recursive Functions

Recursive functions call themselves either directly, in their bodies, or indirectly, via chains of calls to other functions. In any case, you enter a recursive function before you exit it.

At the dawn of computer technology, not all high-level programming languages included recursive functions. ActionScript does, but it limits the recursion depth to 256 levels. At the 256th level, the interpreter suspects that the recursion is infinite, and stops execution. For this project, 256 levels are enough, because there will never be more than 12 moves in the game. You'll never go deeper than the 12th level. In addition, the 15-second time limit will be exhausted before the recursion limit is reached.

When describing recursive functions, many authors use the computation of a factorial as an example. (A factorial is a product of all natural numbers from 1 to N: $N! = 1 \times 2 \times \ldots \times N$). It is easy to implement a factorial using a simple loop. However, not all of recursive functions can be rewritten as loops. In ActionScript, factorial computation looks as follows:

```
function fact(n)
{ if (n < 2) return 1;
  return n*fact(n - 1);
}
```

Surprisingly, it works very quickly, even if you specify

```
trace(fact(100));
```

If you specify a greater value, say, 255, the result will be `Infinity`. If you specify

```
trace(fact(256));
```

you'll see the following message in the **Output** window:

```
256 levels of recursion were exceeded in one action list.
This is probably an infinite loop.
Further execution of actions has been disabled in this movie.
```

I mentioned this situation earlier.

Consider an example of how this function works. Let n be three. If you put `trace(n);` at the beginning of the function, you'll see the following output:

```
3
2
1
6
```

The last line, 6, is the result of computation. At the first call, the `fact` function "sees" that n isn't less than two, and executes the `3*fact(2)` statement. The second call is made with the 2 argument, so the `2*fact(1)` is executed. At the third level of recursion, the function doesn't need to call itself, and returns one. However, it returns this value to itself, to the previous level, rather than to the main program. At this level, the `2*fact(1)` expression turns into `2*1`, and is computed. The result, which is two, is returned to the upper level. The `3*fact(2)` expression becomes `3*2`, and is computed. The result is passed to the `trace` function that displays it.

This might seem too complicated. The human brain cannot think recursively, and it often fails to remember the return point if the recursion level is three or greater. As for the computer processor, it manages recursion easily and doesn't develop a headache.

Now let's return to the project, and apply recursion to the search of the best move. The `isWin` function takes a game position as a parameter and returns one, if the position is wining. If not, it returns zero. To do this, `isWin` declares a local array to store the position. Like other local variables, the array belongs to the current instance of `isWin`. Before the function returns control (to itself), the memory allocated for its local variables is freed up. The execution will continue with local variables of the outer instance of `isWin`, which called its copy. Of course, the code of the `isWin` function isn't duplicated, but new memory is only allocated for local variables.

After `isWin` receives the current position from itself or from the `computerMove` function, it skims through all possible moves in this position and obtains the positions that emerge after the moves. It calls itself repeatedly, passing itself the obtained positions. As a result, a called copy of `isWin` analyzes the position stored in the local array of the calling copy of this function. Suppose `isWin` makes a move, calls itself, passing its local array to the called copy, and receives 1. What is the conclusion? Is the position in the array winning? Nothing of the kind. Surprised? I'll explain this. When `isWin` receives a position, it makes the moves for the opponent of the caller copy. For the opponent to win, he or she should have a winning move in the position. If there is at least one winning move (the called `isWin` function returned one), the position passed to the current copy of `isWin` is losing. Well, when is a position passed to `isWin` winning? When it receives zeroes from all copies of it called during skimming through all of the possible moves. Such a situation indicates that all of the moves in the received position are losing, and, therefore, the caller of the current copy of `isWin` made a winning move. Ooh! The code, however, is quite elegant: A function ten-statement long beats a person in a logical game! In this project, a simple game is implemented, but the function does its job well in any case. This is the power of recursion!

To continue the theoretical digression, I'll tell you that you don't need to pass the array with a position as an argument. All instances of the `isWin` function can work with the same global array. With such an approach, `isWin` should undo the move it made before it returns. It is necessary to restore the position that existed at the moment when the function was called. In each particular game, you should choose the quickest approach. For example, when moves are computed quickly, and the array with a position is large, the second variant is the best.

If you represent a game as a tree of moves, in which nodes correspond to positions, the root node will correspond to the initial position. A few branches (moves) are incident from this zero-level node to first-level nodes, in which the other player can make moves. Other branches are incident from the first-level nodes to second-level nodes, and so on. At a certain level, some nodes don't have incident branches. These nodes correspond to end positions (the board is empty). The `isWin` function starts the tree traverse from the root node, and walks as deep as possible, up to the end node. It then steps back and walks along another branch up to the end. This sort of traverse is called *depth-first* search. Chess programs are based on the same principles. When traversing the game tree, the function doesn't visit all of the nodes, that is, it doesn't analyze all of the positions. If it finds a winning move in a position, it doesn't consider the other moves in this position. It steps back and sees whether the opponent has a counter-move. With such a method, `isWin` estimates the positions, and the estimate gradually moves to the initial position. Finally, when the initial position is estimated, the function completes its work. The estimates for positions on deeper levels are stored in local variables of corresponding instances of the `isWin` function. I could write this function in a non-recursive form, but this would be much more complicated.

11.4.2. *The* computerMove *and* isWin *Functions*

These are the last and the most complicated fragments of code in this book.

Listing 11.13. The computerMove function

```
// The computer's move
function computerMove()
{ // Waiting for a specified time interval
  if (getTimer() < waittime) return;
  // Deleting the wait method of the gameact clip
  delete gameact.onEnterFrame;

  // Skimming through the variants of the computer's moves
  var i, j, k, res, nump, rows = new Array(0,0,0), rows1 = new Array(0,0,0);
  // Assigning the rows and rows1 arrays the numbers of pieces
  // in the rows
  for (i = 0; i < 3; i++)
  { for (j = 0; j < i + 3; j++)
    rows[i] += board[i][j];
    rows1[i] = rows[i];
  }
  // Skimming through the computer moves in the current position
  // starting from the lowest row because there can be more pieces there
  for (i = 2; i >= 0; i--)
  { // Skimming over empty rows
    if (!rows[i]) continue;
    // Making all possible moves in the ith row
    for (j = 0; j < rows[i]; j++)
    { // A move: leaving j pieces in the ith row
      rows1[i] = j;
      // Estimating the move
      res = isWin(rows1);
      // if the move is winning, the opponent will lose.
      if (res == 1)
      { showResult(1);
        // Making this winning move,
        // i.e., removing rows[i] - j pieces from the ith row
        nump = rows[i] - j;
        // Removing the pieces from the board
```

```
        for (k = 0; k < i + 3; k++)
        if (nump && board[i][k])
          { showPiece(0, k, i);
            --nump;
          }
        // It is now the gamer's turn.
        mymove = 0;
        // Hiding the "Thinking..." text
        showThinking(0);
        // If there are no more pieces, the game is over.
        if (!numpieces) showGameOver(1);
        return;
      }
    }
    // Restoring the number of pieces in the ith row
    rows1[i] = rows[i];
  }
  // A winning move wasn't found. Making a random move
  anyMove();
}
```

When preparing to skim through moves, the computerMove function (List-ing 11.13) creates two arrays, rows and rows1, and assigns their elements the num-bers of pieces in the rows on the board. The zero elements of both arrays get the number of pieces in the top row, the first elements get the number in the middle row, and the second elements get the number in the bottom row:

```
for (i = 0; i < 3; i++)
  { for (j = 0; j < i + 3; j++)
    rows[i] += board[i][j];
    rows1[i] = rows[i];
  }
```

The rows array will be used to make moves and pass the resulting positions to the isWin function, and the rows1 array will be used to undo losing moves. The external loop iterates through the ith row, moving from the bottom to top, to remove as many pieces as possible and have more chances to find a winning move quickly:

```
for (i = 2; i >= 0; i--)
  { // Skimming over empty rows
    if (!rows[i]) continue;
```

The internal loop changes the j loop counter from zero to rows[i], which is the number of pieces in the ith row. During each iteration, all possible moves are made. That is, the code first leaves no pieces, then it leaves one piece, then two, and so on up to rows[i] - 1 pieces:

```
for (j = 0; j < rows[i]; j++)
 { // A move: leaving j pieces in the ith row
   rows1[i] = j;
```

Then the res variable is assigned an estimate of the position after the next move is made:

```
res = isWin(rows1);
```

If res is equal to one, the computer won, and the **You lose** message is displayed:

```
 showResult(1);
```

The computer should then make this winning move. To do this, the function assigns the nump (number of pieces) variable the number of pieces in the ith row:

```
nump = rows[i] - j;
```

In a loop, the function finds squares with pieces in the ith row, and removes the pieces until the nump variable becomes equal to zero:

```
for (k = 0; k < i + 3; k++)
 if (nump && board[i][k])
  { showPiece(0, k, i);
    --nump;
  }
```

If no pieces are left after this move, the game is over. Otherwise, it's the gamer's turn, and the computerMove function returns control.

If the function tried all possible moves in the ith row, but failed to find a winning move, it restores the number of the pieces in this row and goes to the next row:

```
rows1[i] = rows[i];
```

If the loop for i terminated naturally, this means the current position is losing, and the anyMove function should be called to make a random move:

```
anyMove();
```

That's all about the computerMove function. Consider the isWin function (Listing 11.14). In fact, it executes almost the same code to skim through possible moves, but it simply returns zero instead of making a winning move.

Listing 11.14. The `isWin` function

```
// Returns an estimate of the move that led to the current position:
// 0 - the move was losing,
// 1 - the move was winning.
function isWin(rows)
{ var i, j, res,
  rows1 = new Array(rows[0], rows[1], rows[2]);

  for (i = 2; i >= 0; i--)
  { // Skimming over empty rows
    if (!rows1[i]) continue;
    // Making the opponent's moves in the ith row
    for (j = 0; j < rows[i]; j++)
    { // A move: leaving j pieces in the ith row
      rows1[i] = j;
      // Estimating the move
      res = isWin(rows1);
      // If the opponent's move is winning, the move that led to the
      // current position was losing.
      if (res == 1) return 0;
    }
    // Restoring the number of pieces in the ith row
    rows1[i] = rows[i];
  }
  // If the opponent's all moves are losing,
  // the move that led to the current position was winning.
  return 1;
}
```

If you have been attentive enough, you noticed that the following two statements:

```
res = isWin(rows1);
if (res == 1) return 0;
```

can be replaced with one:

```
if (isWin(rows1)) return 0;
```

This will speed up the execution a little. (By the way, if you used scalar variables instead of arrays in `isWin` function, the gain in performance would be even greater.

However, don't do this in games where many moves are skimmed through.) This is nice, but you should change this function to allow people to play and have fun. In the current version, if the gamer carefully makes a move other than winning, he or she will get the **You lose** message immediately: The program will warn them that it is pointless to play further. Only when the gamer clicks the **Comp. begins** button, the computer doesn't skim through moves, but makes a random move. If it computed the best first move, the gamer would always lose without making a single move. Like 80 percent of similar positions, the initial position is winning. However, only one move is winning: You should remove two pieces from the upper row. You'll see this after you play with the project in the nim.fla and nim.as files located in the Example\Chapter 11 folder. You'll notice that computing moves takes a certain amount of time (about a few seconds), depending on the performance of your computer.

11.5. Limiting the Depth of Skimming through Moves

The program works well. I would even say it works better than it should. I suggest that you make the isWin function less intelligent.

First, create some additional graphics. This will be the btLevel button to select the game level (1 or 2), and the **Level** text to the left of the button. Begin with the text. Enter the third frame of the main timeline and create a text field using the **Text** tool. The text properties should be as follows: **Static Text, Tahoma, 30 pts, bold**, #0066FF, left-justified. The coordinates of the upper left corner should be X = 258 and Y = 327. Type in the Level word.

As for the button, create a new clip, name it btLevel, and check the **Export for ActionScript** checkbox. Create a layer above **Layer 1**, and name it **Layer 2**. In the first frame in **Layer 1**, draw a rectangle with rounded corners (the corner radius should be 5 pixels). Select the #3399FF color and a thickness of 2 pixels for the outline, and the #FFFFC4 color for the fill. Align the rectangle to the center of the work area. The timeline of this button clip will have four frames: levels one and two, each with a highlight and without. Enter the fourth frame of **Layer 1**, and press <F5> to create a frame and make the object live up to that frame.

In the first frame of **Layer 2**, create a text field with the same properties as the field you created earlier (except that this text should be centered). Type in 1. Align this to the center of the work area, copy everything to the second frame, and change the digit color to #FF6600. Create a blue two in the third frame and a red two in the fourth frame in a similar manner. Attach the following action to all these frames:

```
stop();
```

Let's proceed with programming. In the data section of the main program, replace the semicolon to a comma:

```
// An array to store marks
marked = new Array([0,0,0,0,0], [0,0,0,0,0], [0,0,0,0,0]),
```

and add a few variables:

```
// The game level (1 or 2)
level = 1,
// The maximum depth of skimming through the moves
// (depends on the level)
maxdepth = 6,
// A copy of maxdepth for the isWin function
workdepth = 0;
```

Here, the `level` variable contains what the `btLevel` button reads: one or two. The `maxdepth` variable is the maximum depth of skimming through the moves that is computed from the `maxdepth = level + 5` formula. I found this formula through experimentation. Zero will be assigned to the `workdepth` variable before a call to the `isWin` function, so that the function can determine, to which depth it has dug.

Besides zero and one, the `isWin` function will return a third value, two. It will indicate that `isWin` didn't compute till the final position and cannot estimate the given position. At the beginning of the `isWin` function, you'll increase the `workdepth` variable by one, and compare the result with the `maxdepth` variable. If `workdepth` is greater than `maxdepth`, the function will exit and return two. Before the function exits, it should restore the value of the `workdepth` variable passed to it, that is, it should subtract one from the variable. As a result, `workdepth` will store the current depth or the number of moves made (after the `rows1[i] = j` statement is executed) in every virtual instance of the `isWin` function. Outside the function, the `workdepth` variable is always equal to zero.

Before proceeding to more complicated things, insert the code for the `btLevel` button (Listing 11.15) immediately after the following line:

```
//*** The main program ***
```

Listing 11.15. The code for the `btLevel` button

```
// Placing the btLevel button clip
attachMovie('btLevel', 'btLevel', leveldepth);
btLevel._x = 360;
btLevel._y = 348;
// Defining the onRollOver event handler
btLevel.onRollOver = function()
 { // Going to the frame with a highlighted digit
   btLevel.gotoAndStop(btLevel._currentframe + 1);
 }
// Defining the onRollOut event handler
btLevel.onRollOut = function()
 { // Returning to the frame where the digit isn't highlighted
   btLevel.gotoAndStop(btLevel._currentframe - 1);
 }
// Defining the onRelease event handler
btLevel.onRelease - function()
 { // The level can be changed only at the beginning of the game.
   if (numpieces == maxpieces)
    { // Toggling the level between 1 and 2
      level = 3 - level;
      // Adjusting the maximum depth
      maxdepth = level + 5;
      // Going to the frame where the digit isn't highlighted
      btLevel.gotoAndStop(level*2);
    }
 }
// defining the onReleaseOutside event handler
btlevel.onReleaseOutside = function()
 { // Returning to the frame where the digit isn't highlighted
   btLevel.gotoAndStop(btLevel._currentframe - 1);
 }
```

At the beginning of the program, insert the following lines immediately after the var line:

```
// The depth of the btLevel clip
 leveldepth = 0,
```

The code for the `btLevel` clip is simple: You wrote similar code earlier. Your task now is to display the game level and highlight an appropriate digit, depending on the gamer's actions. In addition, you should toggle the value of the `level` variable between one and two.

In the `computerMove` function, locate the following lines:

```
// Skimming through the computer moves in the current position
// starting from the lowest row because there can be more pieces there
```

Insert these lines before the lines you located:

```
// Setting the depth of skimming through moves
 workdepth = 0;
```

You don't need to reset the `workdepth` variable to zero every time you call `isWin`. As you already know, this variable is always equal to zero outside the `isWin` function.

Listing 11.16 presents an updated version of the `isWin` function, where the depth of skimming through variants is limited.

Listing 11.16. An updated version of the `isWin` function

```
// Returns an estimate of the move that led to the current position:
// 0 - the move was losing,
// 1 - the move was winning,
// 2 - unknown.
function isWin(rows)
{ if (++workdepth > maxdepth)
   { --workdepth;
     return 2;
   }

 var i, j, res, res2,
   rows1 = new Array(rows[0], rows[1], rows[2]);
   for (i = 2; i >= 0; i--)
   { // Skimming over empty rows
     if (!rows1[i]) continue;
     // Making the opponent's moves in the ith row
     for (j = 0; j < rows[i]; j++)
     { // A move: leaving j pieces in the ith row
       rows1[i] = j;
       // Estimating the move
```

```
                  res = isWin(rows1);
                  // If the opponent's move is winning, the move that led to the
                  // current position was losing.
                  if (res == 1)
                  { --workdepth;
                    return 0;
                  }
                  if (res == 2) res2 = 2;
                }
              // Restoring the number of pieces in the ith row
              rows1[i] = rows[i];
          }
    --workdepth;
    if (res2 == 2) return 2;
    // If the opponent's all moves are losing,
    // the move that led to the current position was winning.
    return 1;
}
```

This version of the isWin function differs from the previous in the conditional statement discussed earlier and in the statement

```
    --workdepth;
```

placed before the return. In addition, the "2" estimate indicating that the result is unknown is implemented. This project is located in the nim1.fla and nim1.as files. Make sure to update the code attached to the third frame of the movie:

```
    #include "nim1.as"
```

> If you wish to check for the correctness of skimming through moves, set maxdepth to 100, and edit the code of the orbtLevel.onRelease event handler appropriately. When the maxdepth value is greater than 12, the program should consider moves up to the final position, and win, if possible.

NOTE

You might be eager to start the program and play with it. Go ahead! Surprised? ActionScript is too slow, and 15 seconds aren't enough for it to think over a move. What a pity! Is Flash too silly to play intellectual games?

You, a programmer, should help it. If you analyze the game closely, you'll notice that it is very easy to tell whether a position is winning when only two rows of pieces are left. If there are equal numbers of pieces in the rows, the next move is losing. When the numbers of pieces in the rows are different, the next move is winning if it makes the numbers equal. This rule is used in many games, and is called a *symmetric winning strategy*. In other words, a move that destroys symmetry is losing.

11.6. Adding Some Heuristic

Let's add the heuristic rule formulated at the end of the previous section to the isWin function, and see whether it can speed up playing on the computer's part (Listing 11.17).

Listing 11.17. A version of the isWin function with heuristic

---

```
// Returns an estimate of the move that led to the current position:
// 0 - the move was losing,
// 1 - the move was winning,
// 2 - unknown.
function isWin(rows)
{ if (++workdepth > maxdepth)
    { --workdepth;
      return 2;
    }

  var i, j, res, res2, r0, r1, r2,
   rows1 = new Array(rows[0], rows[1], rows[2]);

  // Assigning the numbers of pieces to scalar variables to speed up
  // the program's work
  r0 = rows[0];
  r1 = rows[1];
  r2 = rows[2];
  // Checking whether exactly one row is empty.
  // In this case, if the other rows contain equal numbers of pieces
  // the previous move was winning.
if (!r0 && r1 && r1 == r2 ||
      !r1 && r0 && r0 == r2 ||
      !r2 && r0 && r0 == r1)
    { --workdepth;
```

```
    return 1;
}

for (i = 2; i >= 0; i--)
{ // Skimming over empty rows
  if (!rows1[i]) continue;
  // Making the opponent's moves in the ith row
  for (j = 0; j < rows[i]; j++)
   { // A move: leaving j pieces in the ith row
    rows1[i] = j;
    // Estimating the move
    res = isWin(rows1);
    // If the opponent's move is winning, the move that led to the
    // current position was losing.
    if (res == 1)
     { --workdepth;
       return 0;
     }
    if (res == 2) res2 = 2;
   }
  // Restoring the number of pieces in the ith row
  rows1[i] = rows[i];
 }
--workdepth;
if (res2 == 2) return 2;
// If the opponent's all moves are losing,
// the move that led to the current position was winning.
return 1;
}
```

Before skimming through the moves, this isWin version checks whether there is exactly one empty row. If there is, it checks whether the other rows contain equal numbers of pieces. If the second condition is also true, the function decreases workdepth by one and returns one.

```
{ --workdepth;
  return 1;
}
```

This indicates that the move that led to the position was winning.

If you failed to understand the conditional statement that combines these conditions, I'll explain it using an example.

```
if (!r0 && r1 && r1 == r2...
```

is equivalent to

```
if (r0 == 0 && r1 > 0 && r1 == r2...
```

In other words, if the top row is empty, and the middle row isn't, and the numbers of pieces in the middle and bottom rows are equal, the function should return one immediately.

Start the game. Eureka! (Perhaps, this is what Archimedos cried running naked through Syracuse with the golden crown in his hands). The program now plays very quickly, and the `isWin` function always wins, even at the first game level, as if there is no limit to the skimming depth. Well, you should adjust the program's mental ability by decreasing the `maxdepth` value. I found a good value (two) through experimentation. Change

```
maxdepth = 6,
```

to

```
maxdepth = 2,
```

in the data section.

In the `onRelease` event handler of the `btLevel` clip, change

```
maxdepth = level + 5;
```

to

```
maxdepth = level + 1;
```

Now the program doesn't think too deep. The heuristic rule is quite handy.

You should now adjust the `anyMove` function so that it doesn't leave positions that can be won easily using the heuristic rule.

To make moves more varied, implement the following idea: Select a random row and a random number of pieces to remove. If at least one piece will be left in this row after this move, make this move. Otherwise, try another random move. To avoid an infinite search, make no more than 50 attempts. If a desired move isn't found after 50 attempts, break the loop and remove one piece from the row with the maximum number of pieces.

Listing 11.18 contains a new version of the `anyMove` function. The comments explain it completely.

Listing 11.18. The new version of the `anyMove` function

```
// Making a random move
function anyMove()
{ var i, j, k,
  n = 50,
  rows = new Array(0, 0, 0);

  // Assigning the rows array the number of pieces in three rows
  for (i = 0; i < 3; i++)
   for (j = 0; j < i + 3; j++)
    rows[i] += board[i][j];
  // Making n attempts to remove k pieces from the ith row
  do
   { // Assigning i a random number, 0, 1, or 2
    i = Math.floor(Math.random()*3);
    // If there are less than two pieces in the row, try another.
    if (rows[i] < 2) continue;
    // Assigning k a random number, 1, 2, or 3
    k = Math.floor(Math.random()*3) + 1;
    // If there are 3 pieces in the ith row, and k is equal to 3...
    if (rows[i] == 3 && k == 3)
     // ...assign k a random number, 1 or 2.
     k = Math.floor(Math.random()*2)+1;
    // If there are 2 pieces in the ith row, assign k one.
    if (rows[i] == 2) k = 1;
    // Removing k pieces from the ith row
    rows[i] -= k;
    // If there are rows with equal to numbers of pieces...
    if (rows[0] == rows[1] || rows[0] == rows[2] ||
    rows[1] == rows[2])
       // ...undo the move.
     { rows[i] += k;
       k = 0;
     }
    // After the move is made, break the loop.
    if (k) break;
   } while (--n);
  // If no move is made, make a simple move.
  if (!k)
   { // Finding the row with the maximum number of pieces
```

```
    i = 2;
    if (rows[1] > rows[2]) i = 1;
    if (rows[0] > rows[1]) i = 0;
    // Removing one piece from the ith row
    rows[i] -= 1;
    k = 1;
  }
// Removing k pieces from the ith row
for (j = 0; j < i + 3; j++)
  if (board[i][j])
  { showPiece(0, j, i);
    if (!--k) break;
  }
// The gamer's move
mymove = 0;
// Hide "Thinking..." text
showThinking(0);
}
```

With this version of the anyMove function, the program makes varied moves, and it is interesting to play against it. However, the game is still for children. This version of the project is in the nim2.fla and nim2.as files.

The projects that implement Nim also have a blue copyright panel and a button with a link to **www.gameintellect.com**. They are necessary if an owner of the book tries to use this game, for example, on his or her site. It is prohibited to sell, rent, or exchange the game, to distribute its source code, or to derive a profit from the game in any other way! The source code is intended only for training purposes.

11.7. Continuation of the Theme

The program works quickly, and you can make it even quicker by replacing the arrays with scalar variables in the isWin function. Why don't you try to make it more interesting and add a fourth row to the game board? In addition, you can implement other game rules, because there are many versions of Nim. For example, one version allows the gamers to remove one or two neighboring pieces from one row. It is called mathematical bowling.

If you fail to write a new isWin function, ask me for help. In any case, a Delphi (or C++) shell will allow you to write a powerful game, because processor code is quicker than ActionScript. This completes my book. I hope it was useful for you. Game over!

CD Contents

The table below lists folders with files containing programs described in this book.

Folder	Comment
\Examples\Chapter 2	Flash project files and graphics files for *Chapter 2*.
\Examples\Chapter 3	Flash project files for *Chapter 3*.
\Examples\Chapter 4	Flash project files and SWF files for *Chapter 4*.
\Examples\Chapter 5	Flash project files, SWF files, and audio files for *Chapter 5*.
\Examples\Chapter 6	Flash project files, SWF files and server PHP scripts for *Chapter 6*. A Web server should run on the local host for the Chapter6.3.swf file to work.
\Examples\Chapter 7	Flash project files, an SWF file, and a graphics file for *Chapter 7*.
\Examples\Chapter 8	Flash project files and executable files for the key generator in Delphi, MSVC++, and Perl and key files for the game.

continues

Continued

Folder	Comment
\Examples\Chapter 9	Flash and Delphi project files and executable files to play Tet-a-Tetris as a Windows application. Shockwave Flash ActiveX component is required for them to work. (This is the Flash Player that comes with the Flash authoring environment, or can be downloaded from Macromedia's site.)
\Examples\Chapter 10	Flash and MSVC++ project files and executable files to play Tet-a-Tetris as a Windows application. Shockwave Flash ActiveX component is required for their work. (This is the Flash Player that comes with the Flash authoring environment or can be downloaded from Macromedia's site.)
\Examples\Chapter 11	Flash project files and SWF files for *Chapter 11*.
\Programs	fontonizer1.01.exe — Fontonizer shareware program. Choose a font for your project without installing it in your system. See how your text looks written in different fonts: Install a font with a single click!
	saveflash_5460.exe — a small shareware program that displays a list of all Flash animations on a Web page, as well as their URLs and sizes, and allows you to save them on the hard disk.
	a_Frigate3_Pro_v30.exe — a powerful shareware file manager with intuitive interface that allows you to work with your computer easily and quickly. Currently, it is the most powerful tool for the work with files. It always takes the lead over the others in using new technologies and ideas.
	awiconsprosetup.exe — a professional shareware icon editor with ready-to-use effects.

Index

A

ActionScript, 2
Active Template Library, 246
ActiveX, 250
ActiveX control, creation of, 247
AddRef, method, 252
Advise, method, 259
Antialiasing, 26
AnyMove, function, 278, 299
Apache
    installation, 158
Arguments, object, 66
Array, 92
    class, 69
    methods, 70
ATL, 246
AtlAxWin, class, 248
AtlAxWin7, class, 248
AtlAxWinInit, function, 247
Autovivification principle, 48

B

Break, statement, 65
BSTR, type, 255
Built-in fonts, 26
Buttons, 105

C

CComBSTR, class, 255
CComPtr, class, 252
Character Spacing, parameter, 186
CheckNK, function, 226
chNK, function, 198

Class:
    Array, 69
    AtlAxWin, 248
    AtlAxWin7, 248
    built-in, 69
    CComBSTR, 255
    CComPtr, 252
    IDispEventImpl, 258
    IDispEventSimpleImpl, 259
    MovieClip, 71
    Sound, 73
Clip depth, 91
COM interface, 249
Command:
    Control | Test Movie, 45
    Create Motion Tween, 38
    Edit | Copy Frames, 90
    Edit | Paste Frames, 90
    Edit | Paste in Place, 23
    Edit | Preferences, 10
    File | Import, 11, 13
    File | Import to Library, 11
    File | Publish, 46
    File | Publish Settings, 10
    File | Revert, 18
    File | Save, 11
    Insert | Blank keyframe, 13, 34
    Insert | Keyframe, 23
    Insert | Layer, 20
    Insert | New Symbol, 12
    Modify | Align | Center Horizontal, 40
    Modify | Align | Center Vertical, 40
    Modify | Break Apart, 15, 27, 36
    Modify | Document, 10
    Modify | Transform, 19
    Modify | Transform | Scale, 43

Move to New Folder, 42
View | Grid, 11
Window | Info, 13
Window | Properties, 28
Window | Save Panel Layout, 11
Window | Scene, 87
Comment, 62
Computer bug, 149
computerMove, function, 288
Conditional statement, 62
Continue, statement, 65
CreateWindowsEx, function, 241
Creating:
   animation
      Motion Tween, 35
      Shape Tween, 39
   button, 29
   layer, 20
   movie, 34
   symbol, 12
   text, 26

D

Data type:
   boolean, 58
   casting, 50
   number, 55
   string, 56
   undefined, 58, 128
Decrypting an SWF file, 224
DefWindowProc, function, 245
Delphi procedure:
   EncodeSWF, 224
   EncodeTopTen, 225
   FormClose, 235
   FormShow, 226
   tetatetFSCommand, 231
DestroyWindow, function, 246
DispatchMessage, function, 244
DispEventAdvise, method, 259

downFigs, function, 135
downOrWaitAction, function, 132
dropFigs, function, 136

E

Edit | Copy Frames, command, 90
Edit | Paste Frames, command, 90
EncodeSWF, Delphi procedure, 224
EncodeTopTen, Delphi procedure, 225
Encrypting an SWF file, 224
enterNameKey, function, 199
enterNameKeyUp, function, 197
Erase, tool, 184
ErrorMessage, function, 241
Event, 75
   button, 79
   handler, 75
   mouse, 78
   movie, 84
   user, 75
exitApp, function, 204
explode, function, 142

F

Flash development environment:
   creating folders, 15
   settings, 9
   timeline, 33
For, statement, 64
FormatMessage, function, 241
FormClose, Delphi procedure, 235
FormShow, Delphi procedure, 226
Function, 66, 104
   anyMove, 278, 299
   AtlAxWinInit, 247
   built-in, 67
   CheckNK, 226
   chNK, 198
   computerMove, 288
   CreateWindowsEx, 241

DefWindowProc, 245
DestroyWindow, 246
DispatchMessage, 244
downFigs, 135
downOrWaitAction, 132
dropFigs, 136
enterNameKey, 199
enterNameKeyUp, 197
ErrorMessage, 241
exitApp, 204
explode, 142
FormatMessage, 241
GetLastError, 241
GetMessage, 244
isDown, 130
isLayer, 138
isWin, 295, 297
keyDown, 120
keyUp, 121, 190
lightning1, 141
MakeFilePath, 255
menuorOver, 192
moveLayer, 147
moveLeft, 149
moveRight, 151
MoveWindow, 241
newFigs, 126, 173, 195
newGame, 281
passing parameters to, 67
PostMessage, 244
PostQuitMessage, 246
recursive, 285
RegisterClassEx, 239
rel, 281
removeLayers, 143
returnHelp, 200
rotateFigs, 151
SendMessage, 244
sendRec, 169
showEnterName, 200
showGameOver, 276
showHelp, 199

showPiece, 279
showResult, 277
showThinking, 276
showTopTen, 201
startGame, 123, 171, 188
SysAllocString, 255
thinking, 277
togglePause, 118
updateScore, 141
UpdateWindow, 243
userMove, 283
waitForAction, 134
WinMain, 239
wipeFigs, 119
youBegin, 277

G

GetLastError, function, 241
GetMessage, function, 244
Global Unique Identifier, 240
GUID, 240
Guide layer, 34

I

IConnectionPoint::Advise, method, 256
IconnectionPointContainer
    ::FindConnectionPoint, method, 256
IDispEventImpl, class, 258
IDispEventSimpleImpl, class, 259
IDL, 254
If, statement, 62
Import to Library, window, 89
Interface:
    COM, 249
    event, 256
    IDispatch, 257, 258
    IShockwaveFlash, 253, 256
    IUnknown, 251
Interface Definition Language, 254
Invoke, method, 257

isDown, function, 130
isLayer, function, 138
isWin, 291
isWin, function, 295, 297

K

Key generator, 209
  in Delphi, 214
  in Perl, 211
Key validation, 226
Key, object, 73
  methods, 74
  properties, 74, 80
keyDown, function, 120
keyUp, function, 121, 190

L

lightning1, function, 141
Linkage Properties, window, 89
Loop, statement, 64

M

MakeFilePath, function, 255
Mask layer, 34
Math, object, 55
  methods, 55
menuorOver, function, 192
Method:
  AddRef, 252
  Advise, 259
  DispEventAdvise, 259
  IConnectionPoint::Advise, 256
  IconnectionPointContainer
    ::FindConnectionPoint, 256
  Invoke, 257
  put_Movie, 254
  QueryInterface, 252
  Release, 252
  Unadvise, 259
MIDL, compiler, 254

Morphing, 40
Mouse, object, 74
  methods, 75
moveLayer, function, 147
moveLeft, function, 149
moveRight, function, 151
MoveWindow, function, 241
Movie:
  button, 21
  clip, 12
  clip instance, 12, 24
  colors, 18
  creating, 34
  current frame, 23
  debugging mode, 155
  importing graphics, 11
  integration into Delphi, 219
  integration into MSVC++, 237
  key frame, 13
  layer, 34
  properties, 10
  registration point, 12
  scene, 15
  symbol, 12
  text, 26
Movie clip, 1
MovieClip, class, 71
  methods, 72
  properties, 71
MSDN Library, 238

N

newFigs, function, 126, 173, 195
newGame, function, 281
Nim, 265

O

Object:
  accessing, 41
  arguments, 66

built-in, 73
Key, 73
Math, 55
Mouse, 74
Selection, 75, 200
String, 57
Object inspector, 220
OLE/COM Object Viewer, 253
Operator
priority, associativity, 59
Overlapped window, 243

P

Parameter:
Character Spacing, 186
PHP, 157, 162
installation, 158
Pixel, 11
PostMessage, function, 244
PostQuitMessage, function, 246
Property:
_parent, 54
_root, 50
put_Movie, method, 254

Q

QueryInterface, method, 252

R

Rectangle, tool, 185
Reference counter, 252
RegisterClassEx, function, 239
RegNow, 209
rel, function, 281
Release, method, 252
removeLayers, function, 143
Renaming files, 220
returnHelp, function, 200
rotateFigs, function, 151

S

Selection, object, 75
method, 75
SendMessage, function, 244
sendRec, function, 169
ShareIt!, 209
showEnterName, function, 200
showGameOver, function, 276
showHelp, function, 199
showPiece, function, 279
showResult, function, 277
showThinking, function, 276
showTopTen, function, 201
Sound, class, 73
startGame, function, 123, 171, 188
Statement, 61
break, 65
conditional, 62
conditional ternary, 63
continue, 65
for, 64
if, 62
loop, 64
switch, 63
while, 64
String, object, 57
Switch, statement, 63
SysAllocString, function, 255

T

tetatetFSCommand,
Delphi procedure, 231
thinking, function, 277
Timeline, 33
togglePause, function, 118
Tool:
Arrow, 17, 18, 22, 23, 28, 36
Erase, 184
Fill Color, 40
Fill Transform, 19

Lasso, 10, 15, 36
Lasso Magic Wand, 15
Paint Bucket, 19
Rectangle, 22, 29, 185
Stroke Color, 19, 23
Text, 28

U

Unadvise, method, 259
updateScore, function, 141
UpdateWindow, function, 243
userMove, function, 283

V

Validating a key, 226
Value:
  boolean, 58
  null, 59
  numeric, 55
  special numeric, 55
  string, 56
  undefined, 58
Variable, 48
  access, 54
  event handler, 85
  name, 48
  of clip, 54
  scope, 50
  type, 48, 49
VARIANT_BOOL, type, 254
VARIANT_FALSE,
  constant, 254
VARIANT_TRUE,
  constant, 254
Virtual functions, 250

W

waitForAction, function, 134
Web server, interacting with, 160, 162
While, statement, 64
Wide strings, 223
Window:
  Bitmap Properties, 14
  Color Mixer, 18
  Color Swatches, 41
  Document Properties, 10
  Import to Library, 89
  Info, 12
  Library, 9, 12
  Linkage Properties, 89
  Output, 45
  Tools, 9
Window | Scene, command, 87
Window classes, 239
Windows program:
  application window, 239, 241
  error handling, 241
  integration of a Flash movie, 237
  loading a Flash movie, 254
  message handling, 243, 245
  message loop, 243
  precompiled headers, 238
  Shockwave Flash window, 246, 248, 249
  window function, 245
  window styles, 243
WinMain, function, 239
wipeFigs, function, 119

Y

youBegin, function, 277